tear here

Three Essential Shutoff

In case of emergency, know the location of these shutoffs:

Main Water Valve

Located near the water meter, usually near an outside wall near the front of the house or in the basement, if you have one (see Chapter 27). Use this valve to shut off water: a) when a pipe is leaking; b) whenever you leave home for an extended period; and c) while making repairs in places where there's not another shutoff. Note: There is probably another shutoff outside, under a steel plate, which a plumber or the water company can operate. Use this valve if your main shutoff does not work, or if the trouble occurs on the street side of the shutoff.

For a private water system, shut off the circuit breaker or switch feeding the pump. Then shut off the valve on the output side of the pressure tank, and release pressure by opening valves at low spots in the house.

Main Electric Switch

Located on the circuit breaker or fuse box (see Chapter 24). In a circuit breaker box, it is the breaker marked "100," "150," or "200." In a fuse box, it is the big black fuseholder marked "main," "60," or "100." In some cases, the main switch is a big lever handle on the outside of a switch box. The main switch should be in the first electrical box that the main electrical feed reaches.

Fuel Line Shutoff

A gas shutoff should be on the gas meter. Look for a big lug resembling a giant screwdriver blade. Turn the lug 90° with a big adjustable wrench or locking pliers. Other gas shutoffs, with smaller steel lugs or brass handles, may be located on gas pipes inside the house. Turn them 90°, across the pipeline. On propane systems, look for a valve on top of the tank.

An oil shutoff is usually a small valve at the bottom of an oil tank, or (if the tank is outside) on the oil line where it enters your house.

Your Essential Tool Kit

- $^3/_8$" variable-speed reversing drill with drill bits and a Phillips bit
- Locking pliers
- Arc-joint pliers
- Adjustable wrench
- 16" pipe wrench
- Hammer
- Wrecking bar
- Screwdrivers (slotted and Phillips)
- 12' tape measure
- Carpenter's square
- Aluminum square
- Hand rip saw
- Block plane
- Utility knife
- Wood chisel
- Nail set
- Hacksaw
- Metal file
- Wire stripper
- Circuit tester
- Soldering iron
- Paint scraper
- Paint roller and pan
- $2^1/_2$" trim brush
- Drywall knife or margin trowel
- Caulking gun
- Two saw horses or plastic milk crates

Your Essential Supply Cabinet

- Paint primer
- Drywall primer
- Wood hole filler
- Carpenter's glue
- Drywall compound or another hole filler
- Pipe joint compound
- Solder
- Flux
- Sandpaper (various grades)
- Steel wool
- Screw-on wire connectors
- Electrician's tape
- Spare outlets and 2-way switches
- Spare fuses (if you have a fuse box)
- Drywall screws ($1^1/_4$", $1^1/_2$", $2^1/_4$", 3")
- Finishing nails (4d "penny," 6d, 8d, 10d)
- Cement-coated sinker nails (6d, 8d, 10d, 16d)
- Roofing nails ($1^1/_2$", 2")
- Assorted drywall anchors or molly screws

alpha books

Your Essential Safety Kit

Goggles

Rubber and leather gloves

Dust mask

Respirator (with cartridges for organic solvents, if you work with them)

Ear plugs or ear protectors

Finding More Tools

Don't overlook friends, neighbors, garage sales, and rental outfits.

The Essential Home Inspection

The roof: From above, look for broken, missing or torn shingles, and loose flashing. Check that the ridge line does not sag. From the attic, if possible, look for stains, fungus, and soft spots that indicate leakage.

Foundation: Look for sagging, bulging, cracking, and decay of masonry, perennial damp spots, and mold building up on the framing lumber or siding.

Interior: Soft spots on floors, out-of-square or jammed windows and doors, major drywall or plaster cracking or decay.

Electrical and mechanical: General condition and age of pipes, wiring, and heating system. Orderly or a mess? Is wiring hanging from the ceiling or well-mounted?

How to Tell if a Circuit Is Hot (Carrying Electricity)

First try to turn the circuit off, using the most logical fuse or circuit breaker.

With your electrical tester, put one prong in each slot of an outlet. Then test each slot against the ground hole (the round one in the outlet). If the tester lights at any point, the circuit is hot.

For a 2-way switch (one switch powers one or more lights or outlets): Turn the switch on. Using a plastic-handled screwdriver, unscrew the outlet cover *without* poking anything inside the box. With your circuit tester, touch one lead to the electric box and the other to the screw terminals on the switch. If the tester lights, the switch is hot. If not, try another ground—like a bare (ground) wire in the box, or the ground hole in a nearby outlet. If the switch is on *and* the tester is definitely touching ground or neutral, *and* you're touching one of the switch terminals, *and* the tester is not lit, then the circuit is cold.

Home Maintenance and Repairs You Should Never Have to Hire Again after Using This Book

Window glass replacement

Stuck window or door

Sticky lock mechanism

Interior painting

Minor foundation or concrete repair

Leaky faucet

Replacing light switches and electric outlets

Simple drain cleanout

Replacing toilet mechanism

The COMPLETE IDIOT'S GUIDE TO Trouble-Free Home Repair

by David J. Tenenbaum

alpha books

A Division of Macmillan General Reference
A Simon & Schuster Macmillan Company
1633 Broadway, New York, NY 10019

This book is dedicated to my father, Frank, who taught me that perseverance, ingenuity, and a passion for improvisation could overcome practically any home-repair nightmare. And to my mother, Frances, a writer who (usually) put up with the delays and the mess.

Screen reproductions in this book were created by means of the program Collage Plus from Inner Media, Inc., Hollis, NH.

Printed in the United States of America

Publisher
Theresa Murtha

Editor
Lisa Bucki

Production Editor
Matt Hannafin

Cover Designer
Michael J. Freeland

Designer
Kim Scott

Illustrator
Judd Winnick

Photographer
David J. Tenenbaum

Production Manager
Scott Cook

Manufacturing Coordinator
Steve Pool

Production Team Supervisor
Laurie Casey

Indexer
Carol Sheehan

Production Team
*Heather Butler, Angela Calvert, Dan Caparo, Kim Cofer, Tricia Flodder,
Aleata Howard, Erika Millen, Beth Rago, Erich J. Richter,
Jenny Shoemake, Christine Tyner, Karen Walsh*

*Special thanks to Mark Genovese and Don Linstroth for ensuring the
technical accuracy of this book.*

Contents at a Glance

Contents

Foreword

Homeowners often face overwhelming fears when something goes wrong with their houses. Many people assume that they must call expensive professionals to solve their home-related problems. There are times when it is best to defer to experienced professionals, but there are also many times when handy homeowners can take control of their own property and save a lot of money.

Have you checked the prices that plumbers and electricians charge these days? If you haven't, let me tell you, they are quite high. The same can be said for other building trades. When you have to call a professional to take care of problems with your home, it is a safe bet to say that you could pay them as much for a few hours of work as you make in a full week at the office.

Can an average person like you really maintain and repair your home without the help of highly paid professionals? In many cases, you can. The odds of success certainly increase for readers of this book. Don't let the title fool you. This book is written in language that so-called idiots can understand, but there is plenty of user-friendly, hands-on advice that will benefit anyone short of a seasoned professional.

I've worked in the building trades for over 20 years. My credentials include building up to 60 single-family homes a year as a general contractor, being a master plumber, and remodeling countless homes. In addition to my trade skills, I'm licensed as a designated real estate broker, and I've written many books about home repair and improvements. Through my experience in these various fields, I've come to know quite a bit about home maintenance, inspection, and repair.

David Tenenbaum demystifies the world of home maintenance and repair and brings the language used by pros down to a level that average people can comprehend easily. When you read this book, you will feel as if you are sitting at the breakfast table and confiding in a friend about the problems with your home.

Many aspects of home maintenance and repair get technical, and there is no way around this fact. However, Mr. Tenenbaum breaks down ominous processes into simple steps, and gives his advice in the context of real-world situations that are both instructive and easy to understand. You will laugh with him as you learn of his mistakes, but most importantly, you will know how to avoid those mistakes in your projects.

The pages of this book are filled with helpful hints and professional guidance. The logical structure of the text makes it easy to find information about any common problems that you might be faced with. People with problems want fast solutions, and this book puts answers at your fingertips. Let me give you a few examples of topics that caught my attention:

➤ Finding trouble before it finds you.

➤ Assessing your needs for professional help, and finding and hiring qualified professionals.

➤ Formulating a plan to fix it or forget it.

➤ Choosing and using the tools you need.

➤ Rolling up your sleeves and getting busy.

➤ Conquering outdoor problems with the roof, siding, and more.

➤ Making repairs indoors—floors, walls, and more.

➤ Taking on mechanical work like electrical repairs, plumbing, and heating.

As a veteran of the trades, I have to say that Mr. Tenenbaum has captured the focus of home repair in a way that anyone can appreciate. Die-hard tool warriors might want a little more detail than what is included here, but Harry and Harriet Homeowner will find this book extremely easy to use and will benefit from it. If you want to avoid paying a contractor for work that you can do yourself, this book is a great place to invest a few dollars. It will be money well spent.

Roger Woodson

Introduction

I don't know how you got interested in home repair. Perhaps it was after buying a house that needed . . . well, let's just say a bit more attention than you bargained for. Perhaps it was after an anxiety attack sparked by paying psychiatrists' wages to a plumber who repaired a drippy faucet and you realized that, on closer inspection, the task was pretty straightforward. Perhaps it was when you realized that you could convert your free time into money.

I do know how I started a lifetime involvement in home repair. It was courtesy of my father, an electronic engineer possessed of the strange notion that he could do almost anything. Wiring? No problem. Television repair? All in a day's work for a guy who designed radar and computers. Carpentry? Well, anything was simpler than TV repair. A new phone line to the study? Sure. A new darkroom in the basement? Sounds like a great winter project (even if we had to drill a ridiculous number of holes in concrete that was hard as . . . concrete).

One of the many lessons my father taught me was that there's a tool for anything—a hammer for pounding nails, a crowbar for pulling them. Sanders, drills, jigsaws, levels, the list never ends, unfortunately. But he also taught me to improvise—to use a screwdriver (within reason) as a pry bar, a hammer as a mallet, a locking pliers for almost anything at all.

I'm not sure exactly what's in your toolbox. But I do know every toolbox needs a tool to make you confident, skilled, and prepared for the predictably surprising problems you'll meet as you become your home's physician.

You're holding that tool.

Where to Find What You Need in This Book

Part 1: You Don't Need Eight Hands to be Handy. Effective home repair is partly a state of mind. To use a hackneyed maxim, you should be prepared—in skills, materials, and tools. Most important is the fixer's mindset: when something goes wrong, you will call yourself before reaching for the Yellow Pages. In this part, I'll talk about planning, about fitting your home repair work into the rest of your life, and then take a close look at the home place—starting with the two critical elements: the foundation and roof. You'll think a bit about whether, in your heart of hearts, you want to tackle certain projects, and if you decide it requires more skills, tools, or time than you can supply, we'll meet the people who are ready to do the projects for you.

In Part 2, Safety, Tools, and Materials: The Building Blocks of Success, I will explain that while the first rule of intelligent tinkering is to save all the parts, the second is not to conclude a weekend project in the emergency room. Thus we'll examine some basic safety rules, and discuss the all-important stupidity factor. Although, in this hyper-electrified era, hand tools seem hopelessly antiquated, you'll be doing most of your repairs with them. We'll sketch out a basic array of hand tools, emphasizing those that are versatile enough to help in many repairs. Then we'll rev up the motor and look at some nearly essential electric tools. Because fasteners—nails, screws, and hardware—can literally make or break a project, we'll take a brief tour of the hardware store, concentrating on some clever inventions that can make your life a good deal easier. And we'll talk about wood, still the basic construction material for the average home.

Part 3, Working Out—Aerobics for Your Home's Exterior, is devoted to essential stuff: the foundation, siding, roofing, concrete, and doors and windows. Talk about important— these are all your house has for protection against the elements. We'll start with the easy stuff (caulking and weatherstripping) and move to broken windows and stuck doors. Then we'll go up to the roof and talk about safety and repairs. Finally, we'll spend a couple of chapters talking about masonry and concrete, two ageless materials that should not be visibly aging in your house.

In Part 4, An Inside Job, we'll take a walk around your interior. If your floor squawks like a frightened hen, or your drywall and wallpaper still show the depredations of riotous children from years ago, you've come to the right place. Fortunately, curing these woes is easier than you think—if you know some professional tricks. And if you have the urge to just paint or wallpaper it all over and start fresh, we'll discuss what kind of material you should be using, and how to best get it onto the wall.

In Part 5, Mechanicals for Non-Mechanics, we'll talk about the hardest stuff—wires, pipes, and heating systems. Remember the old threat from energy crisis days: Let them freeze in the dark? Without your mechanical system, that's just what would happen—when you weren't poaching in the humidity. We'll start with the electrical system, where a determined homeowner can save plenty of bucks. We'll stop by the even-more-intimidating heating system, where a surprising number of money-saving repairs await you. Finally, we'll get our feet wet (heh, heh) in plumbing, where everything seems to leak, unless it's not draining—or doing both at once.

In Appendix A, the Nail It Down Glossary, we'll help you answer vital questions like these: Where does a soffit meet a rake edge? What's a light? (Hint: it's not a kind of beer.) Why is glazing never galvanized? Why does this guy keep asking stupid questions? We'll help you prepare for builder's jeopardy, so you'll never again experience total bafflement at the building-supply house.

Extras

This book is dedicated to the proposition that the human species is defined by the ability to use tools, and the ability to read an instruction book. To help you make the most of this instruction book, I've salted it with helpful signposts. Here's how they work:

Builder's Trivia

The bottom of my toolbag gathers useless junk I just couldn't throw out. Builder's Trivia boxes contain useless junk I couldn't heave out of this book. Some is merely fascinating or thought-provoking. Every now and then, this information will even be practical.

Nail It Down

Knowing the talk of the trade will help you get some satisfaction at the building-supply store. It will enable you to talk with contractors. It will make you feel hip as you call a joist a joist, and distinguish a riser from a stringer.

Handy Hint

Have you ever watched a skilled worker do in 15 seconds something you can't do in an hour? And then realized that it's not just the time wasted, but the fact that the faster job is also better? Look here for pro hints to help even the score with the pros.

Don't Screw Up!

Here you'll find *useful* ideas for keeping your thumbs attached to your hands, your eyeballs in their sockets, and your feet on the ladder.

Acknowledgments

Lots of people have contributed to my handy-guy education. Albin Myher, a kind-hearted auto worker who hired me to build an addition to his house 25 years ago; David Ahlers, a recalcitrant, opinionated, and wickedly judgmental mason who hired me as his assistant 21 years ago; Ron Gedrim, my fiercely intellectual partner in the Wisconsin Barn Board and Beam Company; former Moscow correspondent Henry Shapiro, whose astonishment at finding a journalist capable of manual work did not prevent him from hiring me to fix his house; Orlando Kjosa, a talented carpenter and true friend, who made his last canoe trip entirely too young. And there's Ken Schuster, roofer extraordinaire; Carl Lorentz, a gifted plumber who gets it right the first time and who contributed immensely to the plumbing chapters; and Robert Alexander, a scribbler's guru and veteran wordsurgeon who rose to the challenge of splicing a strand of humor into the tangled thread of home repair.

First among unequals is my wife, Meg Wise, a photographer's apprentice and pillar of support who always assumed I could write books, but is everlastingly impressed that I can replace a garbage disposal.

Special Thanks from the Publisher to the Technical Reviewers . . .

The Complete Idiot's Guide to Trouble-Free Home Repair was reviewed by experts who checked the technical accuracy of what you'll learn here, to help us ensure that this book gives you everything you need to know to begin your transformation into a handy person. Special thanks are extended to the following:

Mark Genovese is a licensed marine engineer and industrial waste water treatment plant operator for an environmental engineering firm. He actively pursues a woodworking hobby and is an assistant SYSOP for CompuServe's Family Handyman Forum. In the forum, he answers home repair questions based on his experience as "super" of several family-owned rental properties.

Don Linstroth has been a campus administrator and Chairman of Apprenticeship in the Wisconsin Technical College System since 1980. He spent thirteen years in the construction trades and six years as an instructor in the Painting and Decorating Apprenticeship Program. He served a Painting and Decorating apprenticeship, has a three-year diploma in building and estimating, an associate degree in civil-structural technology, and a B.S. degree in vocational education. He is a master's degree candidate at the University of Wisconsin-Madison.

Illustration Credits

Computer illustrations by Scott Dougald and David Tenenbaum.

The author wishes to thank the following for their kind permission to reprint artwork: W.H. Maze Company; National Manufacturing Company; Macklanburg-Duncan; Klauer Manufacturing Company, Dubuque, IA; The Glidden Company, a member of ICI Paints; The Kohler Company; Moen Incorporated; Delta Faucet Co.; and Fluidmaster. Other photography by David Tenenbaum and Meg Wise.

Part 1
You Don't Need Eight Hands to Be Handy

I'm always baffled when a brain surgeon who thinks nothing of cutting open the skull of a breathing human being is befuddled when it comes to replacing a burned-out light switch. Or when a teacher who can control, entertain, and even educate two dozen young people blanches at the thought of fixing a leaky roof.

Many homeowners think home repair is some form of rocket science, and instinctively dial 1-555-4REPAIR when they hear the complaints of an ailing house. My friend Kathy, for example, was ready to summon a plumber to replace a leaking sink trap. Instead, I lent her a pipe wrench, and she bought a replacement trap and screwed it into place. She not only saved upwards of $50, but she had the uniquely satisfying experience of being paid to learn something useful.

I think most houses are relatively simple creatures, and you, like Kathy, can do many of the repairs that you've been paying for. In Part 1, I'll explain how to start declaring independence from the home-repair professionals. I'll suggest that you examine your home—from the foundation to the wallpaper—as seen through the steel-rimmed spectacles of a hard-boiled building inspector. I'll talk about professional help—how to find the right specialist, how to compare bids, and how to get a contract that works for you. I'll even try to protect you from the universal tendency to believe you can get something for nothing.

Chapter 1

Getting Oriented to the Home-Repair Hustle

In This Chapter

➤ A realistic attitude toward home repairs

➤ The pros aren't perfect either

➤ When to fix it, and when to leave it alone

This chapter is about Murphy's Law, carpenters' adages, perfectionism, and the "hero-or-wimp" conundrum. It's about why busy homeowners should happily accept some challenges—say caulking windows or replacing their panes—and duck others—like replacing plumbing fixtures or repairing a steep, leaky roof. It's about the decisions you'll face as you ponder an upcoming home project, and about the satisfactions you'll get from tackling it.

I'll begin by demystifying the professionals, who supposedly take a cold, calculating approach to their work. I think it will boost your morale to realize that even the seasoned pros can screw up. Then we'll work on the "who-when-how" decision issues that must precede your first trip to the hardware store—or your call to a pro.

If You've Never Felt Like an Idiot, You've Never Fixed a Home . . .

Carpenters have the best adages—easy to comprehend, steeped in dry humor, and freighted with the wisdom of the ages. My favorite is this absurdity: "I cut it off three times, and it's still too short." Much more helpful is, "Measure twice, cut once." But because houses hide more pitfalls than a Tom Clancy novel, I'll expand on that: "Think thrice, measure twice, cut once."

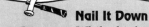

Nail It Down

While this book focuses on "repairs," it also talks about "maintenance." Generally, *maintenance* tasks—things like cleaning, painting, and caulking—are intended to keep the home in good condition, while *repairs* are designed to heal injuries. It's something like the difference between daily exercise and heart surgery: ideally—but not always—the one can prevent the other.

Doubtful? Then listen to a story about the late Orlando Kjosa, the classic "careful carpenter." For years, to save money on renovations or major repairs, and to get expert tutelage in carpentry, I used to hire my skillful, experienced, and patient friend to work alongside me. One broiling August day, Orlando spent five hours nailing in roof rafters to support a new skylight. Then he marked the opening for the skylight, and sawed deliberately, precisely, and idiotically through those same rafters.

It was not, I imagine, a day when any builder would want to be working alongside the customer, yet Orlando was unruffled—he'd been in the home building and repair business long enough to know that anything can go wrong, and everything will go wrong.

I took away a slightly different lesson—that if you've never felt like an idiot, you've never worked on a home. By liberating me from the fear of feeling stupid, that lesson helped me face subsequent projects with a certain black humor. Things will go wrong, but in the final analysis, things will also get accomplished.

Neither Hero nor Wimp: A Sensible Attitude Toward Home Repair

As I've mentioned, my attitude toward home repair was shaped by my father, who believed anything was possible. I can think of a lot of reasons why *you* might want to repair your home, but for me, it's in my blood—I am constitutionally unable to call somebody to repair a faucet or a roof.

Did that sound convincing? Well, it's not entirely accurate: my policy is to try a repair, then, if it resists too much, to call in the heavy artillery. In nine years at my present address, I'm proud to say I've not had to call an electrician. I did hire a drain cleaner to ream out a nasty clog in an underground sewer, a problem that would have taken me far deeper than I wanted to go in the drain-cleaning business.

And I've hired Carl Lorentz, a plumber friend, for three jobs over those nine years. The most recent was after I wasted an hour trying to disassemble a pigheaded faucet. After Carl wrestled with the same piece of recalcitrant metal for a sweaty half-hour, he muttered a dreaded phrase: *I need a special tool.* (Special tools are fetish objects that separate mortals like you and me from home-repair heroes like Carl.) Even with the special tool, Carl spent a couple of hours on that faucet.

I'm trying to explain that home repair is a matter of degree. Particularly when you are getting started, the smartest course is to skim the creamy jobs and hire out the gritty ones. When my roof finally gives out (the signs are there, unfortunately), I'm going to pay a roofer to replace it even though I have nailed my share of shingles (I nailed your share while reroofing a giant barn near Waterloo, Wisconsin, during a stifling heat wave). I'm willing to patch a roof that's not too steep, but I have neither the time nor the back for a whole-house job.

But just as there's no shame in acknowledging your limits, there's no shame in going for what turns you on. If you develop into an eager-beaver roofer, or look forward to augering out drain pipes, I'll stand and cheer. Likewise, if you're only interested in replacing the occasional light switch, or staining the backyard deck, I'm equally enthusiastic. In either case, you'll save some money, learn about your house, and gain confidence for your next task.

One final word on attitude: Even if you think the world is short on heroes, don't be a stupid hero and hurt yourself making a repair (see chapter 6). Even a complete idiot should know when to say "when."

Sorting out the Tasks

Although I won't presume to judge your skills in home repair, I do have some suggestions for jobs that are suitable to various levels of homeowner expertise. (As you read this, keep in mind that the list is not inclusive, and that some building codes require that you hire a licensed plumber or electrician for certain projects.)

Jobs for Beginners

> ➤ Weatherstripping doors and windows (see chapter 11)

> ➤ Replacing window panes (see chapter 12)

> ➤ Lubricating door hinges and locks (see chapter 13)

> ➤ Resurfacing an asphalt driveway (see chapter 14)

> ➤ Painting, staining, and varnishing (see chapters 22 and 23)

> ➤ Replacing outlets and switches (see chapters 24 and 25)

Jobs for the More Confident

➤ Repair on a roof that's relatively flat and low

➤ Masonry and concrete repairs (see chapters 17 and 18)

➤ Fixing large holes in plaster or drywall (see chapter 20)

➤ Installing new outlets or switches (see chapters 24 and 25)

➤ Installing small amounts of copper or plastic pipe (see chapters 27 and 28)

Jobs for a Pro

➤ Replacing windows or doors

➤ Serious drain cleaning

➤ Installing galvanized pipe

➤ Working on high or steep roofs

➤ Working on the fuse or circuit-breaker box

➤ Problems with an air conditioner

Perfect? Or Perfect Enough?

Are you a perfectionist? Does your blood congeal at the idea of leaving a job before it's flawless? I'm sorry to hear that. Perfectionism may not be a diagnosable personality disorder—at least to psychiatrists—but it is a serious obstacle to learning home repair. Nitpickers can find flaws in any repair, particularly their own. (And when they hire people for repairs, they can dramatically increase costs by demanding that the workers spend extra time satisfying their extravagant demands.)

If you're not sure whether I'm talking about you, say "perfect enough" aloud three times. If your teeth are already gnashing, cut yourself some slack. You're just learning to do home repairs, and so you'll probably have to leave some jobs "perfect enough." Consider making a training run on something that isn't obvious—adjust a basement door before tackling the front door, for example.

Then, as time passes, you'll learn what you're doing. You'll gather a better selection of tools and learn to distinguish possible jobs from preposterous ones. Then, when you're ready to play in the major leagues, be sure to say I knew you when you were just learning to pitch.

Save Yourself Some Money, and Have a Good Time

For many people, the prime motivation for doing home repairs is saving money. I wish I could tell you from experience how much you can expect to save, but I don't hire out enough work to know. I do know my annual maintenance bill (on a 1,700-square-foot Cape Cod with garage and basement) usually runs under $500.

Your checkbook should give you an idea of what you're spending. But in my area, the cost of replacing a couple of faucet washers (which sell for less than $1 in the hardware store) starts at $52—the hourly minimum charged by plumbing contractors. A roofing contractor quoted $50 per hour, plus materials, to repair a few leaks in the roof—a job you can usually take care of for about $4, including materials. And while one electrician would charge a straight $35 per hour plus materials to replace a burned-out outlet (without minimum or a trip charge), rates of $45 to $60 for the first hour were much more common.

Granted, you won't be able to make these repairs as quickly as a pro—but even if you take three times as long, you're going to save big money, particularly if you would have to pay for a whole hour for a quick repair, or pay "port to port" for travel to and from the contractor's shop.

Yet the economic imperative is not the only reason to fix your house. Equally important are the primitive gratification of swinging a hammer and the fulfillment you feel as you stand up, sweaty and grimy, and look at a job you've accomplished for the first time. And if you are lucky, you'll feel a certain intellectual thrill from figuring out why the bathtub always ran cold or the paint on the porch railing was always peeling.

And don't forget another advantage: getting the job done in the first place. If the building business is busy, there's a big chance you will have trouble finding a qualified person to take on a small job.

Finally, home repair offers you a chance to experience the most sublime form of education—being paid to be a student. Whether I was farming, salvaging lumber from old barns, or working as a mason and plasterer, I've always believed in learning while earning. And while opportunities to gain wealth and wisdom simultaneously are never as common as they should be, I bet your house has them by the carload.

If It Ain't Broke, Should You Fix It?

Have you ever stirred up a hornets' nest of home-repair trouble, then, while mulling over your options (all of them grim), been advised, "If it wasn't broke, why did you fix it?" This kind of brain-dead "wisdom" sounds reasonable enough, but it ignores the fact that most people don't deliberately stir up hornets' nests—they stumble across them.

I don't find the "ain't broke" rule very useful in home repair, and two disasters explain why. A few years ago, I tried to fix a faucet that was barely leaking, and ended up wrecking something that really wasn't broken (but when I finished, I had a brand-new kitchen faucet with some modern features). More recently, I put off painting a rusting shower stall, which seemed to have many years left. But I took a closer look, and now am going to get an unwanted lesson in installing shower stalls. I guess that's why some people are motivated to maintain their homes—so they don't have to take that kind of time-consuming lesson.

Sometimes, you have no choice—you can't play "innocent bystander" when a leaky pipe is irrigating your basement floor or the outlet behind your refrigerator fuses into a glob of molten plastic.

And even if it "ain't broke," it may not be "factory-fresh." There are shades of gray—a faucet that's dripping ever so slowly may still stain the sink or simply drive you berserk. An electrical outlet that has not yet begun sparking may still have an ominous wobble. In cases like these, you'll have to exercise judgment about whether to haul out the toolbag.

In chapter 2, I'll describe a quick home inspection that may unveil a few repair and maintenance projects. But for now, just remember this: even if it ain't broke, it might still be half-shot.

The Least You Need to Know

➤ In home repair, the perfect is the enemy of the good. Don't be afraid of making a "perfect enough" repair. Remember, rookies usually don't start in the major leagues.

➤ Size up your projects—some are easy and some are hard. Hire professionals for projects that are plain impossible. Your morale and your home will both benefit.

➤ If it ain't broke, it may still need fixing.

Chapter 2

Assessing Your Home

In This Chapter

➤ Seeing "home sweet home" with an expert's eye

➤ Inspecting the roof, foundation, walls, and floors—the bones and sinews of your home

➤ Setting priorities in your maintenance and repair plan

Have you taken a critical look at the home place recently? Have you *ever* looked dispassionately at the various components—the roof, the furnace, the foundation, walls, doors, and windows—of your dwelling? Have you crawled through the shrubbery, or gotten your pants dirty in that miserable crawl space or that hatchway into the attic?

Maybe not—who needs to look for trouble? And chances are you don't consider yourself qualified for the arcane task of inspecting a home. But while "out of sight, out of mind" may be an acceptable attitude about some possessions, it's not reasonable for something as temperamental, weatherworn, and expensive as a house. That's why I suggest taking a level-headed look at your house, with special emphasis on the all-important foundation and roof. If you're lucky, the problems you find will be the kind covered in this book, but even if you're unlucky enough to find more serious trouble, an inspection will probably save you money in the long run because you will catch the deterioration before it gets too serious. And, if you have to hire the work out, you'll have a better idea of who to call first, and what to say on the phone.

A Hyperactive Inspector Is a Homeowner's Best Friend

My friend Josh Martin was calling for some advice. He was about to close on a nice-looking house when his home inspector delivered a 75-page report bursting with phrases like "serious flaw," "needs immediate repair," and "potential liability." For example, the stones on the front path should be replaced lest a tour group of senior citizens trip, fall, and attack his homeowner's policy with a class-action lawsuit.

I read the inspector's report and tried to talk my friend out of buying this hazardous hovel. Nevertheless, Josh and his wife, Rita, ignored me, bought the place, and haven't found any major problems. In fact, they have yet to be sued (although I bet their daughter has tripped on that walk. How long, in today's litigious climate, before she sues her parents?)

Nail It Down

A *home inspector* is somebody who's in the business of assessing the physical integrity and code compliance of existing homes. They are usually hired during the sale of a home, but they can also supply an outsider's impartial view of the need for repairs. Since they will not be making the repair, they do not stand to gain by suggesting unnecessary work.

This story of a zealous inspector obsessed by trivialities is not as absurd as it sounds. In a backward way, it demonstrates what a good inspection can do: If even this paranoid fellow could not find problems with the critical systems—the foundation, structure, and roof—then the house was indeed a solid buy.

I am not advocating that you hire a home inspector, but I do suggest that you look at your place as an inspector might. Sentiment aside, how does the siding and foundation really look? If you were looking for a place that had many "unused miles," would you be impressed?

Should a sane person who already owns a home go searching for trouble? Don't most do-it-yourselfers already have the refrigerator covered with spousal "repair orders"? Because an inspection will take you to new and exotic places (not the Amazon basin or the Paris Opera, unfortunately, but to the crawl space under your kitchen, that barely accessible attic, and up on the roof). These seldom-traveled locations can harbor festering problems that will eventually burst into your consciousness—and your checking account.

An inspection can save money if you find drafts to plug, or peeling paint caused by a buildup of moisture, but its preventive value is most important on the roof. It's one thing to repair a few leaking shingles. It's quite another to replace roof boards, drywall, and rafters that were all rotted by an unnoticed leak. Look at it this way: Whether you inspect or not, you'll wind up making the repair. It's just a matter of how much you'll have to fix—and how much you'll pay.

So even if you have a list of home "to-dos," let's take a quick tour of the major parts of your house. Along the way, I'll discuss problems that a home-repair novice can cure, and problems that indicate the need for professional help.

A Worm's Eye View: Foundation, Basement, and Crawl Space

The foundation—the walls that rest on the ground and support the structure—may look homely (it's usually concrete) but it's the most important part of your house. And that's why your inspection should start at the bottom. From inside and outside, look for crumbling concrete or mortar, and loose blocks, bricks, or stones. Don't obsess about small cracks—they're common and usually harmless. But cracks that are moving, or are wider than about 1/4", can indicate serious settling. Examine the building above the crack: Are the windows and doors jammed or out-of-square? Do the floors seem level? Will a marble roll on its own across the floor? Do cracks on the interior walls indicate major movement? (I've heard of drawing a line or gluing a piece of glass across a crack to see if it's moving, but not having done it myself, I'll just pass the tips along without endorsement.) In any case, you're looking at a structural problem that's beyond idiot territory.

Do you see evidence of ants—like small holes and piles of sawdust—and termite damage—primarily tunnels from the soil to the wood? Keep an eye out for discoloration and softening that signals wood decay, particularly in damp parts of basements and crawl spaces (mini-basements where the ceiling is usually only about three feet high). If you find problems, see chapters 17 and 18 for information about foundation and basement repair.

Up on the Roof

Most roof shingles are designed to last about 25 years, but you should still check regularly for problems. Why? Because you might have cut-rate shingles that are deteriorating ahead of schedule, or perhaps the roofer flubbed the installation. Put a ladder to the edge of the roof, or use binoculars from the ground, and search for torn, missing, or curled shingles. Inspect the sheet metal flashing around skylights, vents, pipes, and chimneys. Is it nailed solidly and tarred as necessary, or is it loose or rusty? Do you see excessive use of tar or silicone on the flashing, indicating that a leak has resisted repair?

Examine the eaves troughs at the bottom of the roof for rust, plugging, and leaks. Also known as gutters, eaves troughs catch water from the roof and route it to the ground, protecting siding and windows from runoff. If you're using binoculars, you may be able to see a build-up of leaves that is probably plugging the gutter, however, binocs won't help you see if the gutters are full of mineral granules from the shingles, a sign that the roof is nearing retirement (see chapter 16). Look inside the house or attic (particularly near the chimney) for discoloration that indicates leakage. Don't ignore leaks—no matter how many reasons you can invent to make them go away, they'll just get worse.

Siding, Windows, and Doors

It may not be obvious until you think about it, but unmaintained siding, windows, and doors can become big repair items. And there's another financial incentive for keeping these items in good condition—lower energy bills. Look for large sections of peeling paint (indicating moisture migrating from the interior); fungus (a speckled discoloration that washes off in a dilute bleach solution); loose siding; delaminating plywood; and poor caulking between siding and windows, doors, trim, and vents (see chapter 15). Also look for eaves troughs overflowing over the siding, a situation that can cause leaks, staining, and decay.

Check for smooth operation and tight, draft-proof fit of doors and windows. Storm windows should be fairly tight and move easily (see chapters 12 and 13).

A Guide for the Inside

Even if the exterior passes inspection, it's a good idea to take a close look inside. Before you worry about surface defects—peeling wallpaper and butchered drywall—look for the structural problems that signal the need for major repairs. Look for crooked lines in floors, ceilings, or walls, which indicate weakening of posts, sagging of beams, or settling of the foundation. Stamp around on floors, feeling for weak spots. If you find these sorts of problems, call a carpenter before more damage occurs.

> **Handy Hint**
> Here's the one good use for cigarettes. Wait for a cold day, light up a coffin nail, and hold it near a closed window or door. The smoke will help you pinpoint drafts.

Other interior problems are unlikely to cause collateral damage, but they can make a good house look dilapidated. Examine floors for stains, gouges, degraded finish, and carpet problems (see chapter 19). Examine the drywall or plaster for cracks, decay, and discoloration (see chapter 20). Check the condition of wallpaper (chapter 21) and paint (chapters 22 and 23).

Mechanically Speaking

Broadly speaking, "mechanicals" are the systems that can't work without wires, ducts, or pipes—things like the plumbing, heating, and wiring systems. And while there's no disguising the fact that mechanical problems can be complicated, expensive, and frustrating, it's usually pretty easy to check the operation of these systems and figure out what kind of action to take.

Take a look at exposed parts of the electrical system (see chapters 24 and 25), particularly in the basement. Is the wiring shipshape—or a spider's web of sagging cables and exposed wires? Do you see a rat's nest of boxes, switches, and cables around the fuse box or circuit-breaker box? (Incidentally, breaker boxes are preferable to fuse boxes, since blown circuit breakers don't need to be replaced.) Look at the rating on the biggest fuse or the main circuit breaker to determine if the overall electrical system rated at less than 100 amps. Any of these signs may indicate an inadequate electrical system and may call for a professional evaluation (see chapters 24 and 25).

Are the outlets the three-hole, grounded type required by many modern electrical gizmos? If not, you may need to update them. Using a circuit tester, check the operation and grounding of all outlets; test all switches for correct operation—these are problems you can generally tackle.

Check that the heating and/or cooling system responds to the thermostat. Examine the condition of ducts, vents, and registers. Do the furnace and air-conditioning units look solid, with sound wiring, or do you see electrician's tape, dangling wires, and a generally disheveled appearance? These signs may mean nothing—or indicate that it's time for a checkup from the heating and cooling doctor (which is usually advisable every few years anyway).

Finally, ask your utility about a free home energy audit. These evaluations, which were popular during the energy crises in the 1970s, will tell you how to stop wasting your heating and cooling money (see chapter 26).

A Word about Priorities

Now that you've gone through the gruesome inspection process, it's time to assess the results. Some problems, like leaking roofs, drafty windows in cold climates, electrical hazards, and plumbing leaks, require immediate attention. Others, like paint and wall-paper glitches, can be deferred.

In general, builders and remodelers start with major problems and work toward the minor ones. If you found structural problems, those come first. For larger projects, it helps to organize your repairs by area of the house or type of task. In other words, do the dining room first, then move to the living room. Or do all the electrical work, then move to the plumbing, and finally the drywall and painting. If you've only got minor flaws, you can approach them in any reasonable sequence.

But don't be tempted to ignore maintenance tasks—the chores that can keep you out of big trouble down the road. Is a railing getting rusty? Then your choices are to paint it now or to replace it later on. Is the gutter getting clogged with leaves? Then you can either clean it in the fall (and think about putting on some screens to keep leaves out in the future), or have water pouring down your siding when the gutters plug up.

Some maintenance tasks—like cleaning gutters, affixing storm windows, and checking caulking and weatherstripping—must be done every year. Depending on your inclination, you might want a list of things that need annual attention. And even if you don't, it's not a bad idea to take a gander at the major home systems occasionally, just to make sure that any decay is under control.

The Least You Need to Know

➤ Building problems generally leave evidence on the surface; in general, the sooner you find and correct a problem, the less it will cost.

➤ Why you should (horrors!) go looking for trouble.

➤ Foundation, roof, and structural problems can reverberate through a building and cause multiple disasters. If you only have time to meet a few parts of your house, start with the bones, the bottom and the top.

➤ Maintenance—the recurring problem of needing to protect your home from decay and the elements—may not be glamorous, but it will save you money in the long run. (Don't believe me? Then tell my neighbor, Doug, who just called to ask for advice about replacing the studs in a wall. Why does he need this? Because an uncaulked window leaked for too long, and now the wood around it is totally rotten.)

WE'LL KNOCK OUT THIS WALL HERE...

Chapter 3

Get a Plan, Stan (Can You Do It?)

In This Chapter

➤ The role of family, job, time, and money in home care

➤ Time-saving ideas for your home fix-up strategy

➤ What you should always bring to the hardware store

➤ Building permits and your friendly neighborhood inspector

So the results of your home inspection were a bit, ah, disappointing? Instead of buried treasure, you found skeletons in the closet? A sagging beam? A crumbling foundation? Extensive water damage? Now it's time to decide what to do about these discoveries, and to assess your tools, time, and skills. Is it possible to undertake the repair yourself? Is it wise? Do you need help or advice? In other words, should you sit on the sidelines, or jump into the game?

I approached my first significant home project in an absolutely gung-ho manner—an equal blend of naiveté and foolish overconfidence. I was trying to undo the efforts of a farmer who, long before, had glued linoleum to the floor *and walls* of my kitchen. Fortunately, he didn't use waterproof paste, but I could never have anticipated how many buckets of water I'd need to slosh on those walls, and how long it would be before the reek of linoleum paste would vanish from the old farmhouse. If I'd known, I'd have thought twice about the job.

Yet as the refinished maple floor in that kitchen proves, there's a lot to be said for a "damn the torpedoes" attitude. Still, I don't advocate closing your eyes before jumping off a cliff—or starting a home repair (acts which can be almost indistinguishable). Since the first step in any significant home project is to examine your skills, I'll start by looking at that issue. Then I'll talk about some relevant social, economic, and legal factors.

Your Skills and Your Project

To decide whether you have the skills for the task, you'll need a better idea of what the task entails. Start by reading the pertinent sections of this book. If you need more information, consult library books that focus on topics I don't cover in detail, or talk with knowledgeable friends.

Once you have a better notion of what the job will require, check these pointers to help decide whether it's for you:

➤ Are you good at solving problems in this field? If you are an ace roofer but a complete zero at plumbing, take this into account.

➤ Do you own—or know where to borrow or rent—the tools you'll need?

➤ Can you get professional advice—suggested for a major project—if you need it?

➤ Can you do the work alone or will you need help?

➤ How soon must the project be finished, and will bad weather hold you up?

➤ How long will it take?

➤ How much of your house will be out of commission (due to shutting off the electricity or water, or because floors are covered by tools or dropcloths)? Some rooms are expendable, but bathrooms and kitchens should not be off-limits for long.

Your Family and Your Project

You imagine that your project won't disrupt your family, because you're not ripping old linoleum out of the kitchen, you're just replacing a "now-you-see-light-and-now-you-don't" light switch. That's great—even if it won't rival the Magna Carta as a contribution to civilization. So you make the ritual trip to the hardware store, assemble your tools, and start shutting off circuits. Then you hear a shriek from your spouse, whose blacked-out computer just devoured three hours' worth of unsaved work while you were randomly snapping off circuit breakers.

That problem could have been avoided if you'd heeded the home-repairer's cardinal maxim: Communicate, communicate, and communicate. At least make sure your family knows—and, if necessary, approves—your plans. In my case, for example, even though I wash most of the dishes, I would still ask my wife to advise on the purchase of a new kitchen faucet. The best bet is to schedule your repair and maintenance projects when there will be a minimum of disruption. (However, keep in mind that if you injure yourself, you'll be happy to have somebody around for assistance.)

Your Job and Your Project

The impact of home projects can extend to your workplace. How will your boss respond when you blame a late arrival at work on an emergency trip to the plumbing supplier for a "bezel-to-bezerk" fitting? Will your boss care that you were trying to save your family another day without running water?

> **Handy Hint**
> If you list the rooms and appliances served by each circuit or fuse (see "Making a Circuit Map" in chapter 24), you can easily shut off only the right circuit. Just to play it safe, use your circuit tester to double-check that the outlet is "cold" before sticking your fingers in it.

As somebody who has scarcely had a boss over the past 20 years, I'd be the last to advise you on handling this peculiar species. But it does make sense to work around job strictures, maximize the use of weekends and vacations, and set realistic expectations, particularly at first. Be sensible.

Your Time and Your Project

If Murphy (the lawgiver) wasn't a fixer-upper, he must have been in the remodeling business. "If anything can go wrong," the wise Murphy told us, "it will go wrong, and at the worst possible moment." That's putting it mildly.

In my experience, the most excusable memory lapse in the building-supply store is guaranteed to require a second trip so you can finally get the *right* reducer to hook up the $3/4$" elbow to the $1/2$" pipe coming from your water heater. The merest error when measuring the thickness of a roof board inevitably results in a second trip to the lumber yard. And saws don't slip—until you're making the last cut on an extremely complicated, one-of-a-kind replacement board.

If you feel obligated to estimate how long a job will take, think hard about how many hours it should require, then multiply that figure by two or three. (For better accuracy, throw some dice. Making estimates is the toughest part of repairing—just ask anyone who does it for a living.)

Tips for Saving Time

There are some ways to reduce your burden under Murphy's Law, and save some time on home repairs. I'll admit that most of the suggestions on the following pages sound pretty pedestrian, but I'll lay them out and let you ignore any or all of them. Generally, I suggest systems that you set up in your spare time; in the midst of a repair, who can be bothered labeling nails or organizing tools?

1. Store your tools intelligently. In chapter 7, "The Bare Essentials: Hand Tools," I've made suggestions for a ready-to-go toolkit. Keep other tools in their places (a pegboard, with its customized hooks, makes excellent organized, visible storage). If you don't need to search for tools, you can get right to work.

2. Use labels. I keep a stack of adhesive mailing labels and a marker in the workshop so I don't have to grope for $1\frac{1}{2}$" drywall screws or 16-penny nails.

3. Store containers with the label facing out. This sounds anal-compulsive, but it saves time and groping around.

4. To avoid extra trips to the hardware or building supply store, keep a supply of extra, broken, and didn't-fit parts on hand (see chapter 9, "Keeping It Together: Buying and Using Fasteners and Materials"). And when you're in the store, why not plan on buying extra nails or screws? After all, you needed them once, so you're likely to need them again, and the dollar price of some extras will probably be cheaper than another trip to the store.

5. Don't lose stuff. This sounds breathtakingly obvious until you squander a quarter-hour searching for a screw that was "here just a minute ago." Remember the advice of conservationist Aldo Leopold: "The first rule of intelligent tinkering is to save all the parts." (Leopold was talking about preventing species extinctions, but his advice derived from the fix-up trade.) Keep tin cans and plastic containers around to hold small parts, and use them, even for a five-minute repair. (Tiny parts can enter the Twilight Zone much quicker than that.)

6. Know what you're doing—by reading this and other books, and talking with people who have been in your shoes. Got a drain that's getting slow? Then mention this casually at the next ice-cream social. Maybe Nelson will stop blathering about his golf score for a millisecond and talk about something useful, like how he fixed a similar problem. Who knows? He might even offer to lend you a pipe wrench.

7. Always bring the dead carcass of whatever you're replacing to the store (unless you're replacing a refrigerator, that is). You may be amazed at how many sizes, features, threads, and materials the store stocks for any particular part; only with the old one in hand can you choose correctly.

8. And bring a list to the store so you don't return half-shopped.

9. Rent those fun, heavy-duty tools, "just like the pros abuse." These macho monsters can shave hours from many miserable tasks, like heavy-duty sawing, drilling into concrete, or tedious nailing jobs (see chapter 8, "The Bare Essentials with Oomph! Power Tools").

10. Don't start an optional plumbing or electrical fix when your relatives are arriving. Ditto for weekends—you'll be lucky if specialty stores are open at all on Saturday, and they are sure to close at noon—just before you drive up with your busted parts.

11. Number and sequence all parts as you take things apart.

Building Codes and Your Job

Once, before starting to build a porch on my farmhouse, I called the township building inspector to ask about a building permit. He wasn't home, so I started the foundation. A week later, he delicately asked whether I was "thinking of getting a permit." As I muttered some half-truths about my heroic efforts to reach him, he cut me off: "I'll be out that way tomorrow, and we'll write one up." He did, and we did, and that was that.

I wouldn't count on such understanding treatment from building inspectors nowadays. These folks are zealots who have memorized codes containing uncountable paragraphs on the size, safety, structure, materials, and use of a living space. Codes or local laws may also govern who can do the work; in some localities, for example, only licensed contractors can do certain electrical and plumbing tasks.

> **Nail It Down**
> A *building code* is a rulebook your municipality uses to govern building construction and repair. A *building permit* is a document issued to a contractor or building owner that allows a project to be started, as long as it adheres to plans on file with the building inspector. When you're done (and perhaps even in mid-project as well) the inspector will come to check that you've followed your plans—and the code.

It's tough to generalize about building codes, since there are at least three in the United States, not to mention codes covering natural gas, electricity, plumbing, heating, ventilating, and air-conditioning. In many cases, you can replace stuff without a permit, but you may need a permit to make a significant change. You are not likely to need a permit to replace a window (a project that novices are not advised to tackle anyway), since that's replacing an existing feature. But you might need a permit to cut in a new window, since that's a structural alteration. In some municipalities, re-roofing requires a permit, particularly if the existing roof must be stripped off. In other cases, a permit may be required if the price of the project exceeds a certain dollar value.

Building inspectors won't give out information from the code, even to the taxpayers who pay their salaries. If you plan to span a certain opening with a 2' × 12' beam, they will tell you whether that is acceptable. But if you inquire what the code requires to span that opening, they'll stay mum. It's maddening, but they do have a rationale: the former question is to check that your plans meet code—an inspector's function—while the latter relates to designing buildings—an architect's or engineer's function.

After repeated dealings with building inspectors, I've concluded that they ask tough questions not just to learn about your *plans*, but also to learn about your *skills*. Once you convince them that you can distinguish a finial from a fascia board, they will be more inclined to "sign off" on your project.

Trouble, with a capital *T*, occurs when an improvement triggers a requirement that the whole room, system, or building be "brought up to code." But that's unlikely to affect your efforts to replace a storm window or realign a door. If in doubt, ask your inspectors, but don't go out of your way to make the job sound bigger than it is. Warding off trouble is one thing; begging for it is quite another.

One final note on building inspectors and permits: after your project is finished, the building *assessor* might want to come visit to see whether the project has increased the value of your house.

Friends and Pros—Vital Sources of Help and Information

Chances are some of your friends do home repair for fun, which makes them potential sources of information or assistance. I have an informal work-trading arrangement with my friend Doug Swaine, who's a recovering general contractor (a fact that must contribute to his relaxed manner). When I needed help installing new kitchen counters, I found that he had actually done it before. (I was confident about bluffing my way through, but his expertise made everything faster and smoother. I'll probably have to repay him eventually on a hideous masonry repair, but that's our deal.)

When it comes to learning from professionals, working alongside them is probably the best option—but there are others. Pay attention next time you hire somebody to work on the house. Which part of the job does the repairer do first? What tools are important enough to live in the toolbox? What special power tools would you rent to do this job? How does a plumber thread a pipe? All these observations—let alone what you can learn from a talkative person—will come in handy down the line.

The Least You Need to Know

➤ If you value your family life, keep the lines of communication open before and during your project.

➤ A little planning, a little luck, and a stockpile of tools and parts will save time on any repair.

➤ Most repairs will not require a building permit, but it pays to check in advance for bigger projects.

HAAAAALP!!

Dial Up for Building Rescue

Let's assume you've rationally decided that your skills, ambitions, and time don't permit you to tackle a problem—perhaps it's an electrical project calling for the special tools needed to bend conduit (the thin pipe that carries wires). Perhaps that little roof leak actually signalled the need for an entire reroofing job, and you simply don't have the time. Perhaps it's a carpentry job that calls for the physical strength of an ox. Perhaps it's clearly beyond your understanding—a plumbing disaster that you just don't grasp.

All these questions present a simple question: Who will do the work? Although I'll devote the rest of this book to helping you handle your own repair projects, I don't intend to abandon you when you reach for the phone book and try to figure out which advertisements are credible and which are pure hocum.

So let's spend a couple of chapters talking about finding the right "someone else." In other words, how to find, evaluate, hire, and live with a good contractor.

Do They Have What It Takes?

Just to bring you up-to-date on the 20th century, even though the people in the home-repair business may have been created equal, some have turned out better than others. When I was in the masonry business, I never left an unsatisfied customer. I returned every phone call and never treated anybody rudely. And despite my affordable prices, my work was flawless.

Just kidding. But I never pulled the kind of monkey business uncovered recently by the New York State Department of Consumer Affairs. In response to a litany of complaints from homeowners, these consumer cops rented a house, mounted some concealed video cameras, summoned 65 contractors for various repairs, and wound up charging 23 of them with fraud. Some were overeager—an appliance repairer who found a towel jammed in a water pump replaced the entire pump, even though it worked perfectly once the rag was fished out. Others were under-eager—a chimney sweep, for example, climbed the roof and returned to the ground without ever touching the chimney (see "Scams" in Chapter 5).

As a homeowner, you have legal protections, even if you don't have electronic spy equipment. Many states require licenses for some tradespeople, such as general contractors, electricians, and plumbers. What this actually means varies from state to state, but it may give you some leverage in a dispute. If the license number is not on the contract, ask to see a copy. But it's better to avoid problems in the first place by "qualifying" your repairer. Start by gathering information from friends and neighbors; make a point of asking who nailed on that beautiful new roof, or who gouged that once-promising oak floor. You can also contact the standard sources—the Better Business Bureau and the local department of consumer affairs.

What Kind of Help Do You Need?

Once, builders were carpenters or masons. Nowadays, the trades have subdivided until you might need a doctorate in construction management to puzzle out the Yellow Pages. As you read the following descriptions of who does what, remember that when the building business is busy, everybody gets picky—carpenters won't do roofing, and painters won't do gutters. When the business slacks off, repairers suddenly find they have forgotten skills.

In cold regions, winter is the slow season for people who work outside, particularly roofers, masons, and painters (although painters may have inside work, and some masonry jobs are enclosed). Electricians, plumbers, and drywallers are less affected by weather, as most of their work is inside. Much of this is common sense: Heating technicians are busiest in fall, and air-conditioning folks in the spring or early summer.

If you find that your repair project is too picayune to interest a builder, try letting a few repairs build up until your list is attractive to somebody who's trying to make a living. Or call a handyperson.

Handymen and -Women

If you've made a dozen calls looking for someone to repair a defective light switch, you're probably ready for an old-fashioned handyperson. These are the people who fill the gap between your skills and those of the big contractors. Generalizing about these folks is not going to help much; about all they have in common is a van, home-repair skills, and experience. To find a handyperson, ask a friend or look on the bulletin board at the hardware store. If you've only got a small project, there's no point going through an FBI-style investigation of someone's skills.

Carpenters

Carpenters do woodwork, everything from repairing wood siding to installing new windows and making doors close smoothly. Carpenters can also help with structural problems, such as sagging beams or rotten posts. Carpenters generally shy away from other specialties, but it's worth asking if one will fix a gutter or a roof leak.

General Contractors

"Generals" are builders—often carpenters—who direct "subcontractors," or "subs." In return for dealing with the inevitable hassles, conflicts, and screw-ups of a big building project, generals receive a percentage of each sub's pay.

It sounds like a hustle—after all, you can tell an electrician where to install an outlet just as easily—but it's not. Generals only work on big jobs, when somebody must anticipate and solve conflicts between the subs. Is the plumber planning to run a hefty drain line where the carpenter wants to put a beam? If so, the general can make a snap decision so the subs can keep working. Generals also have leverage over the subs, who may be working for them on another job next week.

Having said all that, you probably won't be meeting any general contractors in the course of home repairs, which usually involve only one or at most two trades. Nevertheless, it's worth understanding their role, in case you ever contemplate remodeling (in which case, take two Prozac and think it over carefully in the daylight—but that's another book).

Drywallers and Plasterers

Either of these trades (see chapter 20) may be willing to take on repair work, particularly when new jobs are scarce. But don't expect to get help for a small nick in the wall—that's more likely to interest a handyperson. And remember the wild card in wall repair: If the framing is rotten or damaged, the repair cannot begin until the wall is torn apart and repaired.

If a drywaller suggests putting a new layer of drywall over a damaged wall, remember to add the cost of altering moldings and door and window jambs to the cost of drywalling. Repair may be cheaper.

Sparky the Electrician

Electricians deal with most parts of home wiring, from the electric meter to the last outlet. They install conduit, connect the electric meter to the breaker box, and install outdoor and underground wiring. However, electricians are unlikely to work on the following:

➤ The "drop"—which connects the utility lines or buried supply cable to your electric meter (it's usually maintained by the utility company)

➤ Cable television and alarm systems

➤ Phone wiring, which is repaired by you or a phone installer

➤ HVAC wiring—the province of heating and cooling specialists

Hot Shots in the Heating, Ventilating, and Air-Conditioning (HVAC) Business

HVAC folks work on the heating and cooling plant (the furnace and air-conditioner), the controls that tell these machines when to work, and the ducts or pipes that distribute the heat or cold. Some companies may specialize in oil burners or gas furnaces, or in hot-water or steam heat-distribution systems. In certain areas, these trades are licensed. HVAC companies also will perform routine maintenance on your heating/cooling equipment, such as an annual tune-up.

Plumbers, Drain Cleaners, and Other Snake Charmers

Plumbers are the astronauts of the contracting world: they earn stellar sums in return for installing and maintaining the pipes that handle fresh and waste water, venting of drains, and natural gas. Partly, that's because their trucks must be rolling warehouses of steel, plastic, and copper pipe, reducers, and elbows. And let's face it, it's partly because they spend their days doing plumbing.

Septic-Tank Cleaners ("A Flush Beats a Full House")

(Think I invented that one? I wish I were that creative. That's the slogan of a real, live septic-tank cleaner who used to advertise around here.)

The idea behind toilets is simple: "Flush and forget." But that's not always possible if you have a septic tank, a home sewage system which decomposes that-which-you-flush and makes water and sewage sludge. When sludge builds up, it must be pumped out or the system will malfunction—an aromatic and polluting prospect. A periodic pump-out by a septic-tank cleaner is suggested for all septic systems; to protect the groundwater, some states even require pump-outs.

The Original Rockers: Masons and Concrete Workers

Masons build chimneys, fireplaces, and foundations with concrete block, brick, and stone (see chapters 17 and 18). Some will also do concrete work, or at least concrete repair, but don't assume—ask. Some concrete workers specialize in "flat work"—driveways, floors, and steps. Others specialize in form work, meaning foundations and other walls. "Mud-jackers" or "slab-jackers" can raise sunken slabs of concrete in driveways and sidewalks, saving the cost of replacement.

A Primer on Painters

Painting is about the cheapest trade to enter, and simple paint jobs are not exactly rocket science, so painters range from college students to lifers. Some painters make minor repairs to trim or gutters, but all should be prepared to do as much preparation as the job requires (see chapters 22 and 23). Preparations protecting shrubbery, scraping paint, repairing siding and trim, and applying primer can take as much work as the actual painting.

The Top Trade: Roofers

Roofers have one thing in common—they love heights. Some do only shingling; some specialize in tar-and-gravel flat roofs. A roofer will usually detach and reinstall gutters, but whether they will take on a new gutter job might depend on the current demand for roofing.

Exterminators Won't Bug You

Bugs! Most insects play valuable ecological roles in pollination, controlling other insects, and decaying organic matter. But your home is not ecology—in fact, you probably want to remove it from the food chain altogether. Some insect problems can be controlled by changing the conditions in your house so it's less attractive to insects (see "The Enemies of Wood" in chapter 10).

If your insect-control measures don't work, call an exterminator. I suspect exterminators are a mite overzealous when it comes to bugs, but then so are many homeowners. If you're queasy about the chemicals they're using, get information from a library, or from state or federal environmental or health regulators. The exterminator should supply a Material Safety Data Sheet (MSDS), which details the health effects of the pesticides used.

Other Specialists

You thought we were finished? Not in this hyper-specialized era:

➤ Flooring experts usually specialize in tile, carpet, or wood.

➤ Refinishers sand and revarnish wood floors.

➤ Basement waterproofers do what the name implies. Caution: They tend to start with the most expensive solution. See chapter 18, "May We Talk about Your Soggy Basement."

➤ Door and window installers replace doors and windows and install storm windows and skylights.

➤ Garage-door repairers—guess what they do?

➤ Landscape contractors plant trees and shrubs and build decks, fences, and gazeboes.

➤ Phone installers add new lines or repair existing ones.

➤ Siding installers may specialize in aluminum or vinyl.

➤ Gutter installers may install "seamless" gutter, which is formed from a roll of flat aluminum. With fewer joints, seamless gutters should have fewer leaks.

The Least You Need to Know

➤ If you don't want to tackle a problem, plenty of specialists are willing to do it for you, particularly if the project is large enough or you can group several repairs.

➤ Make sure your job falls within the expertise of your contractor.

➤ The best source of information on repairers is friends and neighbors.

Chapter 5

Control with a Contract—and Live to Tell about It!

In This Chapter

➤ Qualifying contractors

➤ The difference between an estimate, a bid, and a contract

➤ How the contract specifies the job

➤ How to protect yourself from building scams

If you are lucky, you've identified reliable contractors who will arrive promptly, do the job right the first time, and charge reasonable fees. With these repairers, you may feel no need for a contract. And for a job costing less than a couple of hundred dollars, the contract may be unwritten (although you should certainly understand the terms in advance).

Larger jobs—and those done by unfamiliar contractors—should be backed by a contract, the size and complexity of which should reflect the scope of the job. For a simple re-shingling, one page might be sufficient. But a bathroom or kitchen renovation calls for a detailed, comprehensive contract, covering carpentry, drywalling, electrical work, cabinets, and plumbing.

In this chapter, I'll describe how to evaluate a contractor, how to negotiate the terms of the job, and how to arrive at a contract. I will also describe how to protect yourself from rip-off artists who prey on homeowners.

Calling All Contractors

Now that you've identified some candidate contractors, it's time to call a few. In general, unless the job is tiny, or an emergency, call three contractors so you can compare their prices and approaches to the job.

On the phone, don't just describe your job and ask about prices. Inquire about the contractor's expertise and experience:

➤ How long have you been in business?

➤ Are you a member of a trade association?

➤ Are you insured?

➤ Are you state-licensed? (If so, the estimate form should carry the license number.)

➤ Do you charge for an estimate? (They shouldn't.)

When the repairer arrives to inspect your job, you'll get a chance to inspect him or her. Do they take a serious look at the project, or breeze through and rattle off a price? Do they explain things so you can understand, or rely on baffling jargon? Are they in a hurry, insisting that you sign for the job right now?

Time and Materials, Estimates, Bids, and Contracts

Home repairers use a variety of systems for charging—time and materials, a flat price, or something in between. No matter what the method, you should not have to pay for time looking the job over or writing an estimate.

Many repairers bill small jobs by "time and materials"—the hours they work, plus the materials they use. If the contractor is honest, you can benefit, because the contractor won't have to pad a fixed price to account for unexpected problems.

Appliance repairers and phone installers commonly levy a "job charge" for the first fraction of an hour, and a lower rate for subsequent fractions. If they cannot finish the job on the first visit, you should not have to pay a second job charge. Many building repairers charge a minimum rate for the first hour, and they may charge from the moment they leave their shop.

Larger repair and remodeling projects should be preceded by some negotiation over price. Amateurs—and some builders—talk about "estimates," "bids," and "contract prices" as if they're the same thing. Before we clarify what they mean, remember that local terminology can differ—be sure you understand what the price does and does not cover.

➤ An *estimate* is a rough guess as to what the job will cost. It may have little relation to actual cost, depending on your choice of materials, what the builder finds when the project begins, and how often you change your mind.

➤ A *bid* is a closer approximation of the cost, after you have selected materials and narrowed your options. It may still be lower than the final price, depending on your changes, the project's surprises, and the contractor's honesty and skill.

➤ A *contract price* is a binding agreement between you and the contractor. It should specify all tasks and materials, and the job schedule, the payment schedule, and what will happen when the predictable surprises arise.

Comparing Prices

So you followed instructions (see "Calling All Contractors," previous page) and got three prices. Will you automatically accept the lowest price? After all, isn't that the point of getting three bids? Not exactly. The bidding process is also a chance for you to size up the bidders. Ask questions. Call references and look at previous jobs, if you're unsure who's going to be best.

Now that the contractors are no longer just voices on the phone, are you confident the lowest bidder will do a good job? Does this person have the best grasp of what's involved? Did the price include all the costs listed in the other prices? Does it specify the same quality materials and brands?

If so, you've saved money and aggravation, and you can start working with the low-price contractor to finalize a contract. But if you have a queasy feeling at this point, take a closer look at the other bidders. Do whatever it takes to convince yourself that you've chosen the cream of the crop. Remember—when the job is finished, you shouldn't feel like taking out a contract on your contractor.

The Contract

Building contracts are largely boilerplate—standard text written by lawyers who work for contractors. Because contracts are written from the builder's perspective, you may want to seek legal advice before signing a contract for an expensive or complex project. And even if you don't hire a lawyer, remember that you can discuss problematic areas of the contract and attempt to change them to suit your needs.

These contracts typically contain six sections: names and addresses of both parties; scope of the project; completion date; payment schedule; signature and date; and general conditions of the work. Although most of the contract is self-explanatory, let's take a look at a couple of sections.

The completion date may not be as early as you'd prefer, particularly if the building business is booming. Even if you don't want to wait several months for completion, you may have to wait a while. But that's not so bad—do you want a contractor who's in demand, or one who can't keep busy?

In the payment schedule, it's best to reserve at least 20 percent—and preferably much more—for a final payment that is due when you are satisfied. If the final payment is too small, it will not give you enough leverage to ensure that the finishing touches are completed. Keep in mind the hidden costs—like interest costs or the price of take-out pizza while a kitchen is being remodeled. You might also consider setting a deadline for completion, with specified penalties for non-performance.

Probably the most important section of the contract is its description of the project. This section should specify exactly what will be done, in terms you can understand (or the contractor can explain). It's not enough to say, "Replace the roof with new shingles." Instead, the contract should detail the steps: "Remove shingles down to bare wood. Replace tar paper and re-roof in 240-lb per square 'mortuary black' fiberglass shingles from Tar Pit Shingle Conglomerate. Install new edging and valley flashing. Inspect all flashing. Remove and reinstall existing gutters. Remove trash when done. Any replacement of rotten boards, and flashing (aside from valley flashing), will be done at extra charge."

The conditions section typically specifies that the work will be done "in a workmanlike manner." While this may sound as concrete as a jellyfish, a court can interpret this phrase simply by asking somebody in the same trade if the work is acceptable. Finally, contracts can specify that disputes be settled by mediation or arbitration (legal negotiation processes that help you avoid a lawsuit), which may save time and money over going to court.

Time to Pay the Piper

After a job is completed, and before you write a check, make a detailed inspection with the contractor. If anything is puzzling, now's the time to ask about it. If anything is unsatisfactory, now's the time to complain about it. The ground rule is this: Don't pay until you're satisfied. And for jobs that take some time to set up, like masonry or painting, don't pay until it's really done.

If your job is big enough to require a building permit, don't pay until the inspector "signs off" that the job meets code standards. The building code is a minimum standard, and a job that's only medium quality will still pass the code. Furthermore, while there's no guarantee that the inspector will notice every flaw, he or she does provide an expert, outside evaluation of the work, which is not something you can afford to ignore. Finally, builders tend to listen to building inspectors, who can make their lives miserable by adopting a nit-picking attitude toward future inspections.

A Word on How Contractors Really Work

Now that you've signed a contract, you sit back and wait for the crew to arrive. And, sometimes, you wait. And even after the work gets started, you find strange absences—say at the opening of trout fishing season, or for no discernible reason. The job is poised for completion, and nobody shows up.

The explanation for this pattern may damage your self-image as the most important customer in the world. Fact is, the builder must start looking for new jobs—visiting prospects, making bids, and drawing up plans—before your project is completed. There's no other way to stay in business.

It's entirely possible that your contractor is working several jobs at once—since the competition will not take over a half-finished job. Is that kosher? I guess it depends on your perspective, but it's a fact of life in the building business, and one you should be prepared for.

Scams

Trust me—no single book could possibly vaccinate you against the human capacity for concocting convincing scams. The usual rule is still the best: if something seems too good to be true, it probably is. Trust your instincts.

Be ready to recognize these standard symptoms of home repair hustlers:

➤ They pressure you to sign right now, and want large amounts of money up front.

➤ They cruise the neighborhood, looking for immediate work "to use up the supplies from my last job."

➤ They are reluctant to give references.

➤ They have a quick answer for everything.

➤ Their explanations raise more questions than they answer.

Many states allow you to renege on door-to-door contracts (including those for repairs) for a few days after signing. If you have that queasy feeling that you've fallen for a fast-buck artist, take advantage of this "cooling-off period."

The Least You Need to Know

➤ You should be able to understand your repairer's explanations. If not, trouble may be on the way.

➤ If you recognize that builders must think about other jobs, you'll be in a better position to work together.

➤ Trust your instincts when it comes to building scams—if it seems too good to be true, it probably is.

Part 2
Safety, Tools, and Materials: The Building Blocks of Success

I hope you didn't expect to get away without buying, begging, or borrowing some tools. Home repair is like hockey—a sport that requires equipment. But because my object is to help you get on with your life, not to make your wallet feel like it got zapped by a hockey puck, I'll emphasize versatility, improvisation, and economy rather than buying tools for the sake of buying tools. Having said that, there's still an argument for buying special tools on occasion—they can pay for themselves in one use. When you ponder the universal tool problem (where can I get my hands on the right ones without bankrupting my family?), don't forget that a friendly neighbor may own just what you need.

Materials are the other thing you'll be buying, so I'll talk about nails, screws, and other hardware, and about wood, the organic heart of most housing. Because your body is your most important tool, I'll start with safety.

Q: What's worse than an accident?

A: An accident that could have been prevented by following safety practices.

Accidents, it turns out, are almost all avoidable, if you use common sense and don't set yourself up by acting stupid.

Chapter 6

Health, Safety, and Common Sense

> ## In This Chapter
>
> ➤ Danger spots—and how to avoid them
>
> ➤ The stupidity factor and accidents
>
> ➤ Keeping away from nasty chemicals

Where to start a discussion of safety? According to some paranoids, frying an egg exposes you to shock hazards from the electric stove, burning hazards from the pan, intestinal hazards from egg-borne bugs, and arteriosclerotic hazards from butter-borne fat. And that's not to mention the danger of slipping on the way to the table or goring yourself with the fork. . . .

That's not my attitude. I'll stress the major safety hazards—the areas you really need to watch. And I'll talk about some attitude problems—primarily the stupidity factor—and certain work practices that grease the skids toward accidents. I'll talk about health hazards you might encounter in your home-repair battles, and discuss a limited but highly effective safety kit which should protect you from most of those hazards. And I'll talk about safe use of ladders, which account for the lion's share of home-repair accidents.

The Stupidity Factor

A couple of years ago, trying to rig up a hoist to lift my canoe, I confidently leaned my 14' ladder against the locust tree along the driveway, and climbed up. Having written a book for painters, I knew I wasn't supposed to do this, but I did it anyway. When I reached the top, the ladder suddenly flipped, and before I could react, we squashed some shrubbery. I was dazed, although fortunately intact.

I could not avoid feeling extremely stupid, but the experience itself taught me the easiest way to prevent such embarrassment: Don't do stupid stuff. If you really must lean a ladder against a tree, find a football lineman to anchor the ladder. Or buy those straps made to secure ladders to trees. Best of all, forget the whole idea.

And the canoe hoist? It didn't work, either. Serves me right.

Because the stupidity factor is behind so many accidents, I'm offering some *suggestions for working safely by controlling the universal human urge to act like a complete bozo*:

➤ Don't work when you are exhausted, distracted, or angry. Any of these conditions can cause you to rush, ignore hazards, or just plain act stupid.

➤ Keep the place neat: coil electric cords so you don't trip on them; stack lumber neatly so it's not strewn all over the place; don't leave boards with nails sticking up, ready to impale you; and store and use sharp tools with caution, so they cut only what they're supposed to cut.

➤ Don't try to do things without first understanding what needs to be done and how to do it.

➤ Get help with big tasks—holding something while you fasten it into place, hauling heavy objects, or holding ladders if you're not sure they are stable enough.

➤ Work with adequate lighting, so you can spot and avoid hazards.

For suggestions on electrical safety, see Chapter 24.

Protect Yourself (No One Else Will)

Do you adore arsenic or crave chromium? Well, neither does wood fungus, the lower life form that gobbles up wood posts, decks, and almost any wood that is constantly wet. That's why most pressure-treated lumber contains the toxic chemical CCA (chromated copper arsenate). So if you don't protect yourself while sawing or sanding treated lumber, you'll breathe a good dose of arsenic and chromium (yum! yum!).

CCA is one of many ways in which repair work can expose you to dust, grit, and toxic chemicals. But because you are not facing a day-after-day, industrial exposure, it's usually pretty easy to shield yourself with prevention, common sense, and protection.

To *prevent* toxic exposure, use a product that contains no toxic materials. For example, if you use the relatively new water-based coatings, you may not need protection against the nasty ingredients in solvent-based paints (but check the label to be sure—some still contain toxic solvents). If I were building a new deck, I'd buy the new pressure-treated lumber that does not contain CCA—not because it would entirely eliminate the toxic exposure, but because it would reduce that exposure.

Another way to prevent exposure is to let George do it. Instead of using a toxic paint stripper, take furniture to a commercial stripper (a company that strips finishes inside tanks). That way, you can forget about protecting yourself against the toxic crud found in most paint strippers.

Common sense tells you to read the label and follow exposure precautions. Use toxic chemicals outside, or at least with the windows open. Common sense also says that since things will go wrong, you should anticipate as many problems as you can and take steps to minimize their impact.

After you have exercised prevention and common sense, you'll want to keep some protective measures available (see the illustration in this chapter of health and safety equipment you should consider having).

> **Handy Hint**
> If you're concerned about the toxicity of materials you are using, ask the store or manufacturer to supply a material safety data sheet (MSDS), which must, by law, be available to users of the product.

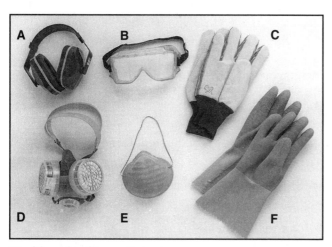

Health and safety equipment

(A) Ear protectors (the kind worn by people who guide jets on airport runways) will dampen the shriek of a circular saw or router. Use them if you like your hearing, or are working indoors, where echoes amplify the noise. Or use ear plugs, which are cheaper and equally effective.

(B) Goggles are helpful for nailing, hammering, sawing, demolishing, drilling, sanding, or any other home repair sport that makes dust, chips, or other flying crud. They are *great* for working overhead.

(C) A pair of leather work gloves is useful for handling rough lumber, working with concrete, and wrecking stuff.

(D) A snugly fitting respirator will protect you against various organic solvents and dusts (buy the cartridge according to the specific hazard you face, like dust or organic solvents).

(E) A dust mask, even this cheapo pollen mask, is used while sanding, wrecking, sawing, and sweeping.

(F) Rubber gloves are excellent for painting, working with paint stripper, and other toxic tasks. Remember—many solvents can pass right through your skin.

Another good safety item is a pair of stiff work boots. For real abuse, steel-toed boots have a steel liner to protect your toes from dropped tools.

Nervous about Leaded Paint?

If your home is at least 15 years old, chances are it has some paint containing lead. (A good pigment, it was used in many types of paint, particularly for trim, enamel, and exteriors.) Lead is toxic to the adult nervous system and much more harmful to children, who can be harmed by tiny exposures. To find out if lead is in various painted surfaces in your home, you'll have to take samples to a public-health or toxicology laboratory.

You can get leaded paint professionally removed, if you have the money (but check local regulations on lead removal first). A better option may be to keep the paint in good condition, and use caution any time you might raise dust, such as by sawing or sanding.

Basic Steps to Ladder Safety

So the leaking thing-a-ma-jubber up near the eaves has put you in the mood for some second-story work? So your roof needs an inspection (and, you pray, nothing more)? What to do? You burrow into the garage, bring out that old wooden ladder, and bet your life some kind of rot hasn't eaten its way through anything important.

Wrong.

You look at the job, clear away any obstacles, then go into your storage area and look over your ladders. You pick out the right one, inspect it for damage, and bring it to the job. You look overhead for electrical wires, and safely raise the ladder. Then you check that the ladder is soundly erected. Finally, you begin climbing.

Remember: One fall from a ladder is one too many. From the vast menu of *ladder safety rules*, these seem most important:

1. Inspect the ladder before using it, to make sure it hasn't deteriorated since you last used it.

2. Make sure the footing under the ladder is solid, so the ladder does not slip away from the wall.

3. The foot of the ladder should be $1/4$ of the height away from the wall. This gives the best stability—the best combination of staying upright without tipping over backwards.

4. Check that your shoes are dry, so you don't slip on the rungs.

5. When climbing, hold your hands on the rails (the long side beams), not the rungs. Then, if you start to fall, your hands will be in position to grip the ladder.

6. Don't climb above the third rung from the top, because you will be unstable and likely to fall.

7. Don't carry more than one hand's worth of stuff, or you won't be able to grasp the ladder securely. If you need more tools or materials, get a nail apron, use bigger pockets, make another trip, or rig up a rope hoist.

8. As my father used to tell me, "One hand for yourself, and one for your work." In other words, hold on with one hand. If you absolutely must work with both hands, wrap one arm through the rungs, to hold yourself in case of a slip.

9. Keep your center of gravity inside the rails, so you don't tip the ladder sideways, and don't lean too far back, so you don't tip it over backwards.

10. Take the time to move the ladder so you can reach the work easily. Leaning to the side is asking for a fall.

Ladders are an excellent place for neighbors to pool resources, since they're used rarely. Another alternative is to discuss a barter with a neighbor who's long on ladders.

In some cases, the ladder you need won't be a ladder at all, but a rented scaffold. Scaffolding is particularly handy for large siding repairs, big tuckpointing (brick-joint repair) jobs, painting, and window replacement. When renting a scaffold, remember to ask about renting planks (the boards you walk on). They cost extra, but they are worth it. Why bother renting a real scaffold and then stand on those old 2 × 10s you've been storing by the compost heap? (Hint: consider renting aluminum planks, which are lighter and easier to handle than wooden planks.)

Handy Hint
If you really must work near electric lines, ask your electric utility to install rubber insulating sheaths over the wires. Utilities hate to have their customers electrocuted, so they may offer the same service to you as they do to professional builders.

What's the Best Ladder for You?

Ladders come in four basic flavors: stepladders, straight, extension, and folding. In all cases, because ladders lean in use, they will not take you quite as high as their length. For example, a 16' ladder will touch a wall at about 15' above the ground. And since you will be standing three rungs below the top, your highest reach will be something just over 15'. Remember, when you put a ladder up to an eave (bottom edge of a roof), it should extend about 3' above the eave to give you handholds as you climb on the roof.

Stepladders can range in height from about 3'—which is ultra-handy for repairing and painting rooms—all the way to the 10' monster some friends and I share for replacing light bulbs on cathedral ceilings.

Straight ladder. A self-explanatory name for an inexpensive ladder that's not very versatile.

An *extension ladder* has two straight sections joined together, giving excellent adjustability in height. Since the sections must overlap, a 20' extension ladder only extends to about 16'. You can use an extension ladder at its shortest setting—half the advertised length. Some extension ladders may be disassembled, so you can use the lower section as a straight ladder. (Don't use the upper section as a straight ladder because one rung is missing to make room for the extension mechanism.)

A *folding ladder* can be used as a straight ladder, a stepladder, or a small scaffold. Folding ladders are convenient but expensive; you'll probably be able to buy an extension ladder and a stepladder for the same price.

In fact, my advice to the average homeowner is just that: get a stepladder and a short extension ladder. (Depending on your house, 16' to 28' should be long enough. Longer ladders are expensive, awkward to handle, and hard to store.) Fiberglass ladders are the safest, because they don't conduct electricity, but they are expensive. I would buy aluminum—it's cheap, light and strong, and although it does conduct electricity, you won't be using your ladder near power lines, *right*?

Raising a Ladder

To raise a stepladder, simply stand it up, straighten the dividers between the sections, and position it so you can reach your work safely. Check the footing by rocking the ladder slightly—all four legs should be on the ground at once. Then climb, staying two steps below the top, and observe the usual don't-lean-too-far rules. A folded-up stepladder can be quite stable leaning against a wall; that's handy for cleaning or repairing ground-floor windows.

Straight or Extension Ladder

I've seen too many people trying to wrestle extension ladders into position with a technique that tries to shirk the laws of gravity. Let's look at an easier and safer technique for raising a ladder.

1. Place the base of your ladder against something solid, like your house, the base of a tree, or the foot of a willing slave. (Direct the slave to push down on the bottom rung with one foot.)

2. Lift the top of the ladder, and stand underneath it. Walk toward the base, lifting the ladder one rung at a time (see the illustration for raising a straight or extension ladder).

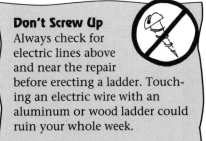

Don't Screw Up
Always check for electric lines above and near the repair before erecting a ladder. Touching an electric wire with an aluminum or wood ladder could ruin your whole week.

The house can be replaced by somebody's foot.

Ladders are easy to move once they are vertical—as long as you keep them near a building *and watch for power lines.*

Raising a straight or extension ladder

3. When the ladder is vertical and near the building, move its bottom into position (see the illustration for raising a straight or extension ladder). Gently lean it against the building.

4. Now check your work. Is the base about ¹/₄ of the ladder's height from the building? Are both feet solidly planted? Are both rails firmly against the building? Give the ladder a slight shake: If it gyrates, something needs fixing. Don't climb until two ends are solidly against the ground and two are against the building.

5. Lower the ladder by reversing this procedure.

Handy Hint
Aluminum siding is easy to dent and scrape. To prevent damaging it with a ladder, pull old gloves over the top rails.

Once an extension ladder is standing up, you could adjust its height with its miserable and barely workable rope-and-pulley system. Because this system is much better for lowering the extension than for raising it, I prefer to extend the ladder a bit more than necessary before I raise the ladder. Then, once the ladder is leaning against the wall, I can easily lower it into position.

The Least You Need to Know

➤ A small kit of safety equipment will take you through virtually every procedure in this book.

➤ The stupidity factor is probably the biggest cause of accidents. It causes you to do idiotic things you would *never* do, idiotic things you *didn't consider* doing, and idiotic things you're *embarrassed* to admit you actually did.

➤ The best antidote to the stupidity factor is to think ahead and work systematically.

➤ Working safely on a ladder is a great way of improving your odds of surviving a home repair.

➤ If safety is boring, then keep your life boring.

Chapter 7

The Bare Essentials: Hand Tools

> **In This Chapter**
>
> ➤ The fundamental hand tools for home repair
>
> ➤ Five versatile tools—your secret weapons for fast, smooth home repairs
>
> ➤ Money-saving strategies for buying and using tools

If the use of hand tools distinguishes human beings from other primates, then some humans are more distinct than others. I'm trying, as delicately as I know how, to say that some people fear tools. My wife, Meg Wise, was once one of them—she probably thought "Vise Grips" was slang for the police unit assigned to control gambling and prostitution. Yet her story shows there's hope for tool-phobes: Early in our courtship, as she helped me nail some flooring, I whined at her to bend her wrist with each swing. With a wicked backhand, she flung the hammer across the room and told me where to get off.

But last year, as we were wrestling with a pipe fitting, I gave her an arc-joint plier to hold the pipe, and after a brief struggle, she demanded a locking plier (AKA "Vise Grip,"), which, I shamefully admitted, was perfect for the job. And if Meg can overcome her fear of tools, so can you.

One of the best ways to overcome this fear is to actually get some tools and learn to use them. And while I have what some people would consider a surplus of tools (I think it's a bare minimum), I've tried, in this chapter, to imagine starting with an empty toolkit. Which would be the most important and versatile tools, the ones that I would buy first? How would I save money on those tools? Could I devise a way to convert normal holidays into occasions for receiving tools?

The Role of Price

> **Handy Hint**
> To quickly bring most of what you need to the site of a repair, store your essential tools in one bag. I let screws and nails accumulate in the bottom of my toolbag, and there's still room for special tools and hardware: the screws and brackets for installing a bookshelf, or the shims and drill for shoring up the basement stairs.

> **Nail It Down**
> *Rip sawing* is cutting with (or parallel to) the grain, and *crosscut sawing* is cutting across the grain. *Rip saws* have coarser teeth than *crosscut saws*, but for occasional use, either will work. If I had to choose one hand saw for all-around rough sawing, I'd choose a rip saw. Why? Simple—it cuts faster.

How much can you spend for tools? Ferrari prices, particularly if you're looking in a specialty woodworker's catalog. But how much *should* you pay for tools? Probably more like Chevy truck. Remember, a good tool may make your job easier, and it *will* last longer, but don't let anybody convince you it will make you a lot more skilled than an average tool.

That said, I must add that many cheapo imported tools have nothing going for them except a bargain-basement price. The screwdrivers twist, the drills break, the files dull, and the saws don't even start out sharp—this kind of economy can get expensive after a while. The best bet is to buy a good grade of tool from an established manufacturer (meaning one you've heard of).

Suggestions for saving money on tools without buying garbage:

➤ Hunt around at rummage and estate sales.

➤ Make a detailed list for friends and family, just in case they want to know what you might need for an upcoming birthday or holiday.

➤ Buy tools in sets—which sell for about half the total price of the individual tools. Although a set may have more variety than you need right now, eventually, when you lose some tools, you'll thank yourself for having bought the set.

Your Basic Toolkit

You can build up a basic toolkit over the years as you take on new projects. Chances are it will contain many of the tools in the following illustrations (Basic pliers and wrenches for home repair; Screwdrivers and so on; Drilling, cutting, and measuring tools; and Construction tools for home repair). (In further chapters, we'll cover specialty tools for repairing roofing, masonry, drywall and plaster, wallpaper, painting, electrical work, and plumbing.)

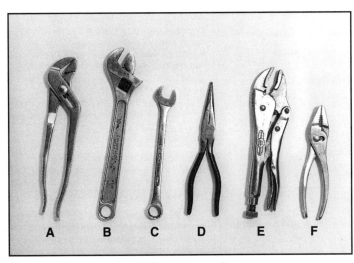

Basic pliers and wrenches for home repair

(A)   The grip of an arc-joint (or groove joint; also know by the brand name "Channel Lock") plier expands to 1¹/₂" and up. It's useful for plumbing and mechanical work.

(B)   An adjustable (Crescent) wrench turns hexagonal and square nuts and bolts. The 10" or 12" size is good for all-around use.

(C)   A combination wrench combines box and open-end wrenches; it holds nuts and bolts better than an adjustable wrench. You're better off buying a set. For the best grip, use the box end; it's less likely to strip the bolt.

(D)   Long-nose (needle-nose) pliers are useful for almost everything; in electrical work, they are the best tool for looping wire to connect to a screw terminal.

(E)   Locking pliers are often called by the brand name "Vise Grip." They can be used for turning nuts (admittedly with some scarring), grabbing other tools, and pulling nails. They also make an emergency vise, clamp, and handle. Get a 10" model for general use.

(F)   A slip-joint plier holds small tools, like a screwdriver or chisel.

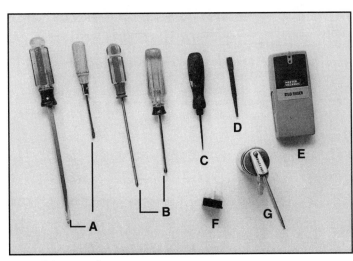

Screwdrivers and so on

(A)   You'll need at least two or three slotted screwdrivers for innumerable tasks. Save money by buying an assortment.

(B)   A couple of sizes of Phillips screwdrivers are essential, but you'll probably use a power screwdriver or variable-speed drill for driving most Phillips screws.

(C)   An awl marks wood and metal. It can punch holes for starting small wood screws, so a drill bit does not wander when it starts.

(D)   A nail set is used to punch finishing nails below the surface and prevent hammer dents in wood. I'd start with an all-purpose ³/₃₂" model.

(E)   An electronic stud finder helps you find support for a shelf, picture, or bracket. They're a bit tricky to use, and I never assume they are correct (see Chapter 20).

(F)   A magnetic stud finder works more slowly, but it's cheaper. When the magnet nears a nail in a stud, it shifts position.

(G)   An oil can is used to lubricate tools, hinges, almost any squeaky metal.

(Penetrating oil, like WD-40, is good for loosening rusted parts. To prevent further rust, you need heavier, less-volatile motor oil like SAE 10 or SAE 10W30.)

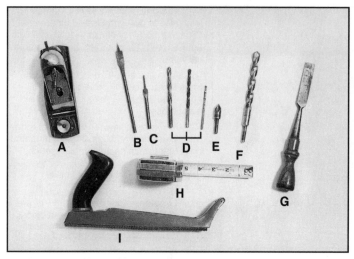

Drilling, cutting, and measuring tools

(A)   A block plane is used for general on-edge, with-the-grain wood removal—such as smoothing the edges of doors, windows, and drawers. It works with end grain found on door bottoms. It's also good for removing saw marks after rip sawing. Hint: Start with a shallow cut, and increase the depth if the plane cuts smoothly. Hold the plane at a slight angle to the direction of travel, which helps it cut more smoothly.

(B)   Spade drill bits come in various sizes. Usually sold in sets, they are used for drilling large holes in wood. Caution: If you hit a nail, the bit will be wrecked.

(C)   A contoured bit matches the taper on wood screws and countersinks the head in one operation. Sold in sets, they greatly simplify the chore of hand-driving tapered wood screws.

(D)   Combination wood-or-metal drill bits make holes for rivets, sheet-metal screws, and bolts. Use them to drill wood if you're likely to hit nails or screws. At the very least, buy a kit ranging in size from $1/_{16}$" to $1/_4$", and plan to buy the $3/_8$" and $1/_2$" sizes early on.

(E)   A countersink removes wood so a flat-head screw will rest flush with the surface.

(F)   Masonry drill bits are sold in various sizes for drilling into masonry or concrete. Buy only the size you need now (each anchor requires a specific size). For a big concrete-drilling job, rent a hammer drill; it cuts much faster.

(G)   A wood chisel ($1/_2$" to $3/_4$" wide) removes wood to make mortises (cutouts) for locks and hinges, and other purposes. Don't bother buying the most expensive one—medium quality is fine.

(H)   A tape measure, sized from 6' to 25', is essential for almost any repair job. 12' or 16' is a good compromise length—small and affordable—but large enough to lay out carpet or bookshelves. A locking tape hold the tape in position while you make a measurement.

(I)   A surform wood rasp will remove wood across or with the grain. It leaves a rough finish but is good for crude door, window, and drawer repair (use a block plane to smooth the surface afterwards).

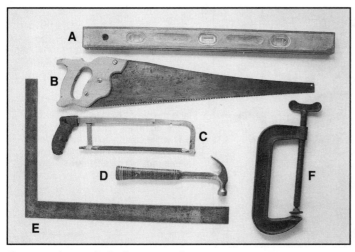

Construction tools for home repair

(A)   A 16" to 24" level is for marking electrical box openings, installing appliances and shelving, and repairing doors. Or substitute a 9" torpedo level, which fits into the toolbag.

(B)   A rip saw is useful f;or cutting with the grain, and for rough cutting across the grain.

(C)   A hacksaw cuts steel, copper, or aluminum. Eighteen teeth per inch is a good blade for general purposes; buy a blade with coarser teeth to cut thick metal ($\frac{1}{4}$" and up). To eliminate vibration and speed the work, place the cut $\frac{1}{4}$" from a vise, locking pliers, or C-clamp.

(D)   A 16-ounce claw hammer is an all-around size for hammering and pulling nails. (Polish the hammer face with sandpaper or emery cloth to increase its grip.) Framing hammers are excellent for pounding big nails; these extra-long, 24-ounce whammers usually have a waffle pattern to grab the nail. But they also make a mess if they hit the wood—don't use them for finish work!

(E)   A carpenter's square is used to measure and mark straight or square (90°) lines. It's helpful for layout work, picture framing, and door straightening, but you may be able to substitute an aluminum square.

(F)   A C-clamp is one of the handiest tools you can own. It will clamp wood for gluing, substitute for a vise, and hold two pieces of wood together as you nail them tight.

Marking from a Tape—Accurately

Accuracy is something that distinguishes real builders from the rest of us. Have you ever marked from a tape measure, and made a line that wandered off toward, say, Nebraska? Later, you couldn't figure out which part of the line was accurate, right? Then you'll have to check out "Marking from a tape" on the next page. Notice that the mark is darkest where it starts (near the tape, where it is accurate). If you mark this way, you can just use the dark part of the mark as your measurement. (You can also make a "V"-shaped mark, with the point of the V at the precise location.)

Handy Hint
Are your steel tools—hand saws, hammers, and squares—rusting? Then occasionally smear on a thin coating of boiled linseed oil. The oil will sink in, darken the tool slightly, and stop rust cold. Unlike motor oil, it won't gum up the tool.

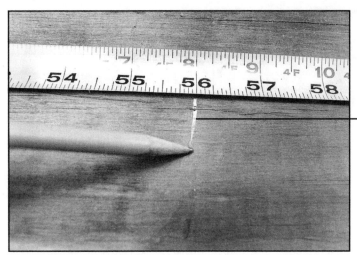

Place the pencil next to the desired dimension on the rule, then quickly pull it away while easing up on the pressure. Even if your mark runs crooked, the darkest part will be accurate.

Marking from a tape

Five Cool Tools You Must Meet

Every handy guy has a set of favorite tools—the overlooked, underappreciated gems in the toolbox. I've put mine on the table in this chapter's illustration showing five cool tools.

A *pointing trowel* is designed to patch masonry, but it's also perfect for working with drywall and plaster. Use it to scrape paint, glaze windows, and ease things apart. Slip it beneath the head of a claw hammer to protect the wood while you pull nails.

A *needle-nose locking pliers* is versatile enough to replace three tools—wire cutters, pliers, and needle-nose pliers. Unfortunately, it's weaker than a regular locking plier for big-time gripping jobs.

An aluminum square (sold under the brand *Speed Square)* guides a circular saw to make a 90° cut. You can slide the saw along the square to trim $^1/_8$" from a board (a job that could otherwise befuddle anybody). It's also handy for marking square lines and angles, and making small measurements ("Basic sawing technique" in Chapter 10).

A *3-pound hammer* is the primordial blunt object. Use it to clean masonry before repairs, drive posts in the garden, pound stakes for concrete forms, and for big-league metal chiseling.

This *wrecking bar* disassembles stuff much more neatly than other wrecking bars because its flat tongue slips under things. Note: Flat steel bars have too much spring; they just jump back at you when you hammer them. This bar has a hexagonal cross-section that makes it much more rigid. I even use it to lift furniture. I place a scrap of wood under the fulcrum, slide the tongue under the furniture, and step on the end. Then I insert a scrap of carpet—pile side down—under each leg, and just slide the furniture across the floor. Bye-bye lumbago.

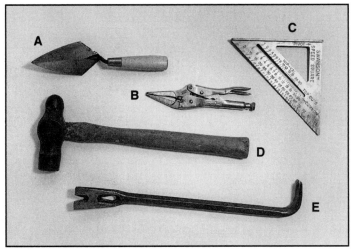

(A)   Pointing trowel
(B)   Needle-nose locking plier
(C)   Aluminum square
(D)   3-pound hammer
(E)   Wrecking bar

Five cool tools

The Least You Need to Know

➤ Many tools are far more versatile than most people realize, which gives you one more reason to buy them.

➤ Your most frequently used tools should be your best-quality tools.

➤ Save time and frustration by keeping your basic tools in one place, ready for work.

The Bare Essentials with Oomph! Power Tools

If you were so inclined, you could squander a bundle on power tools before you even started making a repair—creative designers seem to invent a new electric- or gasoline-powered "labor-saving device" about every week. But since our goal is to minimize the time and financial cost of owning a home, and to give you a little satisfaction in the process, I'll take a different tack, concentrating on the tools you'll really need, and helping you plan a way to rationally accumulate tools without breaking the bank.

As we talk about the four basic electric tools for home repair, I'll discuss whether you really need them, suggest the size most suitable for home repairs, and offer tips for use. I'll talk about how much quality you need, and whether you should buy a cordless model.

Cord or Cordless?

An increasing number of .power tools are sold in cordless models, which is a polite way of saying you'll have to deal with batteries instead of electric cords. I used to think battery-operated tools were toys, until I bought a cordless $^{3}/_{8}$" reversible drill, and it quickly became my mainstay for screwdriving and light drilling. I think I'd be less enthusiastic about a cordless circular saw; I can't imagine its batteries would last very long.

The key advantage of cordless tools, shockingly enough, is that you won't have to mess with a cord (not to mention an extension cord). That means there's less to shlep, less to trip on, and one more outlet for another tool or a light.

But cordless tools have a couple of disadvantages: First, they run out of power. It may be breathtakingly obvious to point out that this tends to happen while you're using the tool, not when it's on the shelf. Then you'll have to wait for a recharge or borrow the blasted thing from somebody else.

Second, cordless tools are not for heavy-duty use. I would not buy a power screwdriver to screw up a roomful stack of drywall, unless I bought a spare battery (but then we're getting way beyond idiot territory). But if you're more interested in driving a few screws for a new bookshelf, that's exactly what cordless drills are designed for.

> ### Builder's Trivia
>
> "Contractor quality" means almost nothing—except a high price. Homeowners should not waste money buying tools designed for day-in, day-out work. Consult *Consumer's Report* or another rating service for advice on tool quality for the kind of service you expect to use.

Variable-Speed, Reversing Drill (Doubles as Power Screwdriver)

The drill has always been the first power tool to buy, simply for drilling holes in wood and metal, and wire-brushing to remove paint and rust. A variable-speed drill will drive slotted screws, but the bit tends to slip; Phillips heads, which are found on drywall screws and elsewhere, are infinitely easier to drive.

In the last 10 years, these cheap, strong drywall screws have revolutionized home repair and increased the importance of variable-speed, reversing drills (see "Electric drill and saber saw," on following page). Screws, unlike nails, won't crack plaster or drywall. They work in places too tight to swing a hammer, and they're easy to remove. Drywall screws do a lot more than just fasten drywall to studs; they also secure hardware and repair wood. You could even use them to build a doghouse.

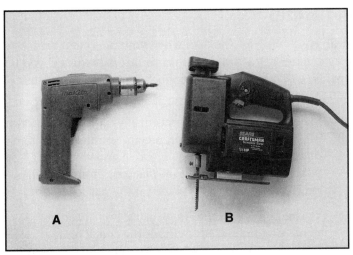

(A) The ³/₈" cordless, variable-speed, reversing drill is the all-around hero of home repair, used for drilling, screwing, polishing, and sanding.

(B) A saber saw makes curvy cuts a breeze, and can even cut a straight line once in a while.

Electric drill and saber saw

Electric drills are sized by the maximum opening of the chuck (the rotating clamp that holds the bit). Power, weight, and price all increase along with chuck size. The common sizes are ¹/₄", ³/₈", and ¹/₂"; for home use, I'd buy a ³/₈" model first. If you need a bit with a diameter that's larger than the chuck, buy one with a reduced-diameter shank (that's the part gripped by the chuck).

Thrilling Drilling Tips

Drilling may seem utterly straightforward, and for the most part, it is. But if you're new to the sport, take advantage of my hard-won experience by scanning this list of suggestions for getting the most from your drill.

➤ If your hole is slightly too small for a wood screw, carefully wobble the drill while it's running. Don't get too aggressive, or you'll break the bit.

➤ Breaking too many of those little (¹/₈" or smaller) wood bits? Then do what the pros do—use a finishing nail instead. They're cheap, so you can replace them when lost or bent. Just cut the head off with a hacksaw or wire cutter. And although finishing nails are not very accurate, that's not important for most pilot holes (which allow a wood screw to penetrate wood).

➤ A small power drill with a wire brush is the best tool for removing rust from tools, railings, etc. Run it at top speed. Hold small pieces in a vise or locking pliers while brushing, and wear safety glasses.

Test Your Mettle: Drilling Metal

When you first start drilling metal, you'll long for the days when your opponent was mere wood. Metal, particularly steel, hates being drilled. To get to first base in steel you'll need more technique, and sharper bits. Fortunately, brass, copper, and other soft metals are not nearly so challenging.

> **Handy Hint**
> Steel comes in many flavors, or hardnesses. That's why a steel hacksaw can cut a steel bar—because it's harder. It's also why you may get nowhere cutting or drilling steel. Ordinary tools cannot cut the kind of hardened steel found in locks, tools, springs, etc.; all you will do is waste your time and dull the tool.

➤ Make a small dimple to prevent the bit from wandering as it starts. In soft, thin metal, hammer a nail to make the dimple. In thick metal, hammer a center punch (a hard, pointed tool that looks somewhat like a dull pencil and that's made for the purpose).

➤ Tighten the bit in the chuck using two or three tightening holes. This tightens the chuck more effectively, because the gears are in better alignment when you move to the second tightening hole.

➤ Use a faster rotation speed for smaller holes, and a slower speed for large holes.

➤ To make holes $3/16"$ and larger in thick metal, drill a pilot hole first with a smaller bit, then enlarge the hole. And cool the bit with some motor oil to prevent heat from damaging it.

➤ Keep bits sharp, or buy new ones.

➤ Don't try to drill hardened steel, which you'll find in tools and some hardware. If a sharp drill won't cut the metal, back off—it's probably hardened.

Can You Get By without This Tool?

If I had no power tools, a drill would be my first buy. You can use a hand drill for a few small holes in wood, or a brace and bit (which is expensive) for large holes. But you need a power drill to drill metal, or to drill many holes, or to do wire-brushing. And to drive screws, you'll need a variable-speed, reversing drill.

En Garde—and Other Tricks with the Saber Saw

A saber saw is a portable jig-saw; by driving a small, straight blade back and forth, it can make straight or curved cuts. Always push down while cutting to prevent vibration, and press forward with light pressure as you start. Once the saw is fully in the cut, you can press harder. For a straight cut, run the saw along the aluminum square (see Chapter 7, "Five Cool Tools You Must Meet") or another type of square (see the figure "Electric drill and saber saw," earlier in this chapter).

This economical saw may come with many features, none essential:

➤ Variable speed: Helpful for cutting plastic or even cellulose ceiling tile, and for starting cuts.

➤ Adjustable angle: The blade can be angled to about 45° from the base, but it may be difficult to return it to exactly 90°. Use a square (see Chapter 7) to set the blade at 90°.

➤ Pivoting blade: A handle on top allows the blade to pivot 360° while cutting—so you can cut your way into a corner. This feature helps you orient the tool so you can see the blade while cutting, but make sure the blade locks into position for straight cuts.

Can You Get By without This Tool?

This is an optional but handy tool, best for occasional cutting, intricate work like repair of "gingerbread" trim on a Victorian house, or installing electrical outlets in drywall.

Belt Sander

Belt sanders move a 3" or 4" wide sanding belt, bulldozer-track fashion. They are great for removing a lot of material; for heavy-duty refinishing, smoothing the edge of a door, or removing paint (although paint may clog the belts, which are expensive). Some sanders need a drop of motor oil on the front roller with each use. A model with a 3" × 24" belt should be plenty for home work (see "Sawing and sanding the big-time way," on following page).

Make sure to install the belt in the direction indicated by the arrow inside the belt, or the belt will tear apart. If you're doing more final finishing than rough wood removal, consider an orbital sander, which moves sandpaper in an egg-shaped pattern better suited for finish work.

Can You Get By without This Tool?

Probably. But if you ever need to smooth some gouged wood, or straighten the edge of a door, then you're a prospect for a belt sander. (However, a rented power planer is the ideal tool for trimming a door.) And if you do much refinishing, an orbital sander will start to seem pretty useful pretty fast.

Circular Saw

A circular saw, often called by the trade name Skil-saw, has a circular blade and is a standard tool at construction sites. You can adjust the depth and angle of the cut. Some saws stop instantly when you release the trigger; that's a nice safety feature, although the blade guard usually snaps down and covers the blade pretty effectively (see below).

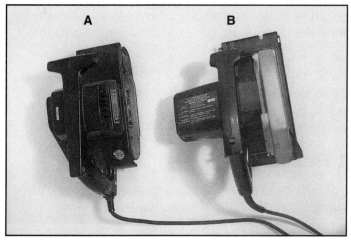

(A)   A belt sander is a heavy-duty answer for flattening wood and removing paint. Use it with care, as the wood comes off quickly.

(B)   A circular saw is essential for cutting plywood and particle board, and is handy for general sawing; it will even cut brick. (But don't be a doofus—get a blade designed to cut brick!)

Sawing and sanding the big-time way

In general, adjust the blade so it penetrates the wood by about $1/2$"; cutting deeper just strains the motor and makes sawing more dangerous. With the right blade, you can cut some bricks and concrete blocks (although it's a dusty, noisy job, rather low on the recreational scale).

A circular saw may be the most dangerous tool in a home workshop. Read and follow the instructions, particularly regarding eye protection and setting up the cut. Don't work in cluttered areas, or in low light, or when you're tired. In short, don't act stupid with a circular saw in your hands.

Some Sharp Words on the Blade

You can buy dozens of blades for a circular saw, but you can probably get along with two. The first is a fine-toothed plywood blade, which also cuts paneling, particle board, and wooden siding. The second is an 18-tooth, carbide-tipped blade, which cuts 1" and 2" lumber. Carbide teeth stay sharp much longer than regular steel teeth.

If your saw starts smoking, making a hideous shriek, and cutting crooked, the blade is dull. Dull blades can also singe the wood (making it difficult to finish), damage the motor, and draw so much current that they blow a fuse. Have I convinced you to avoid dull blades? Good. But how? Avoid nails.

However, even normal cutting will dull a blade eventually. Non-carbide blades are surprisingly easy to sharpen with a decent metal file. Hold the blade in a vise and sharpen the underside of those teeth that angle away from you. Then flip the blade, reclamp, and sharpen the other teeth. Good carbide blades can be professionally sharpened, but cheap ones can be replaced.

Can You Get By without This Tool?

A hand saw will work fine for cross-cutting a few 2 × 4s. But to cut many boards, or rip saw a long plank, or cut plywood or particle board, get a circular saw. Most have a $7^1/_4$" blade diameter, which is adequate for virtually everything you'll attempt.

Power-by-the-Hour—Renting Big-Time Tools

One of my favorite rhythm 'n' blues songs recorded one singer's plaint: "Got to find me a part-time love." That's how I see renting tools—as an opportunity for part-time love—the kind of love you don't have to maintain, repair, or store (not to mention buy in the first place).

Even though I have a decent collection of tools, I've rented chain saws, wood splitters, post-hole diggers, concrete mixers, and an electric jackhammer over the years. (I even rented a hefty hammer drill to drill through a brick wall. The drilling went fine, until I hit a backing wall of 8" solid concrete. From there on it was strictly Alcatraz work.)

> **Handy Hint**
> If you rent a tool on Saturday morning, chances are a one-day fee will take you through the rental yard's opening time on Monday—so you'll get almost two days for the price of one.

Tool rental yards should have most of the goodies listed in Table 8.1. Some of these tools are suited for large jobs, but that's the point—this is where you get pro equipment. Even if you don't exploit these tools to their limit, you've still have lightened your load. Tool rental outfits may also rent ladders, scaffolding, and extension cords.

Table 8.1   List of rental tools; and uses

Tool	Uses
Nail gun	Repeated nailing, as of siding or roofing
Hammer drill (AKA rotary hammer)	Drilling holes in concrete, blocks, and brick
Electric hammer	Small jackhammer for demolishing concrete, brick, block, and pavement
$1/2$" drill	Drilling metal, concrete, or large holes in wood
Right-angle drill	Drilling large holes in confined spaces (as between studs or joists)
Screw gun	For large-scale screwing, as in drywall or decks
Reciprocating saw (AKA "Sawz-All")	Cutting flush to a surface; cutting into walls, ceilings, roofs; and cutting steel pipe, angle-iron, and flat stock. Ideal for remodeling work.
Power miter box	Sawing consistent, accurate 90° cuts or miters in lumber up to 4×4
Table saw	Accurate rip sawing of wood, plywood, etc.
Power planer	Smoothing edges or end grain of doors so they swing freely
Radial arm saw	Fast, accurate crosscut sawing of material up to 24" wide
Diamond tile saw	Cutting bricks and tile
Pipe wrenches and threader	Cutting, threading, and assembling steel pipe
Pipe auger (snake)	Cleaning clogs from drain pipes
Power grinder or wire brush	Polishing metal, removing paint or rust, and cleaning brick joints for tuckpointing
Paint sprayer (air or airless)	Spray-painting large areas, indoors or out
Portable generator	Supplying 120-volt electricity in remote locations
Floor nailer	Invisible (blind) nailing of hardwood flooring
Masonry nailer	Shooting hardened nails into masonry and concrete with a powder charge

Tool	Uses
Compactor	Compressing earth while building patios or foundations
Air compressor	Driving air tools, such as nailers, staplers, and air-powered paint sprayers
Power washer	Washing the house, especially before painting or staining
Power wheelbarrow	Moving heavy loads of sand, soil, and concrete
Concrete mixer	Mixing (gasp!) concrete (get one with a trailer hitch if you have a way to pull it)
Power trowel	Finishing large, flat concrete work
Post-hole digger	Digging holes for fence posts, basketball poles, signs, and lights
Pumps	For drying out basements and other low areas

A Friend in Deed Is a Friend You Need; or, How to Borrow Tools without Losing Friends

Rental outfits are not the only source of tools—friends can be equally valuable, and much more affordable. But before you ask Joe to borrow his pipe cutter, consider the fable of Doug and David. David used to borrow drills, hacksaws, even the occasional sledgehammer. I didn't mind—after all, there was no point in his wasting money on something he'd only need once in his lifetime. But that's how long it seemed to take for David to return my tools—a lifetime. I've quit offering, and he's quit asking.

At the other extreme, when my friend Doug borrows my reciprocating saw, he does it in high style: He asks ahead of time, so I can make plans. Then he borrows it for the minimum time, and sometimes checks that I've not suddenly found a need for it. And when he does return the saw, I usually find a couple of new blades in the case.

More Tool-Borrowing Etiquette

➤ Don't ask to borrow a tool you can't control. For example, I don't lend out my chain saw, but I'm happy to lend out a miter box or an electric drill.

➤ Return the tool—quickly, and in good condition.

➤ Offer to repay the favor by working alongside your benefactor.

➤ As you amass your own tools, offer to lend them in return.

The Least You Need to Know

➤ When it comes to electric tools, choose carefully and buy the most versatile ones first.

➤ Just because you'll need a tool once in a while does not mean you should buy it. Try borrowing from a friend or renting.

➤ A variable-speed, cordless $^3/_8$" drill is the obvious first choice for an electric tool, but it's important to understand your needs first. Cordless is not for everybody.

Chapter 9

Keeping It Together: Buying and Using Fasteners and Materials

In This Chapter

➤ How to select and use nails, screws, and anchors

➤ Identifying and choosing hardware for repair projects

➤ Time-saving hints for using fasteners

Fasteners—the generic term for nails, screws, and anchors—are like the joints in your body. They aren't exactly the structure, but structure is not possible without them. Almost every home repair project—replacing a bookshelf, patching the roof, or hanging a lava lamp—calls for fasteners at some point, which means you'll want to know what the hardware mavens are selling.

In this chapter, you'll learn that nails have . . . well . . . come a long way in the past few years, as manufacturers finally figured out that one size does not fit all applications and that the main job of a nail is not to split the wood. At the same time, screws have taken their rightful place as a fast, versatile, and non-destructive fastener. Not to be outdone, manufacturers of other hardware have put on their creative hats and come up with some novel answers to the age-old problem of holding it all together. Finally, we'll finish up by discussing a somewhat unorthodox approach to buying materials—one that gives you a fighting chance of having the right item "in stock" when you need it.

Bang, Bang, You're Nailed

Nails are the oldest wood fastener around, unless you count bark and vines that once were used to bind wood together. But old needn't mean old-fashioned—a glut of new nails has reached the market in recent years—and for good reason. Common nails, long the industry standard, had a nasty habit of splitting lumber. Today's nails are less likely to split and more likely to grab. Some are almost as strong as screws—but faster to drive (see the illustration in this chapter that displays types of nails you may need). Here are the most common kinds of nails you'll use in your home repair projects:

Builder's Trivia

Nails are sized by an archaic and baffling system of "pennys." Basically, 4d (4 penny), is $1^1/_2$" long, and 16d is $3^1/_2$" long, and the other sizes vary between those lengths. Fortunately, most nail manufacturers recognize that this is gibberish to the average homeowner, and list nail length in inches.

Pole barn: Tough and springy, up to 6" long; rings on the shank prevent pulling out (meaning you should never put one in the wrong place!).

Roofing: A galvanized, big-headed nail for asphalt shingles. The nail should sink at least $^1/_2$" into the roof decking.

Sinker ("coated"): A lighter version of the common nail which causes fewer splitting problems; for 2" lumber, a cement coating makes it easier to drive and improves the grip.

Box: A light-duty nail for assembling thin wood, it's almost split-proof.

Siding: A galvanized (rust-resistant) version of the box nail, available up to $3^1/_2$" long, for fastening wood siding.

Ring shank: This medium-duty nail has rings on the shank for a better grip.

Spiral: This heavy flooring nail obtains a kind of screw grip that resists pull-out and reduces squeaking; use a galvanized version outdoors.

Drywall: A thin, big-headed nail for fastening drywall and plaster lath.

Paneling: A skinny, hardened nail for wood paneling; buy a color that matches the paneling.

Finishing: A thin, inconspicuous nail for door trim and baseboard.

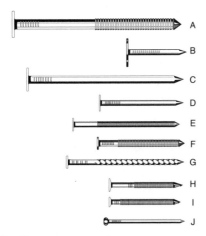

(A) Pole barn
(B) Roofing
(C) Sinker ("coated")
(D) Box
(E) Siding
(F) Ring shank
(G) Spiral
(H) Drywall
(I) Paneling
(J) Finishing

Type of nails you may need

Screwing Up Again, Eh?

When it comes to fastening, screws have three advantages: they're strong, they're secure, and they're removable. Most screws must be driven into a pilot hole, but drywall screws seldom need one. (Pilot holes, incidentally, are preliminary holes drilled to guide the screw and prevent splitting in the wood.) For small wood screws, you can "drill" the pilot hole with a finishing nail.

Wood, drywall, and sheet metal screws have a thread tailored to their particular material. Machine screws and machine bolts must be screwed into a nut that has the correct thread. Compared to wood screws, machine screws and bolts are stronger, less likely to pull out (particularly if you use flat washers with them), and more homely. Wood and sheet-metal screws are made with straight (slotted) or Phillips heads. Many are available in galvanized (rust-resistant) steel. For a price, you can buy solid brass, which is much more attractive, but weaker, than steel (see the illustration in this chapter of screws that may come in handy). Here's a brief description of each of the more useful kinds of screws:

> **Handy Hint**
> Smear hand soap on wood and drywall screws before driving. This will reduce friction and save your palm—or the batteries in your drill. And remember this simple rule (which applies to the top of a screw, as you face it): Right makes tight.

Round-head: Attaching hardware to wood.

Oval-head: A decorative version of the round-head.

Flat-head: Mounting hinges.

Drywall: Attaching drywall, and dozens of other uses. Sold with Phillips head, from $7/8$" to $3^1/_2$" long. It has no taper and drives easily with a power screwdriver.

Lag: For heavy-duty fastening; comes with a square or hexagonal head up to about 6" long.

Sheet metal: Joining sheet metal; doubles as an emergency wood screw.

Machine screw and nut: Fastens all the way through a joint. Note: The nut and screw must be the same diameter *and* have the same number of threads per inch.

Machine bolt and nut: A heavy-duty version of the machine screw, it's usually sold with a hexagonal head. Again, these are sold in "coarse" and "fine" threads. Fine threads are smaller, so there are more of them per inch.

Flat washer: For reinforcing wood and sheet metal before fastening with machine screws or bolts. They make a stronger joint, prevent leakage, reduce friction, and let you use a small bolt in a large hole. In other words, keep some around—they're that handy.

Lock washer: To prevent machine nuts from loosening; used mainly where vibration will occur, as on autos and appliances.

Builder's Trivia

Wood screws are sized by a number system, running, for our purposes, from a small #4, in even sizes, through a chunky #12. Each size is also available in a number of lengths. Thus, a package might say "$1^1/_4$" #12 screws." For average home repairs, #8 and #10 will be most useful.

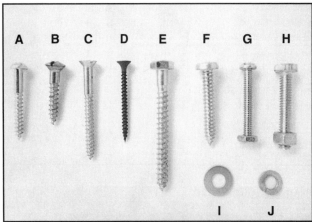

(A)	Round-head
(B)	Oval-head
(C)	Flat-head
(D)	Drywall
(E)	Lag
(F)	Sheet metal
(G)	Machine screw and nut
(H)	Machine bolt and nut
(I)	Flat washer
(J)	Lock washer

Screws that may come in handy

Anchors

So you're trying to hang that gilt-framed black-velvet painting on plaster or drywall, and you can't find any studs to support the art? You could see the section in Chapter 20 called "Six Ways to Find a Stud." Or you could get a wall anchor. Many varieties are available, but the general routine is the same: drill a hole, insert the anchor, drive the screw into the anchor (if it's a separate piece), and tighten. To fasten to concrete, use a lag shield on a lag screw (it's a nuisance, but it really holds). Here's how to use each of the anchors:

Nylon anchor: A quick, cheap anchor, good for light jobs.

Winged nylon anchor: Fast but more expensive, for heavier-duty fastening.

Molly-screw (expansion) anchor: Requires a large drill hole and cumbersome to fasten, but it's strong. Drill a hole, insert the anchor, and tighten the screw. Then remove the screw (the anchor remains in the wall), stick the screw through the thing you are mounting, and tighten it back into the anchor.

Spring toggle: Drill a hole, insert the screw through the object to be mounted, thread it into the anchor, and slip it into the hole and tighten. The wings automatically expand to grab the wall.

Lag shield (concrete anchor): Drill a hole in concrete with a special masonry drill, insert the anchor, insert a lag screw through the object and into the anchor, and tighten.

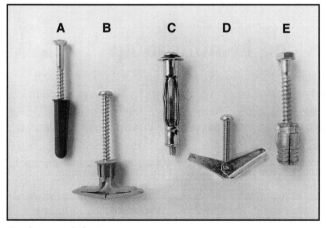

(A) Nylon anchor
(B) Winged nylon anchor
(C) Molly-screw (expansion) anchor
(D) Spring toggle
(E) Lag shield (concrete anchor)

Anchors and their uses

65

Glues

Over the past decades, industrial chemists have invented a shelf-load of glues and cements, but you can probably get by with the ones listed in Table 9.1.

Table 9.1 Glues and their uses

Name	Uses
Carpenter's or white	For porous materials: wood, cloth, and paper. This basic workshop item is perfect for fixing split wood, building or repairing furniture, and so on. The joint must be nailed, screwed, weighted, or clamped for $1/2$ hour, while the glue sets.
Contact	For gluing and repairing countertops and other flat materials. This cement grabs instantly, so you've got to align the parts perfectly in advance.
Construction	Sold in tubes for caulking guns, this stuff can be combined with nails to make an extremely strong joint.
"Super" or "Krazy"	Fast-setting glue makes strong joints in metal, ceramics, glue and some plastics. Use with care—it can bond your skin. Although nail-polish remover can probably take it off your skin, it's smarter to use gloves when working with this stuff.
Epoxy	A heavy-duty, two-part cement for metal, glass, ceramic, wood, and concrete.

Hardware Basics—Types and Identifications

Choosing hardware can be simple: You take the busted part to the store and replace it. But if you don't know what you need, or the store doesn't have a replacement, consult the following illustrations of door hardware (Table 9.2) and other hardware (Table 9.3) for suggestions. Remember: *Always* take the broken piece to the store—you may confront an unimaginable mix of sizes, finishes, and styles.

Table 9.2 Door hardware

Item	Description
	Butt hinge: For standard doors, sized up to 4" long. These hinges must be installed in a recess, or mortise.
	Strap hinge: Doors and gates in yard, basement, and garage.

Item	Description
	Tee hinge: Can only be used where the door and trim are flush with each other; usually found in garages and yards.
	Semi-concealed hinge: Mainly for kitchen cabinets; the hinge is screwed to the back of the door.
	Doorstops: To prevent a door from damaging walls and woodwork, a doorstop may be (a) screwed to the baseboard or (b) slipped over the hinge pin.
	Door straightener: Prevents sag in a wooden screen door.
	Storm door closer: Closes a door slowly without slamming.
	Hook and eye: For quick, easy, light-duty locking of a door.
	Barrel bolt: For quick, easy locking of door.

Table 9.3 Other hardware

Item	Description
	Corner iron: Reinforcing furniture or installing shelves.
	Joiner (strap, tee, and L): Reinforcing furniture and shelving.
	Shelf bracket: Installing shelves.
	Continuous (piano) hinge: Strong attachment of folding shelves or lids of boxes.

Table 9.3 Continued

Item	Description
	Pull: Replacing or updating drawers and cabinet doors.
	Chair and corner brace: Strengthening leg attachment on chairs and tables.
	Sash catch: Securing individual sash in double-hung windows.

Builder's Trivia

Good hardware stores have much more than nails and nuts. Many stores keep a huge set of drawers with fasteners in every conceivable size, shape, and material, and curiosities like bizarre brackets for folding furniture. Hardware stores may also cut glass, repair screens, cut and thread steel pipe, and sharpen knives, scissors, and other tools.

A Word on Acquiring Materials

Your mother—or whomever it was that indoctrinated you with the myth that cleanliness was next to godliness—will hate me for this, but I'll say it anyway: Don't throw stuff away. When you rip apart a wall, save good wood and any electrical boxes and outlets that are modern and in good shape. When you take apart old plumbing, save the good fittings. These odds and ends can save time and money—an electrical box can cost $3, and a trip to the building supplier can devour 90 minutes (if you count driving, parking, and wandering around gape-mouthed in search of a size-7 snarf hinge in antique brass finish).

Another way to save time is to buy extra nails and screws. Ten dollars' worth of sorted and labeled fasteners can eliminate countless supply trips.

Finally, there's the prospect of shopping on the curb. Are you too proud to poke around in the trash, looking for a good 2×4 and a sheet of plywood for a basement shelf? Not me. I consider the curb a public utility—kind of like clean water. On garbage nights, I drive slowly, scanning for large piles of goodies. I don't think of it as trashpicking, but as a 24-hour store where every item carries a money-back guarantee.

The Least You Need to Know

➤ Always bring the broken part to the store when you buy a replacement.

➤ Hardware is available in a bewildering variety of types, sizes, and finishes, for virtually any task.

➤ Buy some extra screws and nails for each project; eventually your collection will save trips to the store.

➤ Use small jars (baby food) as an inexpensive way to organize your fasteners.

Wood: Its Care and Handling

Let's face it, wood is so good that if nature hadn't evolved trees, we'd probably be trying to invent them. That's difficult. Despite enormous effort, nobody has perfected a substitute, and wood—whether in boards or as some chopped, sliced, and glued derivative—remains the material of choice for building houses.

But while we see wood as a strong, beautiful material, fungi and insects see it as food or a place to call home. Nails, unfortunately, see wood as something to split. In this chapter, you'll learn to exploit wood's strengths and overcome its weaknesses. You will also learn to speak the misleading language that's used to describe lumber, and you will be introduced to "manufactured wood products," which no longer means just plywood.

What's in a Name? Nominal Size, True Size, and Other Lumber Lingo

Walking into a lumber yard is like dropping through the looking glass, where nothing is what it seems. Once upon a time, a 2 × 4 measured 2" × 4", but this simple, straightforward approach is hopelessly antiquated. These days, lumber is named with a bald-faced swindle called "nominal size." Nowadays, the ubiquitous 2 × 4 has shrunken to $1^1/2" × 3^1/2"$. Why? Because it's cheaper for the manufacturer—but not necessarily better for you.

Like three-card monte or the shell game, the swindle has rules:

➤ Lumber is identified by thickness × width × length, so if you wanted an 8-foot 2 × 4, you'd ask for a 2 × 4 × 8.

➤ For framing (or "dimension") lumber (with a nominal thickness of 2"), subtract $^1/2"$ from each nominal dimension to find the actual size. Thus, subtracting $^1/2$ from each dimension of the 2" × 4" gives you a piece that's $1^1/2" × 3^1/2"$.

➤ The actual thickness of nominal 1" lumber is $^3/4"$.

➤ The actual width of nominal 1" lumber is $^3/4"$ less than the nominal width (a 1 × 10 actually measures $^3/4" × 9^1/4"$).

➤ You can find boards that are actually 1" thick. Just ask for "five-quarters." (Did anyone claim this was going to make sense?)

➤ Believe it or not, Ripley, but the length of lumber is stated accurately—a 10' board will be 10' long—or maybe a couple of inches longer!

➤ Just to keep you guessing, plywood, paneling, and drywall are sold in full dimension: a 4 × 8 sheet measures 4' × 8'.

Lumber is graded under a confusing system that's mostly irrelevant for our purposes. The best stuff, with no knots, is called "clear," "select," or "No. 1." Straight-grained, comely, and costly, it's used mostly for molding and other places where appearance is more important than cost. "No. 2" lumber, AKA "common," is cheaper, and suitable for most uses where the Queen of England is not expected.

In the brave new world of lumber, you will meet these "manufactured wood products":

➤ *Plywood*, a sandwich of thin sheets glued at right angles, is a stable, strong, and versatile flat material, used for shelving, roof decks, and furniture. The best grade is "A" and the worst is "D." Plywood rated "X" is suitable for exterior use. If the plywood will be visible, ask for "good one side"—the knots will be plugged for a smoother surface. And pay attention to the number of plies—three, the minimum, is much weaker than five or seven plies.

➤ *Oriented strand board* is similar to plywood, but it's made of wood fragments glued together. It's cheap and homely, and is used increasingly for roof decking and other sheathing purposes.

➤ *Particle board* is a strong, dense pile of glued sawdust that's used for subfloors, shelving, furniture, and counter tops. It's generally used inside, although some siding is made of particle board.

> **Handy Hint**
> When buying lumber, pass up the first few pieces in the stack and look for the good boards below them. How to distinguish good lumber? It's straight when you "eyeball" it from the end. It's neither twisted nor knotty. Generally, once you reach the good wood in a pile, you'll find what you need pretty quickly.

The Enemies of Wood

For such an amiable material, wood has an outsize share of enemies: sunlight, water, fungus, and insects. To control these enemies, you've got to know their *modus operandi*, and you've got to stay vigilant.

Outdoors, unprotected wood starts degrading almost as soon as it's exposed to the elements. Ultraviolet light from the sun strips off the surface, causing the wood to turn gray. Rain causes swelling, dryness causes contraction, and cracks develop, giving water and mold access to deeper wood. The wood dries out more slowly, making it that much more hospitable to attack by decay organisms (see Table 10.1).

Table 10.1 The six plagues of wood and what to do about them

Plague	Nature and signs	Geographic location	Location in home	Cures
Dry rot	A fungus that consumes the cellulose of wood, leaving a soft skeleton that reduces to powder. Look for wet, powdery, flaky, or discolored wood.	Humid climates	Under roof leaks, in damp basement, near cold-water pipes with condensation. May soften wood for attack by insects. Important: eats only damp wood.	Figure out where moisture originates and cure that problem.

continues

Table 10.1 Continued

Plague	Nature and signs	Geographic location	Location in home	Cures
Carpenter ants	Large black ants which tunnel through wet wood and rigid foam insulation. Look for piles of sawdust beneath the tunnel openings.	Widespread	Under roof leaks, in damp basements or crawl spaces, in wall cavities, etc.	Dry out the damp areas; call exterminator if problem persists.
Termites— subterranean	Look for tunnels running up the foundation— these termites can't stand sunlight (unless they are swarming through the air while mating).	Widespread	Starting from the bottom up.	Keep wood out of contact with soil; look for tunnels on foundation; call exterminator if problem persists.
Termites— dry wood	Do not require contact with ground; can enter through gaps in siding and attic vents; leave droppings which look like tiny seeds.	Southern states	Near doors and windows.	Call exterminator.
Termites— damp wood	Usually attack wet wood, but may spread further.	Pacific Northwest	Damp wood	Call exterminator.
Wood-boring beetles	Often called "worms," look for wormholes.	Widespread, especially in older basement beams.	May enter in a load of firewood or from a nearby tree.	Call exterminator if problem is widespread and active (as shown by new sawdust on floor).

Dry rot, which attacks damp or wet wood, earned its misleading name because the rotten wood looks dry. Dry rot is easier to prevent—by keeping the wood dry—than to cure, so see "Home Ventilation—Why and How," in Chapter 11, and "May We Talk about Your Soggy Basement?" in Chapter 18.

Carpenter ants and termites are colonial beasts; you get one, you may soon have a million. If you stay alert for signs of these silent villains, you can deal with invasions before they get too bad.

Although exterminators will happily spray poison on insects, calling the bug-killers should be a last resort. Start by changing conditions to make the house less hospitable to insects. Carpenter ants, for example, burrow only in wet wood; you can send them packing by closing the leak that's soaking the wood. Extermination also raises health concerns: Chlordane, used for termite control until 1988, is a persistent, carcinogenic pesticide, and although newer pesticides are less hazardous, who's to say they are perfectly safe? On the other hand, if you're forced to choose between extermination and watching your house be gnawed to death, that's an easy choice.

Treated Lumber

Industrial chemists have responded to the threat fungi and insects pose to wood by inventing pressure-treated lumber, which is universally used for decks, steps, and other outdoor or below-grade work. The most common pressure-treated wood is a greenish variety treated with chromated copper arsenate, called CCA. CCA is relatively safe, unlike two earlier preservatives, pentachlorophenol and creosote, which are now restricted due to health concerns. Nevertheless, CCA contains the toxic chemicals chromium and arsenic, so you should cut it with care. Work outside, and wear a dust mask to avoid

Nail It Down
To a builder, *grade* is not something on a report card—it's ground level (not to be confused with "ground zero"). Something that is *below-grade* is below ground level, whether it's actually in contact with the earth or not.

breathing sawdust, and a long-sleeve shirt (some people report skin irritation from working with this stuff). Think of it this way: "If it's green, it's mean." Don't even try to burn green wood, since that could release arsenic-laden vapors. If this discussion is giving you the heebie-jeebies, look for the new varieties of treated wood that don't contain arsenic or chromium.

And even though treated wood is not appetizing to bugs, it does require attention, as I learned when sunlight and rain began darkening and splitting the deck in my backyard (see "Treating Decks," Chapter 14).

Cutting Remarks on Slick Sawing Techniques

Handy Hint

When you cut plywood or paneling with a circular saw, even with a fine-toothed plywood blade, the top side will splinter. If the plywood must look good, you'll have to cut with the good side down. Imagine the piece backwards, then mark and cut from the back. Don't bother doing this if you don't care about appearance; the splintering will not weaken the wood.

Cutting wood accurately sounds easy—until you try it. Then you notice that the saw binds in the board, or it wanders from the line, or it doesn't cut at all. That's when you realize you need a sharp saw and good technique.

Saw horses are the traditional way to support wood while sawing, but I prefer plastic milk crates; they're easier to store, better for cutting plywood, and helpful for supporting other stuff you repair—from cabinets to lawn mowers.

Arrange the supports so the cut-off piece can fall free. If you saw between supports, the board will sag, the saw will bind vise-like, and you'll get a crooked cut at best and an injury at worst (see "Basic sawing technique" on the following page). And, be sure to get a speed square to guide your circular saw (see "Five Cool Tools You Must Meet" in Chapter 7). Fast, facile, and fiendishly accurate, it's a carpenter's best friend.

1. Keep the cut reasonably close (within 6") of the support, and use enough supports to hold the work securely.

2. Push the raised edge of the square against the board, then mark your cut (see the photo below).

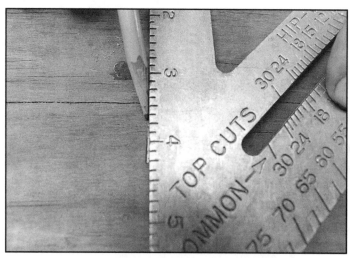

3. Slide the square aside and move your circular saw into position.

4. When the blade is exactly where you want it, slide the square tight to the saw's baseplate.

5. Pull the trigger and slide the saw along the square (see the next illustration). Once you get the hang of it, you won't need to watch the blade—just hold the square in position.

When marking your cuts, the pencil, not the edge of the square, should be on the cutting line.

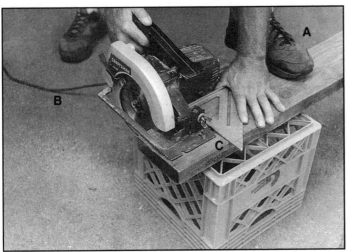

(A)   Firm support close to one side of the cut, with foot pressing the wood down.

(B)   No obstructions or snarled extension cords.

(C)   Saw glides firmly along the square.

Basic sawing technique

6. For a wide board, stop cutting halfway, move the square to the other side of the board, and finish (or, if you're feeling rich, buy a 12" aluminum square).

If you're cutting a long piece from a board, it will split when it falls unless someone holds it. If a servant is not available, use a third support about as high as the other two, or slightly shorter (if the third support is too tall, it will push the wood up and bind the saw).

Handy Hint

Cutting molding for a 45° miter (the kind you see at the corners of door trim) is tricky—just take it from somebody who repeatedly cuts moldings backwards. Now I stand in the room where the molding will be nailed, and mark the location of the cut, *and* its angle, on the molding.

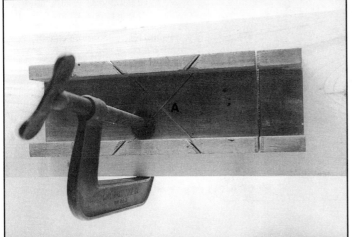

Clamp the miter box to a workbench, or fasten it with drywall screws to something secure, like a workbench or a hunk of 2 × 10. Otherwise, it's going to wander and cause more problems than it solves.

Sawing with a miter box

For cutting small pieces, such as molding, use a miter box. You can buy or rent a miter box with metal guides to hold the saw, but I use a simple wooden model with a small back saw. A back saw has a stiff back and is made for accurate cutting with a miter box.

Hammering for the Ham-Handed

When I was a kid, the county fair offered a prize to anybody who could whump a big nail into a knotty 2 × 4 with three whacks. That's when I learned that although hammering may look Neolithic, it's a tricky knack. In case you didn't get to the county fair, heed these suggestions:

➤ Use a natural swing, and flex your wrist.

➤ Try to hammer downward. Nailing overhead is tiring and clumsy; if you must, drill a pilot (prepatory) hole for the nail (or use a power-driven screw).

➤ Nail the thinner piece to the thicker one—nail the siding to the stud, for example, and the plywood to the floor framing.

➤ Use a nail set (see Chapter 7, "Your Basic Toolkit") to prevent hammer dents in finish work, or if you can't quite reach the nail with the hammer.

➤ For a better grip on the nail head, clean corrosion from the hammer face with sandpaper.

➤ Get good support behind the work. If you must nail into something that springs back, use a screw or secure the boards with a C-clamp, or see "Nailing to a moving target," below.

Nailing to a moving target

My friend John Christenson showed me this amazingly effective trick for nailing to a wobbly post. Hold something about as heavy as your hammer—like another hammer (A) or a pipe wrench—behind the nail. As long as it bounces back when you hit the nail, the backup weight will absorb the blow, and you'll have a tight joint.

Why Wood Splits—and How You Can Prevent It

One of the biggest drawbacks of wood that comes directly from a tree (I'm not talking about plywood and similar products) is that nailing tends to split it. Wood splits between the grain (the fibers that are vertical in a living tree) because the "glue" bonding the fibers is weaker than the fibers. Splitting is a real problem in old, dry wood.

To minimize splitting:

➤ Drill a pilot hole through the top board; this is almost a requirement for hardwoods like oak and hard maple.

➤ Use a small nail. Use box or sinker nails instead of common nails—they are much easier to drive, and stronger because they cause less splitting.

➤ Dull the nail by hammering the point so it cuts the grain instead of splitting it.

➤ Use plywood or oriented strand board instead of regular lumber. This stuff may be ugly, but it won't split.

➤ Space your nails across the grain—don't put them all into the same grain fiber.

➤ Avoid nailing near the end of a board (if you must, drill a pilot hole first).

Instead of overnailing to make a superstrong wood joint, use one of these tricks:

➤ Apply glue to the joint before nailing, so you can use fewer nails.

➤ Bolt the joint and use flat washers on both sides.

➤ Use a sheet-metal or strap-iron mending plate (sold at lumber yards and hardware stores); or

➤ Glue and then nail or screw a triangular reinforcer (called a gusset; made from scrap plywood) to the joint.

Nail It Down
Pilot holes are not down-at-the-heels bars where airplane pilots get soused between flights. They are holes drilled to help screws and (sometimes) nails get where they are going.

Toe Nailing

Toe nailing—nailing diagonally through one board into another—is your only choice if you can't get behind a joint to nail straight through. Toe nailing is usually used for construction, not repairs, but it's a handy trick to know. (If you have trouble toe nailing, substitute a drywall screw in an angled pilot hole). You may have to hold the upper piece still by placing your boot or a temporary block of wood behind it.

1. Punch a dent in the upper board, about 1¹/₂" from the end, with the hammer and nail held almost perpendicular to the wood.

2. Hold the point in the hole you just made, but angle it steeply toward the bottom piece, and hammer it tight (see the illustration for toe nailing). If you're smashing the wood with the hammer, use a ¹/₈" nail set.

(A) Toe nailing is almost impossible if the pieces don't meet soundly. Cut the pieces correctly or use a shim to get good contact.

(B) Make sure the nail is angled steeply at the second board or you'll just push the top piece to the side.

Toe nailing

Filling Holes in Wood

Handy Hint

Lumber yards sell wood shims—they resemble long wooden wedges—which are great for filling gaps before nailing. Place one shim atop another, and slide them together until they're the right thickness. Nail through the shims, and cut them off if needed.

Like people, wood can show its age. But you won't need a plastic surgeon to repair the occasional hole, scratch, or dent in wood. Instead, you need a can of wood filler and a couple of tricks. (If you're planning to stain the wood, or to put a clear finish on it, make sure to choose a filler that will absorb stain.)

1. Clean the surface with a putty knife, utility knife, small trowel, or sandpaper. *Make sure nothing remains above the final surface level.* Otherwise, the patching material will bulge out and you'll need to do too much sandpapering afterwards.

2. Mix up some wood filler and push it firmly into the hole.

3. Scrape the patching flush with the knife almost perpendicular to the surface (see the next illustration), and allow it to set a while. Scrape with the grain of the wood.

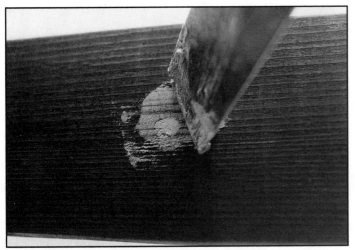

Filling holes. To prevent a big sandpapering chore afterwards, scrape off all filler from the surface of the wood.

4. If needed, press another coat into place.

5. Wait a while until the patch is partly hardened. Moisten a rag and rub the surface to remove extra filler and avoid sandpapering. dampen the rag (use water for water-based filler, and solvent for other fillers). Repeat after an hour to remove any hazy filler remaining on the surface.

6. If needed, lightly sandpaper the patch when it's completely dry to level it.

7. Prime and paint.

The Least You Need to Know

➤ Moisture, insects, and fungi are wood's number-one enemies.

➤ Wood is easy to saw—if you use a sharp saw and good support.

➤ The right nail, and the right technique, can simplify nailing and prevent splitting.

➤ Glue, screws, and reinforcing plates are helpful alternatives when nails are not strong enough.

➤ If you're trying to restore beat-up molding or surfaces, wood filler is your best friend.

Handy Hint
I buy wood filler in powder form and mix it with water when I need it. Powder seems less convenient than ready-mixed filler, but that stuff dries out in the can while powder lasts forever on the shelf. When mixing, add water slowly—a little water goes a long way.

Part 3

Working Out—Aerobics for Your Home's Exterior

The exterior of your home—the foundation, siding, caulking, windows, doors, and roof—is the first part your friends see. It's also the first part the weather sees. The exterior is supposed to keep everything and everybody inside warm, cozy, and dry (or cool, cozy, and dry—depending on where you happen to live). But if your house is past toddlerhood, I'll bet its skin has developed problems—wrinkles, sags, leaks, and even blemishes.

Hollywood stars buy facelifts all the time—and why should your home get any less pampering? In this chapter, we'll talk about giving the old place a minor facelift. Even if you're not planning a Hollywood audition, its appearance and durability will only benefit.

CAULK-GUN FIGHT!!

Chapter 11

Skin-Tight: Caulking, Weather Stripping, and Ventilation

In This Chapter:

➤ Your caulking and weather stripping—is it up to the job?

➤ Where, how, and when to caulk and weather strip

➤ How to protect your home from moisture buildup

In college, I rented an old brick farmhouse with a little problem called winter. The big chill was particularly severe in the kitchen, where six battered doors and four dilapidated windows supposedly kept the weather at bay. So I cut my teeth on caulking and weather stripping in a house where you could fly a kite on a blustery January evening.

Log cabins were once chinked with straw, mud, and clay—low-tech materials that kept some weather out. Nowadays, these organic materials have been replaced by caulking (the gooey stuff that squeezes into cracks) and by weather stripping (the flexible seals for doors and windows). Caulking and weather stripping don't just keep out annoying things like rain, wind, cold, heat, insects, and noise. They also offer a quick return on your investment—in the form of lower utility bills. They often pay for themselves in less than a year.

Unfortunately, these modern sealers are so effective that they can cause a problem which would have been inconceivable to log-cabin dwellers: a buildup of moisture inside the home. So I'll also talk about home ventilation in this chapter.

Where and When to Caulk

A good way to learn about controlling heat and moisture, and where better caulking is needed, is to obtain a home energy audit, courtesy of your local utility (see Chapter 26). Or spend an hour on a particularly hot or cold day looking for drafts.

You'll need to caulk almost anywhere dissimilar building materials meet. That's because when the temperature changes, different materials expand and contract at different rates creating cracks which can only be sealed by a flexible sealer, like caulk.

Outdoors, caulk:

➤ At the joint between the foundation and siding (if you can get to it).

➤ At cracks in the foundation (see "A Word on Foundation Repair," Chapter 18).

➤ Around windows, doors, faucets, and other openings in siding.

➤ Around chimneys, vent pipes, and vents in the roof.

➤ Note: In brick houses, don't caulk the small, regular holes just above the foundation, or above doors and windows. These "weepholes," designed to allow moisture to escape the wall, must be left open.

Indoors, caulk:

➤ At cracks around exterior door and window frames.

➤ Where pipes or wires enter, as under a sink or tub.

➤ At floor joints near a tub or toilet (to prevent spills or condensation from damaging floors and walls).

Spring and fall are ideal caulking weather, because it's warm enough to meet the minimum temperature requirement of caulking, surfaces are dry, and you won't get broiled (caulking in the heat of summer is 100% slavery). Sadly, caulking won't flow or adhere well in cold, damp weather, even though winter is when you are most likely to feel motivated to cure drafts.

Caulking Materials

So what are you going to use in that caulking gun? The short answer is the best stuff you can afford. The lifetime of caulking rises quickly along with its price, so unless you actually enjoy caulking (you know who you are!), buy stuff that will last 5 to 10 years. See Table 11.1.

Table 11.1 Use the right caulk for the right job

Type	Lifetime	Notes
Oil base	1–2 years	Cheap, not durable, prone to shrinking and cracking.
Latex base	5–10 years	Use indoors. Not very flexible; should not be used on joints that are moving (large gaps in the old caulking indicate movement).
Acrylic	10 years	Flexible. Use indoor and out, cures quickly, cannot be painted.
Butyl	5–10 years	Exterior use, especially on concrete, metal, or masonry. Water resistant, good for places where water may collect. Cures slowly.
Silicon, polyurethane, other "elasto-meric" caulks	20–50 years	Exterior and interior. Very flexible and durable. May not adhere to paint, or may need primer before caulking. Some can be painted. Some are transparent; others are white, black, brown, or gray.

Caulking Cracks

Caulking is real idiot-proof work. First, you clean the crack. Then you pump the caulk into place. Finally, if you're feeling ferociously fastidious, you smear it flat. While many tasks merely *sound* easy, this one truly *is* easy. About the only complication is deciding that caulking is more important—today—than going canoeing or reading a book.

You'll need a paint scraper, screwdriver, trowel or other cleaning tool, brush, caulking gun, caulk, utility knife, ladder, and rag. Buy your caulk before start-ing—each variety has limitations on temperature and how big a crack it can fill. To do the job:

Don't Screw Up!
If you're planning to paint your caulking, make sure to use a paintable variety. Some of the most durable caulks cannot be painted (although the transparent versions will be hard to see even if they aren't painted). Even if a caulk can be painted, it will need to cure for a while first.

1. Clean the crack with a tool and/or stiff plastic brush. Remember that any surface irregularities will show up in the caulking—if you want the caulking really smooth, you'll have to remove any bumps at the edge of the joint. Drive in any raised nails.

Keep steady pressure on the caulking gun, and try not to let bulges form if the gun snags on an obstacle. Remember— it's much easier to make a smooth application than to fix it afterwards.

2. Remove all the dust. If the crack is very deep, see "Are You Extremely Cracked?" later in this chapter.

3. Put the tube in the gun, cut the tip of the tube at an angle, and pierce the seal with a long nail. Make a broader opening in the tip for wide cracks.

4. Start caulking, holding the gun at an angle, and pressing the tip against the crack.

5. Move the gun steadily along the entire crack, gradually squeezing the trigger. Release pressure just before the end of the crack, since the caulking will ooze out for another few seconds. If your gun has a pressure release, push it just before the end of the crack.

6. Optional: Smooth the caulk and press it into place with a moistened finger, the handle of an old toothbrush, or a rag dampened with whatever solvent the manufacturer specifies.

Are You Extremely Cracked?

In my house, some cracks are more like glacial crevasses—they seem to extend down toward the center of the Earth, and they could suck up entire tubes of caulking without accomplishing much except wasting money. To fill these cracks, I've got to stuff a backing material in with a trowel or putty knife so the caulk has something to press against. You can buy fiberglass made for filling cracks, or just rip some material off a roll of fiberglass insulation—just make sure no packing sticks out when you're done. Spray cans of urethane foam insulation are excellent for sealing and backing up caulking, but the foam expands so much that it tends to rise above the surface; and it's very difficult to cut it back.

If the crack is slightly too wide for your caulking, try this trick: On the first pass, aim the gun at one side of the crack, giving the caulk a good grip on that side. Let the caulk harden a bit, then caulk the narrower crack remaining.

Weather Stripping

What's the best weather for stripping? A summer thunderstorm, when the cool rain relieves the muggy heat, and housebound neighbors won't notice you splashing, bare-bunned, in the cloudburst.

But the best weather for weather stripping is a mid-winter storm. Only then can you appreciate how much frigid air can move through cracks in doors and windows. But since it's a trifle difficult to weather-strip an open door when it's 20° outside, it pays to keep on the lookout for cracks during warmer weather.

Nail It Down

Jambs are not something you want to get out of—they're the 1" wood members that encase doors and windows.

Weather stripping has improved immeasurably over the years. Old windows and doors didn't even have the stuff, while their modern counterparts have an array of impregnable plastic and magnetic barriers. (The improvement in weather stripping alone may justify the expense of replacing drafty windows, but that's not our province here.)

Many varieties of weather stripping are being sold these days; do yourself a favor and avoid the ineffective foam tape and felt varieties. This stuff looks ugly, works poorly, and dies in a couple of years—some economy. In some cases, you'll have to contact the manufacturer to replace an intricate weather stripping.

Table 11.1 Weather strip varieties

Item	Description
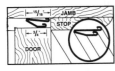	*Compression weather strip* nails to the jamb; the vinyl gasket folds up slightly when the door closes, making the seal.
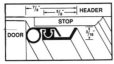	*Tubular gasket*—a plastic tube with a strip that's nailed or screwed to the stops; slots allow easy adjustment to the door. The vinyl gasket is replaceable.
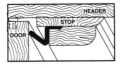	*Vinyl-wood stop*—a wood strip with vinyl weather stripping, nailed to the jambs. The door folds the vinyl slightly to make the seal. This style can be nailed to the existing stop, or replace the stop.
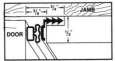	*Magnetic weather strip* (for steel-clad doors only). The weather strip slides into a notch in the jamb, and the strip magnet pulls the weather strip to the door, for a very tight seal. You may have to contact the manufacturer or distributor for an unusual variety.

One of the most versatile weather strips is a Vee-shaped strip of flexible plastic that's glued on one side. Use this so-called "Vee-strip" in door and window jambs or stops —it adheres tightly to clean surfaces even in cold weather. The only tool you need is a utility knife.

Various sweeps, shoes, and thresholds are sold to prevent wind and rain from gusting below your door.

Table 11.2   Door bottom solutions

Item	Description
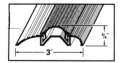	The gasket threshold is the basic door-bottom sealer. Makes a good seal, but you may have to remove the existing threshold and/or saw the door to exact length. After a few years, you can pull out the vinyl gasket and replace it.
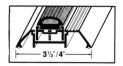	An adjustable-height threshold has set screws to take up the slack of an uneven gap at the bottom of the door. Good for an inaccurate door gap.
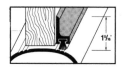	An aluminum and pile door sweep is easier to install, but may not seal as effectively as a gasket threshold. Note that the sweep must contact a relatively flat portion of the threshold.
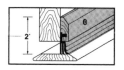	An oak and vinyl sweep can be stained or painted to match the door trim. You don't need to saw the door bottom, but the sweep is visible from the inside, and it may have trouble riding over a carpet or an unlevel floor.
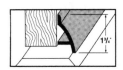	A drip cap, in aluminum, vinyl or brass, keeps the rain out.
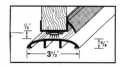	A combination drip cap, threshold, and door sweep is a comprehensive solution to door woes.

Insulation

Want to stay warm? Want to stay cool? Then you'll need insulation—keeping out drafts with weather stripping is not enough. If you need insulation in walls, that's generally a pro job, because somebody's got to bore holes in the walls and spray the insulation in. But foundations, crawl spaces, and accessible attics are all places where you can save money by insulating.

The effectiveness of insulation is rated by "R-factor"— the higher the R-factor, the more insulating power you get. Usually, the R rating applies to the thickness of the insulation product it rates, but you may occasionally see an "R per inch" rating, which describes a type of material. In other words, a 2" foam sheet, rated at R-8, would have an R per inch value of R-4.

> **Don't Screw Up!**
> When choosing weather stripping for a door bottom, do not underestimate the challenge of cutting the door accurately enough to make a gasket threshold work. Measure several times before you remove the door from its hinges; mark with a knife, not a pencil; and use a straight edge to guide the saw.

The most popular varieties of insulation include fiberglass, foam, and blown cellulose. Inch for inch, polyurethane foam has the best insulating value, but it's somewhat more expensive, so if you don't care how thick the insulation is, it's better to buy thicker, cheaper material. One of the big advantages of fiberglass is that you can stuff it into irregular spaces to seal them; I've used it to fill gaps between the joists around the edge of the basement.

Foam won't rot or stop insulating if it gets wet, but it will retain humidity in the building, and thus contribute to damaging moisture buildup. Most other insulation materials lose insulating power if they get wet (see the next section about ventilation), and some, like cellulose, can even rot.

When applying insulation in older homes, be sure to follow your building codes—don't just throw the stuff anywhere. For example, you can't cover up old knob-and-tube electrical wiring (see Chapter 24). Likewise, don't cover vents in the soffit (the lower edge of a roof), which are designed to allow moisture to escape from the roof.

Home Ventilation—Why and How

Caulking, weather stripping, and insulation keep the weather out, and they hold moisture in. This moisture, from breathing, cooking, washing, and bathing, causes problems in winter, when it migrates through your walls toward the colder, drier conditions outside. If this moisture condenses inside the walls, it can peel paint and rot wood, plaster, and drywall. Condensation on windows can wreck your winter view, ruin paint, and rot the sash.

In Southern Florida and other places where humidity and fungus are constant problems, the best solution to humidity may be whole-house air-conditioning. But in most other climates, simpler measures can reduce the moisture problem. Start by operating exhaust fans in the kitchen and bathroom. Run a dehumidifier in the basement in the summer. For suggestions on dampness below stairs, see Chapter 18, "May We Talk about Your Soggy Basement?" Aside from roof vents (see below), most long-term solutions to moisture buildup, like installing vapor barriers in walls, are virtually impossible without remodeling.

Roof Vents

One of the best ways to allow moisture to escape is attic and roof vents, which have the fringe benefit of cooling the house by allowing hot air to escape the attic.

Handy Hint
Here's a quickie fix for a kitchen vent fan that's spinning slowly due to a grease buildup. Cut off the electricity, remove the filter, and remove the screws securing the fan. Squirt WD-40 on the fan shaft near the motor, spin the blade by hand, reinstall everything, and turn on the circuit. WD-40 will soften the grease that's dragging on the fan shaft, and you'll have a like-new fan.

Any do-it-yourselfer can vent a shingle roof that's not too steep. To ensure good circulation, put vents in the soffit (beneath the eave) and near the ridge (peak of the roof). The ventilator package should explain how many ventilators your house needs.

Aluminum soffit is usually vented with tiny slits. You can install round ventilators into wood soffit with a hole saw or a right-angle drill. Drill between each rafter and push the vent into the hole. You'll need good ladders, and goggles to shield your eyes from flying crud.

To insert a roof ventilator under the shingles near the ridge, you'll need chalk or pencil, hammer, saber saw or keyhole saw, drill and bits, a trowel, ventilator, roof cement, and roofing nails.

When you cut the opening for a roof ventilator, hold the saber saw firmly against the roof to prevent vibration.

Work slowly with the trowel to minimize damage as you separate the shingles.

1A. If you can get in the attic: Locate the ventilator from below by punching a nail through the midpoint between the rafters about 18" below the ridge. Use this nail as a center point for the hole. Go to step 2.

1B. If you must work from above: Locate the rafters by pounding on the roof and looking for the place with maximum bounce. Then center your hole between two rafters.

2. Place the ventilator on the roof—centered between the rafters or on the nail from step 1A—and mark the opening (not the outer dimension) on the shingles with chalk. (Some ventilators come with a template for this hole.)

3. Start the hole with a $^3/_8$" drill for a saber saw or at least $^1/_2$" for a keyhole saw. Cut through the entire roof thickness to remove the hole.

4. Slip the trowel under the shingles above the hole to loosen the cement bonding them to each other. Clear away the debris.

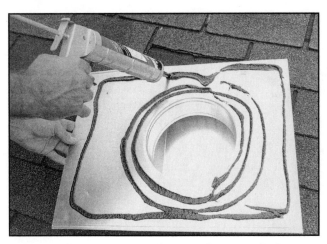

5. Coat the bottom of the ventilator base with roof cement and slip it under the shingles.

6. Nail the ventilator in place and coat visible nail heads with cement. Squirt a line of cement under the shingles you loosened in step 4 and press them into the cement.

Theoretically, you don't need any roof goop on the bottom of the ventilator, but it's better to overdo things than have to return to fix a leak.

The Least You Need to Know

➤ Caulking and weather stripping offer about the fastest payback of any home repairs.

➤ Since most of the expense of caulking is the labor of installing it, you might as well pay for material that will last for several years.

➤ Insulation can save money and make the house more comfortable at the same time. But like everything else, it's got to be chosen and installed correctly.

➤ Moisture accumulations can damage paint, wood, drywall, and plaster. To improve the ventilation in your home, operate whatever vents you already have, and consider installing vents in the roof.

Chapter 12

A Transparent Guide to Windows

> ## In This Chapter
>
> ➤ How to keep your windows swinging or sliding
>
> ➤ Removing and replacing glass, step-by-step
>
> ➤ What to do when your insulated windows turn traitor

If you want some air, light, or a view, a window beats a solid wall, but when it comes to staying out of trouble, I'd bet on the wall any day. Windows leak. They break. Their glass sags with age. Even insulated windows, which are great for keeping cold weather out, eventually get cloudy. And some windows can't be opened without a fullback shove.

Windows come in many styles and shapes—they slide up and down, they slide side to side, and they swing from the top or side edge. The double-hung window is still one of the most common, so let's get acquainted with some window lingo (see the illustration of parts of a double-hung window).

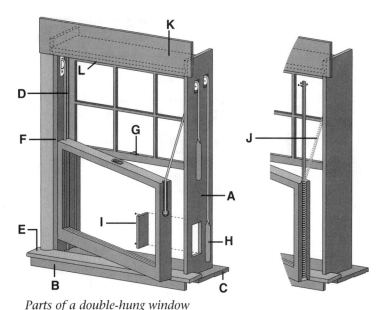

(A) Side jamb
(B) Apron
(C) Sill
(D) Inside stop (parting stop)
(E) Stool
(F) Outer stop
(G) Meeting rail
(H) Sash weight or counterweight (in some windows)
(I) Pocket and cover (in some windows with sash weights)
(J) Counterweight spring (in some windows—replaces sash weights)
(K) Head jamb
(L) Muntins

Parts of a double-hung window

Unsticking Stuck Wood Windows

Why is a wood window like a jazz quartet? Because they both love to jam. Yuk yuk. No more two-liners—I promise. But seriously, windows do get stuck, a problem that is most serious when caused by a shifting foundation. Although you might be able to stop this movement, repairing it is beyond idiot territory. Still, it's worth having someone do it, because foundation movement can also crack the plaster (see "A Word on Foundation Repair," in Chapter 18). Here, we'll talk about windows that are jammed or painted shut, are swollen with moisture, or have poor counterweights or balky mechanisms.

Jammed or Painted Shut

Don't Screw Up!
Before you apply megatons of force to any window, double-check that the lock is open, and that a nail or another security device is not holding it closed. Don't use hammers, levers, or other primitive force on the sash (although you may need a hammer to remove the outer stop). There's glass there!

Amazing as it may seem, people actually paint windows shut—by slobbering paint into the cracks between the moving parts (the sash) and the fixed parts (the jambs and stops). To free a stuck window, you'll need a hammer, trowel or putty knife, and a paint scraper. You may also need a plane, a belt sander with fine sandpaper, a drill, and some nails.

1. Slip a putty knife or trowel in the cracks between the sash and the stops, and between sash and sill. Run the tool around the whole window, wiggling it and trying to move the sash.

2. Press up with your hand at the middle of the lower sash. If the sash moves at all, concentrate your efforts where it's still stuck.

3. If the window refuses to move, remove the outer stop (the molding that forms the channel for the sash). Use a hammer to tap a wood chisel and/or stiff trowel under the molding to remove it. See the "Wood Sash" section later in this chapter for more advice on pulling this molding without trashing it.

4. Remove the sash without letting the counterweight ropes or straps disappear into their holes.

5. Clean out the sash channels and lightly sandpaper or plane the edges of the sash where it binds. If there's a lot of extra paint, use a paint scraper or a very light touch of a belt sander, using medium sandpaper.

6. Reinstall the sash and reconnect the counterweights. Drill new nail holes and renail the stops slightly looser than before. (If you use the old holes, the stops will return to the position where they jammed the window.)

7. If you repaint the window, use paint sparingly, and paint the parts separately so paint does not bridge the gap and put you back where you started.

Moisture

Damp weather swells wood, particularly if it's not protected by a sealer. If a window sticks only occasionally, you may want to live with it. Otherwise, try these suggestions:

➤ Paint the sash with water-resistant paint.

➤ Try the suggestions in "Jammed or Painted Shut," on previous page. If you must trim the sash with a saw, planer, or belt sander, don't get too enthusiastic, particularly in damp weather. Otherwise, when the humidity drops, your window may rattle and admit drafts.

Poor Counterweights

Suppose the window opens, but you can't be bothered calling Arnold Schwarzenegger every time the smell of fried fish makes you yearn for fresh air. The problem may be a detached counterweight. These metal weights are suspended in hidden channels behind the jambs to balance the weight of the sash and make it easier to open. A double-hung window has two counterweights for each sash (see the earlier illustration).

To remove the counterweights, follow steps 3 and 4 in the preceding procedure for opening a jammed window. Detach the ropes from the sash and look for a removable rectangular cover (it may be painted over, but you'll see an outline if it's present). Use a wood chisel and screwdriver to remove the cover, then rehang the weight with a new cord.

If there's no cutout, you can't access the counterweights without at least tearing off the window trim. At that point, I would get rid of the ropes and go to a hardware store to buy a spring kit to support the sash.

If you're working on an aging, drafty double-hung window, consider replacing the sash, glass, and sliding channels with a kit that gives you essentially a new window, with spring supports, modern weather stripping, and the ability to clean all the glass from the inside. These kits, which must be ordered for your window size, are a comprehensive solution to window woes, but they're much cheaper and easier than replacing the entire window.

Balky Mechanism in a Casement Window

Casement windows may not have counterweight problems, but they still know how to stick. To loosen a casement window, oil the mechanism and hinges with penetrating oil, such as WD-40 or Liquid Wrench, followed by motor oil. If that fails, carefully release the mechanism and repeat the process. You may need to use repeated applications of penetrating oil, and a few light whacks of a hammer, to loosen the mechanism. But don't break anything; you may have trouble finding a replacement mechanism.

Keeping in mind that there are many designs out there, here's how to remove and reinstall one type of casement window sash:

1. Open the sash part-way and figure out how to release the opening mechanism, which is located on the bottom of the sash. In the window shown in the top photo at right, the bar slips down and out when it's opposite the arrow on the channel of the opening mechanism.

2. Detach the sash from the top and bottom mechanisms by sliding the catch securing the pin to the side, using a screwdriver (see bottom photo at right).

3. Carefully slide the sash to the side, so you can pull it from the track. Disengage the bottom first, then get a firm grip on the sash before disengaging the top.

4. Reinstall by reversing these steps.

Feeling Rather Stuffy?

If your double-hung windows have the usual kind of "combination" aluminum storms, chances are the screen only covers the bottom half. To get better ventilation (particularly

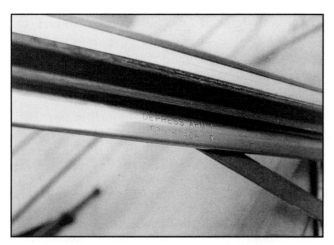

Adjust the sash until the bar is located at the arrow, and push down (you may have to hunt around to figure out how to disassemble your window if it's different from this one).

Pull out the sliding catch, and the pin will drop out of the slot. Slide the sash to the side and remove it.

on upper stories), remove the upper aluminum storm, take it to a window-repair store, and have a screen made to the same size. After you install the new screen above the existing screen, you'll be able to open both sashes, allowing hot air to escape from near the ceiling.

Replacing Glass

Way back when, I hit a line-drive home run in front of hundreds of college classmates. Unfortunately, my delight was terminated by the painful, costly crash of the softball tearing through a beautiful leaded window. But when it comes to breaking windows, I've found that utter stupidity works as well as softball heroics. Last winter, I attacked a housefly on the window with a magazine. The fly merrily escaped— but the pane went straight to the trash can. What a pain!

Wood Sash

To replace broken glass in wooden sash, you'll need gloves, goggles, a small trowel or putty knife, a hammer, new glass, glazier's points (the tiny nails that hold the glass in place), boiled linseed oil (or primer or diluted exterior alkyd paint), a small brush or rag, and glazing compound. If the window is accessible from outside, you might be able to fix it in place. Clean out all the glass, and start with step 4. Here's what you need to do to replace that pane if you must remove the sash first:

1. Remove one outer stop (the vertical strip of molding inside the jamb that holds the sash in the channel). Starting at one end, slip a trowel under the molding, near a

nail, and pry the stop slowly away from the jamb. If a nail head comes up, pull it, protecting the wood with the trowel blade or a scrap of wood. Move along the length of the stop—don't concentrate in one place—and pry with the hammer and trowel in unison to minimize damage (see Chapter 20 for more on the correct way to pull molding).

2. Remove the lower sash and detach the counterweight ropes or spring lifts. Don't let the ropes disappear into the jamb.

3. If you're replacing the upper sash, remove the parting stop by repeating step 1 (even more delicately—this stop is harder to remove). Once the sash is out, you're in a good position to install weather stripping; at least clean the channel so the sash operates smoothly.

4. Wearing gloves and goggles, place the broken sash on a garbage pail. If the pane is mostly intact, lay a rag across it and beat it with a blunt object (see the illustration for this step). Remove the shards and scrape the seat (where the glass meets the wood) with an old wood chisel, paint scraper, small trowel, or putty knife. Remove all glazier's points with pliers if they don't pop out.

Be careful when removing the pane of glass. Be sure to wear goggles and heavy-duty gloves.

5. Cutting glass is no job for complete idiots, but hardware stores and glass companies have the tools and expertise to do it safely and accurately. Bring the actual dimensions of the opening, and explain that they are the dimensions *of the opening,* not the glass. Let the glass company figure out the actual size for the new pane.

6. Paint the seat with boiled linseed oil, primer, or diluted house paint so the glazing compound does not dry too quickly.

7. Press a small bead of glazing compound in the seat to seal the pane from behind, then press the new pane into the bead and seat it securely.

8. Gently but firmly press glazier's points into place with a trowel, putty knife, or wide screwdriver. Remember, this is no time for a Hercules imitation!

Use linseed oil or exterior primer to seal the seat for the new pane of glass.

Smooth the glazing compound with the trowel. For the final pass, grease the trowel with a little boiled linseed oil so it doesn't pull out the glazing compound.

9. Distribute glazing compound on the seat and press it to make a smooth coat (see photo). When you're almost done, lubricate the trowel or knife with linseed oil and glide it along the edges, leaving a smooth seal behind.

10. Reassemble the window and reconnect the counterweight ropes or spring lifts. Carefully renail the outer stop—it should be tight to the sash without binding it. In dry weather, the stop should be a bit loose, so when it swells in humid weather, it will not bind.

11. Let the glazing dry for about a week, then prime and paint it.

> **Handy Hint**
> The best window-cleaner is also the cheapest. Splash some ammonia in warm water. Dip a ball of old newspaper in the solution and clean the glass. Dry the glass with a clean ball of newspaper, then recycle the soggy paper.

Metal Sash

If you can't access the glass from outside, you'll need to remove the sash. See the section about removing casement window sashes earlier in this chapter for suggestions. You may have to hunt around, starting at the operating mechanism, to figure out how to remove it. Then follow the directions for replacing a pane in wood sash, steps 4 through 9, above. Instead of glazing points, use the clips that hold the old pane, or buy replacements at a glass company. When reinstalling the sash, lubricate the hinges and operating mechanism.

To replace a broken pane in a sliding aluminum window, either:

➤ Remove the sash, clean out the broken glass, and take the frame to a glass company for replacement; or

➤ Take the sash apart by removing the little screws at the corners. Measure the size of the glass, and have one cut for you. If the rubber gasket holding the pane is in good shape, reuse it. Otherwise, buy a replacement.

Insulated Glass

Insulated—or double-pane—windows are a boon for people in northern climates—since they eliminate the innumerable leakage and cleaning problems of the combination of interior and storm windows that is needed to keep winter out. But like most technological fixes, these windows raise problems: When the seal around the edge of the glass leaks (and it will eventually), condensation will cloud the glass.

> **Don't Screw Up!**
> For safety purposes, doors must be glazed with clear plastic like Plexiglas, or with safety glass. Safety glass breaks into tiny, harmless fragments, it's quite heavy and expensive, and must be ordered, as glass companies cannot cut it. Although Plexiglas scratches easily, it's cheap and easy to replace.

The only cure is to replace the clouded glass, but you don't need to call the glass company to the house for that. Instead, you can yank out the sash and order replacement glass (local glass companies cannot cut insulated glass). Be sure of the length, width, and thickness before you order; if you order the wrong size, you'll have to toss the glass. If you're not sure of these dimensions, you can remove the sash (see the information in "Balky Mechanism in a Casement Window," earlier in this chapter) and have a glass company measure the glass with calipers. Then, when your glass is ready, you can remove the sash again and install the new pane, or have the glass gurus install it for you.

But remember to plan ahead—glass companies do not stock many sizes of double-insulated glass, and ordering it from a manufacturer can take several weeks. You might be able to shorten this wait by going directly to a manufacturer, if one is nearby.

The Least You Need to Know

➤ If humidity is jamming your windows, fight back by cleaning and carefully planing or sanding them, and then sealing the wood.

➤ Opening a window that's painted shut requires patience and a light touch with the tools.

➤ You can save big money, and look like a real hero, by replacing broken panes, but it's best to have a glass company or hardware store cut the glass.

➤ When insulated glass clouds up, it needs replacement. You can take the sting out of this process by removing and replacing the sash by yourself. Remember to plan ahead—you'll need to order the glass, which can take as long as a month.

Chapter 13

An Entry-Level Treatise on Doors

In This Chapter

➤ Sticks, squeaks, and sags—the enemies of a blissful entry

➤ Solving problems with storm doors

➤ How to install a deadbolt lock

Talk about underappreciated—nobody notices doors until they turn bad. But unless your house is fresh out of the box, I guess you are noticing your doors more than you'd like. Maybe they won't close without a ligament-wrenching shove. Maybe they won't lock without a King Kong crank on the key. Maybe they squawk like a first-year clarinetist.

Doors cause so many problems that I'm surprised nobody has figured how to eliminate them. But at least designers have invented ways to make them work more smoothly—better hinges, better hardware, even better doors. So if you're getting tired of shouldering your way into your house, looking like a cross between Elliot Ness and The Fridge, let's get some medicine for door diseases.

They Don't Have to Stick

When it comes to sticking, doors find plenty of causes—dry hinges, loose hinges, hinge mortises cut too deep, the list goes on and on. But except for structural shifting, which can wrack a doorway out of square, and a warped door, which generally needs replacement, every one of these problems is within idiot territory. So let's start curing the typical causes for sticking doors.

Builder's Trivia

Like people, doors are either left- or right-handed. Stand with the door swinging toward you, and look at the hinges. In a left-handed door, they will be on the left, and vice versa. You'll need this information to order a pre-hung door (one that's assembled with its jambs).

Dry Hinges

Cars have stickers to remind you when they need a lube job (don't tell me you ignore these reminders, too!). Door hinges don't have stickers; instead, they use an annoying screech to indicate it's time for an "oil change." Fortunately, the job is simplicity itself. You'll need an old flat-bladed screwdriver or a long nail, a hammer, penetrating oil if the pin is stuck, and an oil can and rag. Just follow these steps:

1. Examine the hinge. If there's a hole at the bottom, under the pin, you've got an "anti-rising" hinge—go to step 4. Otherwise, continue with step 2.

2. For a *standard hinge*, pound up on the lip of the pin with screwdriver and hammer (see left-hand photo on facing page).

3. If the pin refuses to budge, spray it with penetrating oil, swing the door a few times to loosen the pin, and try again. Remember, the pin always gives way—sooner or later. Go to step 5.

4. For an *"anti-rising" hinge,* place a 3" finishing nail in the hole, and pound up with a hammer (see right-hand photo on facing page). After the pin rises a bit, it will pop right out.

5. Leave the pin part-way out, and release the other hinge pins.

6. Remove the door, taking care not to scrunch your fingers.

7. Oil each pin with motor oil, sliding the pin through the rag until it's thoroughly coated. Oil the parts of the hinge that rub against each other; then wipe off oil.

8. Move the door back into place, and partly insert the top pin.

9. Insert other pins and drive them into place.

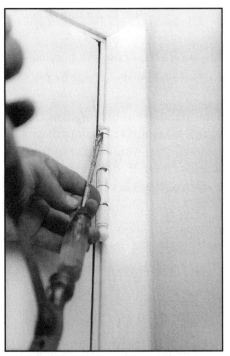

Old-style hinge pins must be battered into submission with this "el crudo" technique. Unfortunately, there's no way to save the paint.

An "anti-rising" pin comes loose with much more sophistication; there's a hole in the bottom for a nail.

Loose Hinges

Give door hinges some credit—if you'd been slammed 10,000 times, you might be coming loose, too. If you've got a door that's threatening to leave its moorings, you can probably trace the problem to loose screws holding the hinges. If the screws are loose, the latch side (the side away from the hinge) may be chafing on the jamb, and you may be able to lift it a fraction of an inch.

Loose hinge screws are easy to cure, and it doesn't hurt to check and tighten them every few years. Save this job for when you're feeling compulsive, or have no other pressing repairs waiting in line (yuk-yuk!).

Don't Screw Up!
"Hollow-core" doors, commonly used in interiors, are essentially two sheets of thin paneling separated by strips of cardboard, glued on edge. It's easy to fasten something like a hook or a shelf to the perimeter of a hollow-core door, because there's solid wood backing up the paneling. Otherwise, you'll need to use expanding-type hollow-wall anchors (see Chapter 9).

To cure loose hinges, you'll need a screwdriver; a hammer; wood glue; and a dowel, golf tee, or wooden matches. Follow these steps:

1. Try to tighten the screws. Ask somebody to lift the latch side, or use a flat prybar and a block of wood to raise it with your foot. If the screws tighten securely, you're done. If they slip in their holes, continue.

2. Find some longer flat-head screws of about the same diameter as the originals. Test to see if they will grab good wood (if they reach the 2×4 behind the jamb, they will be solid). Caution: If the screws are too big in diameter, they won't sit flat in the hinge, and may jam against each other when the door closes. If the screws work, replace them all and you're finished. If the screws jam or don't get a good bite, continue.

3. To reinforce the screw holes, pull the hinge pins, remove the door, and remove hinges from the jamb.

4. Coat golf tees, dowels, or wooden matches with wood glue and tap them into all oversize holes.

5. Oil the hinges (see the preceding section to learn more).

6. After the glue has dried, position the hinges and *carefully* mark the center of each hole with a nail or awl. Drill a new hole for the screw, then reattach the hinge and rehang the door.

Builder's Trivia

Doors are sold based on dimensions in feet and inches. Thus the common 32" wide by 80" tall door is called 2' 8" by 6' 8". Why? I hoped you'd ask. Simply because it's more complicated.

Hinge Mortise Problems

Hanging doors—mounting them inside the jambs—is a tricky business. If the hinges don't sit in an adequate recess (a mortise), the door will be reluctant to close. But if the mortises are too deep, the door will be reluctant to close. This sounds like a Zen koan but it just reflects the delicate nature of doors.

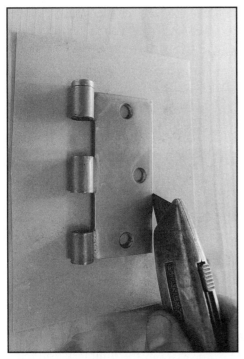

When repairing overcut hinges, if you hold the hinge firmly in place, you can't help cutting an accurate shim. Hint: cut on a double layer of cardboard, so the knife can cut cleanly through the top layer.

Examine the hinges. They should be flush (level) or a hair above the jamb. If the mortises are too shallow, the door will probably rub at the latch side. You'll have to remove the hinges and chisel a deeper mortise.

If the mortises are too deep, the door will tend to spring open as you close it, and you may see a wider gap on the latch side than the hinge side. Fortunately, this problem is easy to solve if you have a screwdriver, utility knife, an awl or a nail, and some cardboard from a cereal box.

1. Examine the hinges to see if the mortises are too deep on the jamb, the door, or both.

2. Remove the hinge pins and set the door aside.

3. Remove hinges that are too deep and place them against a thin piece of cardboard. Using the hinge as a template, cut several shims (see the illustration for this step).

4. Place the shims into the mortises, punch holes for the hinge screws, and rescrew. The shim should be invisible.

5. Test the cure; if cardboard is too thick, try several sheets of copier paper.

Oiling Door Latches and Locks

Molly, my neighbor, came over the other day, fuming that her husband had left her a door key that didn't work. I volunteered to try the key anyway (which seemed safer than dragging out a ladder for some second-story work). With a bit of persuasion, the key turned the bolt, and my neighbor stepped inside with a gratified "thank-you." For my part, I was pleased that nobody had thought to put any oil on that lock for years—otherwise, how would I have played neighborhood hero?

It's about as simple as this: When metal meets metal, you need lubrication, whether factory-applied or done-yourself. If you ever have trouble getting your key to turn the lock of home sweet home, or if your door latches are sticky, it's time for a lube job. You may be able to spray white lithium grease or penetrating oil into the latch and keyhole, but if your lock is quite old, or extremely sticky, you'll need to take the mechanism apart and oil it. You'll need a screwdriver, some motor oil, and a rag; when you have them in hand, follow these steps, being sure to number or lay out the parts in order so you can reassemble the blasted thing with minimal pain:

1. To disassemble the latch or lock mechanism, remove knobs or locks from both sides, and the shaft connecting them, then pull out the latch or bolt mechanism from the edge of the door.

   The details will depend on the exact type of mechanism:

   ➤ On older doorknobs, loosen the screws on one knob; then unscrew the knob from the threaded shaft. The remaining knob and shaft will pull out in one piece.

   ➤ On newer doorknobs, push the tab coming up from inside the knob with a screwdriver while pulling the knob slightly, and pull off the knob. Then pull the other knob off with the shaft.

   ➤ For deadbolts and other locks, remove the screws holding the inner faceplate, or *escutcheon*, then pull the lock apart.

   ➤ After the faceplate is removed, the tumbler assembly on some deadbolt locks must be unscrewed from the lock (use a key to twist out the tumbler). You may need a long hex (*Allen*) wrench to loosen a set screw inside the mechanism.

   ➤ On some doorknobs, the knob and escutcheon come off in one piece after you remove two screws from the inside.

2. At the *edge* of the door, remove the two screws holding the latch mechanism and pull it out (if the latch is not secured by screws, just pull it out).

3. Oil all moving parts, turning them occasionally to get the oil between the metal parts (see the illustrations showing how to oil a doorknob or door lock mechanism). Put some oil on the key and work the lock a few times.

4. When you reassemble the mechanism, don't overtighten the faceplate. This can distort the parts and cause the lock to grind or even seize up.

5. Wipe off extra oil and reverse these steps to assemble. If any wood screws are loose, see suggestions in "Loose Hinges," earlier in this chapter.

Planing a Sticking Door

Wet wood swells and dry wood shrinks. And that can cause nightmares if you have alternating wet and dry seasons. If you plane a door so it works perfectly in wet weather, it may turn into a real pygmy when the weather dries out. To plane a sticking door, you'll need a hammer, screwdriver, pencil, and hand plane. You may also need a power planer, particularly to plane end grain. (Caution: if the bottom of the door is dragging, it's likely that the hinges are loose—something we dealt with earlier in this chapter.)

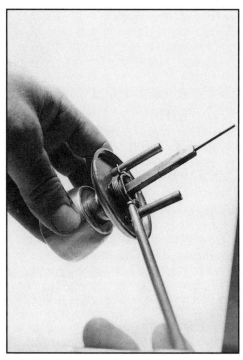

Put motor oil on the moving parts of the door mechanism and rotate them so oil gets into the dry spots.

1. In wet weather, mark the side of the door where it chafes against the jamb with a pencil (don't mark the door edge; you will be removing that wood). If you can't locate the jam, turn on a strong light behind the door, or slide a paper in the gap until it sticks.

2. In dry weather, remove the door, remove lock and latch (see "Oiling Door Latches and Locks," earlier in this chapter), and plane the door. Don't remove too much wood. To plane the end grain, rent a power planer and plane from the edges toward the center of the door. (Although a hand planer is adequate for planing with the grain, a power planer is faster and surer here too). Concentrate your planing on the marked areas.

3. Rehang the door (without installing the latch hardware) and test. The door should swing absolutely free, and the gap between it and the jamb should be uniform.

4. Seal the door edges (paying special attention to end grain) with a clear sealer or water-resistant paint, to slow its absorption of moisture. Reinstall hardware, and hang door.

Screen Door Straightener

If you are as much a fan of simplicity as I am, you'll love the screen door straightener, a gadget with two rods joined by a turnbuckle. To raise the latch side and square up a sagging screen door, just screw the straightener onto the door at a 45° angle and tighten the turnbuckle.

1. With the straightener almost fully extended, hold it against the door and drill the first screw hole. The straightener should extend from about halfway up the hinge side to the outside bottom of the latch side. Insert a screw halfway.

2. Install the rest of the screws and tighten.

3. Tighten the turnbuckle until the door is square and swings smoothly.

4. If the door is really rickety, install L-shaped brackets on the corners as reinforcements.

Adjusting a Storm Door Operator

Storm door operators are those tubes that slowly close storm doors—at least that's what they are supposed to do. In fact, they sometimes slam, as one did on my wife's innocent ankle last month. And sometimes—invariably during the storm of the century—they fail to close. Most people don't know you can adjust the speed of closing, but you can.

Find the speed adjustment. Some operators have a screw. On others, you must detach the operator at one end, turn the tube, and reconnect it.

Tightening the screw or the tube should slow the closing action, and loosening should speed it up.

Unfortunately, you may need a different position in summer, when the storm door is only holding a screen, and another in winter, when the heavier storm window is in place. You could change the setting twice a year, but I compromise. Life is too short to mess with this gadget that often.

They've Gotta Stay Closed

So far we've been talking about doors that won't close. But there are times when you don't want them to open. Nights and vacations both call for working latches and good "deadbolts." (These are not acolytes of a rock 'n' roll band, but locks with squared-off bolts that resist jimmying.) Let's check out some repairs.

So Your Door Doesn't Latch?

When a door fails to latch because the spring-powered doohickey does not slip into the striker plate (the plate on the jamb that grabs the doohickey),

➤ The latch may be too sticky to spring into position (see "Oiling Door Latches and Locks," earlier).

➤ The striker plate may be too deep in the jamb. Unscrew the plate and stick some cardboard shims under it.

➤ The pocket under the striker plate may be too shallow, so the doohickey can't seat. Remove the plate, and drill and chisel a deeper pocket.

➤ The latch may not align with the striker plate. Look for off-center scratches on the striker plate. If the latch is slightly off-center, remove the striker plate, hold it in a vise, and file away some metal. (Don't try to move the plate; it will return to the same place when you attach it through the old screw holes.)

➤ The door will not close sufficiently (the marks on the plate are centered, but the latch won't grab unless you shoulder the door). Use a file to remove metal from inside the striker plate.

> **Don't Screw Up!**
> You can buy deadbolts that can only be opened with a key—from either side. These locks are dangerous, and should not be used on exterior doors. Why? Because in a fire, you may not be able to find the key quickly enough.

Installing a Deadbolt

Say you're feeling insecure at home—at least you have company. But what should you do? The obvious solution is to upgrade the door locks by installing deadbolts (see the illustration for installing a deadbolt). Many doors have windows, which could allow an intruder to break the glass, and reach through and open the deadbolt. That's why I place new locks more than an arm's reach from windows, if possible. Although locks mounted this low may be a bit awkward to open, they are more secure.

> **Handy Hint**
> Metal-clad doors have advantages—in terms of stability and durability, but must they look like tank armor? Sorry, I'm getting off the track. I meant to explain that it's easy to drill through the thin metal cladding to install locks and doorknobs.

To install a deadbolt, you'll need a screwdriver, hammer, chisel, electric drill (the bigger the better), $7/8$" bit, $1^1/2$" bit (you may do detter to buy a hole-saw kit, with replaceable bits), the deadbolt kit, and lipstick or toothpaste (seriously!). (Sometimes, lock-installation kits include a $7/8$" spade bit and a $1^1/2$ or $1^1/4$" hole saw.)

Drill from both sides for a cleaner cut. Make sure to hold the drill square to the door.

Holding the drill horizontal, carefully drill all the way into the opening made in step 1.

1. Using the template supplied with the lock, drill a $1^1/_2$" hole for the handle and latch mechanism. When the bit starts to show on the far side of the door, finish the hole from that side—to prevent splintering (see the illustration for this step).

2. Using the $^7/_8$" drill, bore in from the edge of the door to meet the first hole (as shown in photo).

3. Place the latch mechanism in the $^7/_8$" hole and carefully trace its outline on the edge of the door. A utility knife gives a finer line than a pencil.

4. Carefully chisel along this line, deep enough to receive the latch plate. Make the mortise flat, so the latch can sit flat.

5. Mark holes for the two screws that hold the latch in place. Using a nail or awl, punch a mark so the drill starts in the center of the hole.

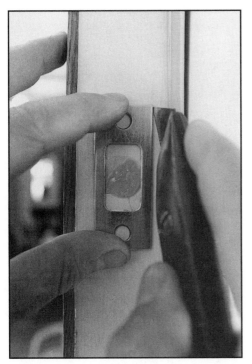

Take your time while positioning the strike plate—this is the only tricky part of the procedure.

6. Drill two holes and screw the latch into place.

7. Assemble the mechanism per instructions. As you tighten it, make sure the bolt operates smoothly.

8. Now for the tricky part. Apply lipstick or toothpaste to the edge of the bolt, close the door, and open the bolt to mark the jamb.

9. Position the striker plate carefully over this mark (as in photo) and mark the area to be removed with a utility knife. Chisel out a mortise for the plate, then drill and chisel a deeper mortise for the bolt. Screw the plate into place and test the bolt.

> **Handy Hint**
> To replace a door and jambs, look for "pre-hung" doors, which are sold pre-assembled to their jambs and hinges. Pre-hungs are relatively easy to install in a doorway, although you must remove the molding and jambs first. Unfortunately, if your doorway is an odd dimension, a pre-hung probably won't fit.

The Least You Need to Know

➤ Doors stick for a lot of reasons, few of which are serious enough to daunt an eager homeowner.

➤ Don't plane doors excessively, particularly in wet weather; you may remove too much wood.

➤ Balky door latches may call for some improvising, but you can usually revive them.

➤ Deadbolts are easy to install, although you may have to buy two jumbo drill bits to put in the first one.

Work for the Yard-Bird

If you think you can shirk your home repair obligations just by lounging in the back yard, I've got news for you: sunlight, snow, rain, and fungus exact their heaviest toll outdoors, and the yard is ideal territory for rot, decay, and rust (did I hear anyone mention moral decrepitude?). But it's also a place to save money—in tomorrow's repair bills, and in next year's replacement bills.

Even if you'd rather be napping in the hammock, or just plain asleep at the switch— the forces of decay are happily rotting, rusting, and ruining your outdoor possessions. So finish slurping that beer and let's go out for some yard work.

Painting Outdoor Metal

I'm sure chemists have another way to explain it, but it seems the iron atoms in wrought iron and steel have a sick fascination with oxygen—a fascination which winds up in the unhappy marriage of iron and oxygen we call rust. Aluminum also oxidizes on the surface, but the oxide sticks around to do something useful—namely protecting the metal from further oxidation. That's why aluminum doesn't need as much protection as iron and steel.

Even well-painted iron and steel will rust eventually, and if you can't entirely prevent it, at least you can delay it considerably, and pass your dwelling on to its next owner in reasonably good shape.

To paint iron and steel, you need to get the surface as clean as you can, get the metal dry, and put on a rust-inhibiting primer. You'll need a scraper, an electric drill with a wire brush, goggles, primer and paint (liquid or spray), and dropcloths or masking. For a superior job, get a propane torch or heat gun to warm the metal before painting. Don't paint on a windy, rainy, or cold day. Here's how to clean up the rust and apply the paint:

1. Scrape big globs of rust, then put on your goggles and wire-brush all loose rust. If your drill has variable speed, run it at flat out (as shown below).

2. Use sandpaper if you want to smooth paint at the margins of the repair.

3. Mask the surroundings as needed.

4. Warm the metal, particularly in damp conditions, to remove entrapped moisture. If you use a propane torch, move it rapidly across the surface so you don't damage the existing paint. Don't get the metal too hot to touch.

Wearing gloves and goggles, wire-brush with your drill at high speed to clean up rust. Note the two-handed grip—needed because the drill tends to wander.

5. Spray metal primer onto the warm, bare metal, overlapping onto painted areas. Keep the can a steady distance from the work, and move it parallel to the surface (not in an arc). Lay on a thin coat, then repeat (see the photo on facing page).

6. When the primer is dry, paint the whole thing with finish paint.

Since some kinds of metal enamel take weeks to harden, don't schedule any railing-climbing exhibitions for a while.

"All Hands on Deck—Prepare to Be Boarded!" (How to Replace Rotten Deck Boards)

Ah, wooden decks—the delightful replacement for front porches, the staging ground for innumerable barbecues, the whining ground for mosquitoes, and the forefront of your home's battle against the elements.

Deck boards can go bad for any number of reasons—from poor original quality to subsequent abuse and neglect. If the deck is *screwed* down, you're in luck: simply unscrew the damaged board, cut a replacement to the same length, and screw it down. You'll need rustproof deck screws, a power screwdriver, and a pilot drill bit.

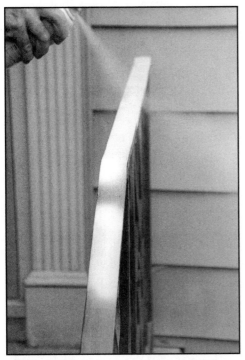

Spray metal primer with quick strokes to avoid buildup. Return several times to each area—even a few seconds of drying reduces sags.

Deck boards that are *nailed* down are more difficult to remove and replace. You may need a saber or keyhole saw, an aluminum square, a pencil, a hammer, a pry bar, a chisel, replacement board, scraps of treated 2 × 4 or 2 × 6, and galvanized deck nails. It will be very handy to have a circular saw and a C-clamp.

Start by sizing up the problem. It's easier to remove whole boards, but if the damage is small, you can replace only a portion of a board. Since that's more complicated, we'll cover it here. Follow these steps:

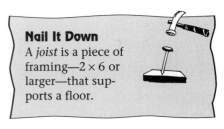

Nail It Down
A *joist* is a piece of framing—2 × 6 or larger—that supports a floor.

1. At the end of the section to be replaced, mark a square cutting line on the board. Sight down from above and make the line directly above the *edge* of a joist. Sawing at the edge allows room for the saw blade while leaving the good piece of decking nailed to the framing.

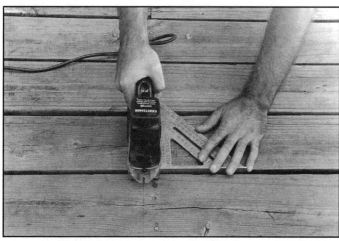

Cut straight and square along the line. Don't let the square slip.

Gouge around the nail head with a wood chisel until your hammer can grab the nail head. Then pull it.

2. Cut along the line, preferably with the saber saw. Use the aluminum square to make a straight, square cut (see the illustration for this step).

3. Pull as many nails as possible. If you have a small wrecking bar called a "cat's paw," hammer it under the nails and pull them. If not, gouge around the nail head with a wood chisel (while avoiding the nail), then pull the nail with a hammer or wrecking bar (as shown in the photo).

4. Once most of the nails are out, pry the board out with the wrecking bar, using shims to protect nearby boards.

5. Cut a section of 2 × 4 or 2 × 6 about three times as long as the width of your board. (If the board you removed was sound 2" lumber, use a piece of it). Place this "nailer" against the joist where you sawed out the old board. If you have a C-clamp, clamp the nailer into place as you nail it. Drill pilot holes or start the nails before putting the nailer into place, or use screws.

6. Fasten the nailer to the framing, with the top of the nailer against the bottom of the deck (see left-hand photo on facing page).

7. Cut the new board to length and nail into place. Drill holes for nails at the ends to prevent splitting (see right-hand photo on facing page). Finish per suggestions in "Treating Decks," on page 122.

Start the nails into the nailer, then C-clamp it tight to the bottom of the surrounding decking while you finish nailing.

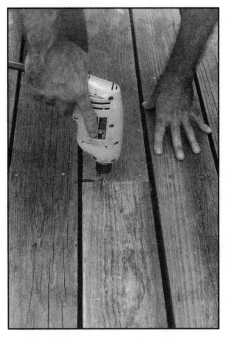

At the ends of boards, a pilot hole will prevent splitting.

Treating a Deck or Stairway

Chances are your outdoor deck or stairway is made of treated lumber—the faintly green stuff that's so full of poison that even bugs and fungi won't sink their teeth (or the fungal equivalent) into it. Treated lumber is great stuff. It lasts forever. It never needs painting. It's like, permanent.

Wrong. Treated lumber may be repellent to insects and fungi, but it won't last forever unless you paint, stain, or otherwise adorn it. Sadly, if you want it to last a long time in good condition, you'll have to do this every year or two.

Why? Because when water seeps into wood, it causes expansion and cracking, and eventually splitting. And while sunlight helps keep wood dry, its ultraviolet rays also degrade wood. Just as you need sunscreen at the beach, your deck (and other outdoor wood) needs sunscreen too (see "Treating Decks" later in this chapter).

Swab the Decks!

If you're like me, you've shirked your duty to protect your backyard deck (or any other outdoor wood). And now you've got a funky deck, a dirty deck. So you've got to do what I just did—use deck cleaner to brighten and clean the wood before staining. (Although deck cleaner may sound like a backyard version of Love Canal, the stuff I used was pretty non-toxic once it was mixed with water. Still, it's expensive, and if I am more diligent about protecting the deck, I won't need to use brightener again).

To clean a dirty deck, you'll need a bucket and a brush with stiff bristles or a garage broom. (Must I remind you to read the instructions on the deck cleaner you buy?)

1. Sweep the deck with a broom.

2. Mix the cleaner per instructions and apply to a small portion at a time.

3. Work it back and forth with a brush (I used a garage broom, which worked faster, and was much easier on my back than a hand brush).

4. If you've got stains, try removing them with a dilute solution of household bleach.

5. Hose off and allow the wood to dry for at least 24 hours before staining.

Treating Decks

Now that you've repaired and cleaned the deck, it's time to protect it. Don't be tempted to use paint; it's not flexible enough to expand and contract as the wood responds to changes in humidity and temperature. Instead, use a water-repellent treatment to protect against water absorption and ultraviolet light and forestall warping, swelling, and cracking. Many of these products will stain the wood in the same operation.

I'd suggest using a product with a low percentage of volatile organic compounds (VOCs), which cause ozone smog. Low-VOC coatings are not just good for the environment, they're good for you—you won't smell that refinery stench as you use the stuff, and you will be able to clean your tools in water instead of paint thinner.

Outdoor wood needs a new protective coating as soon as raindrops start to sink in. Choose a warm day when leaves are not falling and rain, dogs, and children are not in the forecast. You'll need a 2" paintbrush, a roller with roller pan, and a garage broom (or the short-bristled broom sold for coating asphalt driveways). To save your back, think seriously about using a roller extension handle or a sprayer. The wood should be fairly dry (although some products do not require absolute dryness). Here are the steps for treating your deck:

Apply deck coating with a roller, but don't lard it on—this stuff is supposed to penetrate, not sit on the surface. Brush out the coating after a few minutes with a clean garage broom or a stiff-bristled brush.

1. Clean the deck; use a brightener (described earlier in this chapter) if necessary.

2. Using the 2" brush, cut in near the house, cracks, and other non-rollable areas. Do not get too far ahead of the roller.

3. Apply the coating as indicated on the can. I used a roller; buying a sprayer just for this purpose seemed too extravagant.

4. After two to five minutes, brush away puddles and drips.

5. Roll the end grain again, since it absorbs lots of water repellent.

6. Clean up tools and keep traffic off the deck. Do not re-recoat unless the label directs.

In the Tar Pits—The How and Why of Resurfacing Asphalt

When I first decided to coat my asphalt driveway, I knew I'd arrived in the suburbs. Asphalt is a mix of gravel and asphalt binder which, in the ideal world, would last forever, but in the real world, suffers from water and frost damage. Although asphalt is high on most "I'll-do-it-next-year" lists, the stuff needs occasional treatment, and this quintessentially suburban job is a surprisingly simple way to help your asphalt reach a ripe old age. (For information on concrete repair, see Chapters 17 and 18.)

Asphalt coating is cheap and easy to apply—and hardly as grubby as it might seem. Again, using a "low-VOC" product will minimize the environmental cost of maintaining your driveway. You'll start by cleaning off weeds, fixing and filling cracks, and finish by putting on the black goop. You'll need a garage broom, square shovel, trowel or hooked tool, hose with spray nozzle, wide brush, plastic milk container, gloves, knife, crack-filling compound, and surfacing compound (which covers about 100 square feet per gallon). Once you've gathered what you need, follow these steps:

Spread the asphalt coating from one end to the other, using a homemade extension to the brush sold for applying asphalt goop. Don't stretch the coating too thin, or you will leave gaps that become surprisingly obvious later on.

1. Cut around the perimeter of the driveway with the shovel to remove grass and weeds.

2. Clean the cracks with a trowel or a hooked tool.

3. Sweep the driveway thoroughly, then flush the cracks with the hose at full pressure.

4. If the surface is oily, clean it with household cleaner. Flush the driveway clean with a hose.

5. Fill deep cracks with sand to about $1/2$" from the surface, then drench the sand to settle it.

6. Apply crack-filling compound per directions on the container, then trowel it flat for better adhesion. Let the filler dry. Put on a second coat if the cracks reappear (guess what? They will!). Give the filler 24 hours to dry.

7. For the actual coating, choose a moderately warm day; preferably not a stifling one, with no rain forecast. Cut the plastic jug to make a ladle, and use it to pour the surfacing goop onto the driveway. Brush the goop out, but not too thin (see the photo above).

8. Protect the driveway from traffic for 24 hours.

The Least You Need to Know

➤ Hot, dry metal is quite receptive to paint, which can delay the return of rust.

➤ Treated lumber needs the protection from rain and ultraviolet light that it can get from a water-repellent, ultraviolet-resistant coating.

➤ If water soaks into the surface of outdoor wood, it's time to renew the water-repellent treatment.

➤ If your deck is old and dirty, use a brightener on it before coating.

➤ Filling cracks and resurfacing asphalt driveways is no-brainer, big-payback work for homeowners.

Chapter 15

Beauty's Only Skin Deep—Care and Healing for Your Siding

In This Chapter

➤ Maintaining vinyl, aluminum, wood, shingle, hardboard, and plywood siding

➤ Fixing popped nails

➤ Replacing damaged plywood siding

Siding may seem dull, but it can conceal nasty surprises. Shortly after I moved into a house with new aluminum siding, a board blew loose. Then, a few days later, I received further proof (was any needed?) that Murphy's law also applies to siding: the stuff started to peel from the whole side of the house. It turned out that the contractor had saved time and money by using nails that didn't quite reach the studs—a brilliant bit of false economy that forced my wife and me to waste a beautiful evening renailing the siding.

Still, not much goes wrong with siding that's properly installed and maintained. But if you fail your house-painting auditions, or let moisture build up behind the siding, you can expect trouble. With siding, as elsewhere, it's smarter to prevent problems than try to solve them.

Wood Shingles

Wood shingles—they're usually made of cedar—are a traditional siding material. Shingles are sometimes left unpainted; near the ocean, they weather to a beautiful gray. But if you want longevity, it's probably better to give shingles occasional treatment with a water-repellent, ultraviolet-light inhibitor (see "Wood Shingles and Shakes," in Chapter 16, for information on these treatments). To replace wood shingles in siding, adapt the technique for replacing asphalt roof shingles (see "Presto-Chango Shingle Replacement," in Chapter 16).

> **Don't Screw Up!**
> Peeling paint, mold, and carpenter ants in your siding all indicate one thing: moisture. Excess humidity, whether it comes from outside or inside, is probably the biggest danger to your siding (and the structure beneath it). Moisture is a lurking disaster that must be fixed before you repaint or re-side (see Chapter 11, "Home Ventilation—Why and How").

Lap Siding

Wood lap siding, also called clapboard, comes in various styles and is often made of cedar or redwood. Like all wood, lap siding needs paint, stain, or a water-repellent treatment every few years. Good eaves and functional gutters will help reduce water damage.

Hardboard lap siding is a form of particle board, formed to resemble wood siding, and primed at the factory. Paint new hardboard as soon as possible, because the primer degrades in sunlight.

Plywood Siding Repair

Plywood siding comes in several textures and thicknesses. About the only way to wreck this strong stuff is to neglect your obligation to paint or stain it. Once water gets inside plywood, decay is sure to follow, in the form of delamination and destruction. Pay special attention to cracks between the sheets, since the end grain absorbs an outsize share of water.

To repair plywood siding, you'll need a circular saw with a plywood blade, a carpenter's square, a level, a pencil, a nail set, a hammer, tin snips, nails, aluminum flashing, replacement siding, and two scraps of 2 × 4.

1. Mark out a rectangular cutout around the damaged area. Vertical cuts should run down the center of studs (nail holes reveal the stud locations). Use a level to mark all lines so the cutout is rectangular.

2. Punch nails on the cutting lines beneath the siding with a heavy nail punch so they don't wreck the saw blade. (If you have a cat's paw—a small, nail-pulling crowbar—you can try to pull the nails, but that's likely to damage the siding.)

3. Fit a circular saw with a plywood blade. With the saw adjusted just deep enough to penetrate the siding, saw along the lines.

4. Pull any nails holding the damaged piece and remove it.

5. Cut a piece of new siding about $^1/_8$" smaller in each direction, matching the grain and pattern.

6. Buy "Z-bar" flashing to make sure rainwater does not seep into the plywood through the horizontal joints. Or make a strip of aluminum flashing for the top. Mount a 2 × 4 in a vise. Hold the sheet metal over the 2 × 4 and bend it with a second block of 2 × 4.

7. Slip the flashing under the existing siding above the repair, and nail it into place through at least two studs (see the illustration).

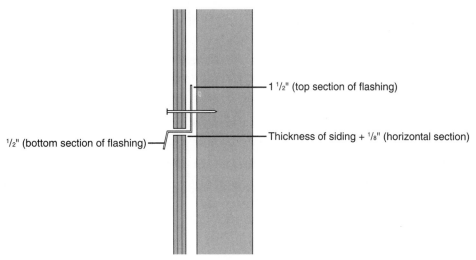

Flashing on top of plywood siding. Nail the top section of the flashing into two or more studs. Note the lower section does not rest against the siding. Paint the flashing to match the wall.

8. Slip the new plywood under the flashing and nail into place with galvanized ring-shank nails.

9. Caulk the seams, allow the caulk to dry, and stain or paint the siding and flashing.

Aluminum and Vinyl Siding

Vinyl and aluminum are cheap but durable replacements for wood. Aluminum, which tends to dent easily, is factory painted. If it needs repainting, find primer and paint made for aluminum. Consult the paint can for cleaning instructions; to clean a whole house, I'd want to rent a power washer.

Vinyl siding is becoming more and more popular, and comes in many styles and textures. Because it is dyed rather than painted, it can't chip (although it can fade).

Repairing aluminum and vinyl are pro jobs, particularly since they are hard to cut without special tools. You may have extra siding available; check around in the garage, basement, and attic to see if somebody stashed some siding for repairs.

Popped Nails

You won't see nails at all in aluminum and vinyl siding, but you will see them in wood siding. And if they "pop" above the surface, you'll see them all too clearly. What to do?

If only a couple of nails have popped, pound them back in place with a hammer and nail set, fill the holes with exterior putty, prime, paint, and forget. If the nails don't grab, pull them out and drive in a siding or deck screw, slightly larger and longer than the nail.

But if a whole section of nails has popped, you may have a structural problem—like warped studs or a shifting structure, and renailing probably won't help. It's best to find and cure the root problem. At least replace the nails with screws, which will knit the structure together more soundly, and may prevent things from getting worse.

The Least You Need to Know

> ➤ Siding is pretty durable stuff, and siding damage is often a side-effect of other problems, like structural movement or moisture build-up.

> ➤ Small repairs in lap, shingle, and plywood siding are easy, assuming you can reach the damage and find repair material.

> ➤ Plywood and hardboard siding desperately need protection against the weather. Don't skimp on paint or stain.

Chapter 16

Gimme Shelter— and Other Advice on Repairing Roofs

In This Chapter

➤ Detecting, isolating, and repairing roof leaks

➤ Replacing rotten roof boards

➤ Gutter maintenance and repair

We've reached the chapter I've been awaiting. Now that we're talking roof, I won't have to convince you about the value of preventive maintenance—even a complete idiot understands why a house needs a working roof. Roof leaks can be sneaky; by the time you recognize one problem (a leak) you may have a bigger problem—damaged drywall and framing caused by a silent but deadly drip, drip, drip. Call it the homeowner's water torture.

Until this point, I haven't asked you to look for trouble—if you live in a house, trouble knows where to find you. Now, however, I will suggest that you look for trouble, because the best way to avoid the water torture is to look around once in a while, and to follow the roofers' advice: Think like a raindrop. But before we start doing that, we'll get our feet wet by learning the anatomy of roofs.

Roofing Lingo

Roofers, like everybody else, are entitled to a private dialect. The following illustration will clarify the key terms you must know to handle the roofing jobs in your future.

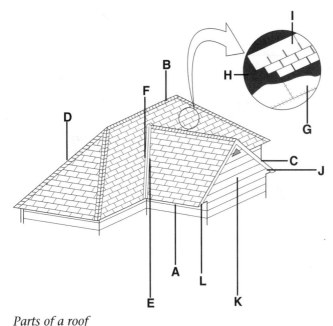

Parts of a roof

(A) Eave—the lower, horizontal edge.

(B) Ridge—the horizontal line along the peak.

(C) Rake edge—the slanting edge.

(D) Hip—where two roof planes meet in a convex angle.

(E) Valley—where two roof planes meet in a concave angle. (Valleys can be " open," meaning the shingles are cut off to expose the flashing material, or " closed," in which case the shingles cover the flashing.)

(F) Valley flashing—metal used to seal the valley. (Should be present in open and closed valleys.)

(G) Sheathing (decking)—the plywood or boards nailed to rafters.

(H) Roofing felt (underlayment)—gives a final seal in case the shingles leak.

(I) Shingle—usually 12 × 36" total size, with 6" showing.

(J) Fascia—vertical face of rake edges and eaves.

(K) Gable—area under a peaked roof.

(L) Soffit—horizontal section under an eave or rake edge.

The Basic Principle of Roofing . . .

. . . is that water runs downhill, and upper parts of roofing overlap lower parts. Most parts of a roof are that simple (but not where roofs intersect a chimney or another roof).

But because shingles, flashing, and everything else on a roof expand and contract in response to changes in temperature, a repair that looks solid today may turn flimsy in a year or so, particularly when wind blows the rain almost horizontal. Thus, a bit of overkill is acceptable, even wise, in a roof repair.

Most roofing shingles are made of a fiberglass mat, soaked in asphalt, and covered with colored, sunlight-resistant mineral granules. These shingles last fifteen to twenty-five years, depending on their quality and the environment on your roof. When you start seeing lots of mineral granules in the gutters, your roof is showing its age and will soon need replacement.

Roofers don't talk about the slope of a roof in degrees or percentages. Instead, they talk about "roof pitch" (this is *not* what happens when a roofer tries to sell you a shingling job you don't need). Pitch is measured in "rise over run," the number of inches in height gained every time you move 12 inches horizontally. Knowing the pitch can help you decide whether you want to walk on the roof. (The 4–12 pitch found on ranch houses and many new homes is pretty flat. A tolerable pitch is 6–12, but if the roof is much steeper, you need a pro.) Roofing contractors and suppliers also can use pitch to calculate roof area from floor-plan dimensions of a house.

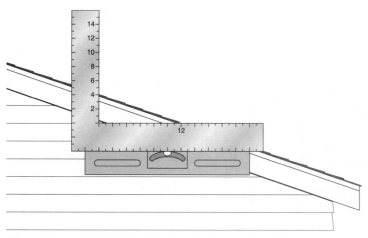

Measuring roof pitch. Pitch is simply the number of inches a roof rises per foot of horizontal "run." Use a level and a square to measure pitch, with the horizontal leg held at 12 inches; the pitch shown is 4–12.

To measure your roof pitch you'll need a ladder, a level, and a carpenter's square. Stand on a ladder leaning against the rake (slanting) edge of the roof. Move the 12-inch marker on one leg of the square to the edge of the roof. Use the level to make this leg horizontal. Read the rise where the vertical leg meets the roof (see the illustration of measuring roof pitch in this chapter). To estimate pitch on the ground, hold a board against the siding, and ask somebody to tell you when it's parallel with the rake edge. Then use the above technique to measure the rise.

Special Tools and Materials

Roofing doesn't call for much in the way of tools. You could get fancy and rent a nail gun to put on a new layer of shingles, but for repairs a hammer will do just fine (see the illustration for roofing tools and materials).

Handy Hint
Roof cement can get stiff in the can, particularly one that's poorly sealed. To rejuvenate tar when it's still somewhat flexible, *carefully* spill in a little mineral spirits or gasoline, then stir until the stuff has the consistency of a tar pit.

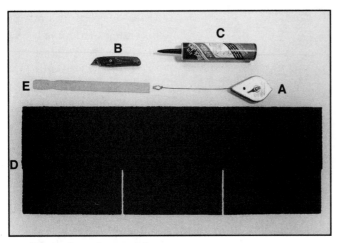

(A)   Chalk line—Used to draw long straight lines, for starting or finishing shingling. Pull the line out, stretch it tight above where you want the line, pull it up, and snap.

(B)   Utility knife—Cuts shingles (from the back if possible).

(C)   Roof cement (aka "tar")—Seals gaps and nailheads, and holds old shingles down. Also sold in cans.

(D)   Asphalt shingles—The primary roofing material. (Nails go just above the slot between the tabs, so the nail heads will be covered by the next course of shingles.)

(E)   Paint stirrer (for applying tar)—Trowels work great, but you'll have to clean them afterward.

Roofing tools and materials

Not Looking for Trouble? Then How Will You Find the Leak?

If you're lucky, a roof leak will announce itself. Maybe a section of drywall will fall into your living room when your boss is just starting dessert, or some black crud will start oozing down the chimney on Christmas Eve.

Handy Hint
You can check for leaks around flashing, if you don't mind making them temporarily worse. Spray a hose thoroughly around the base of the chimney, from all conceivable directions, while a lackey looks inside the house (in the attic if possible), to check for leaks. There's always the chance you'll "detect" a leak that really doesn't exist, but it's a good diagnostic trick.

Sadly, as my friend Steve Sinderson learned, roof leaks can be far more subtle. Steve's a former carpenter who asked me to help him find an inscrutable, occasional leak in his living room. We spent half a befuddled day on his roof and grew desperate enough to saw out a strip of roof decking, which taught us absolutely nothing. Although the chimney flashing seemed tight, in the interest of thoroughness we did re-tar and refasten it with screws. To our surprise, that fixed the roof.

Steve figures the culprit was windblown rain entering under the loose flashing. Windy rain is nasty, because it negates the basic principle of roofing by blowing water sideways, even uphill. As we learned, wind causes nightmare leaks, because roofs that work fine when water obeys the basic principle can fail when water disobeys it.

Patrolling Your Roof from Inside

Even if your attic is only accessible through a hatchway, I'd suggest you occasionally visit the dust and cobwebs living up there, preferably after a downpour. Look for dampness, mold, or discoloration, which indicate that the wood is starting to rot, or soft spots, which are actual rot. Pay special attention to brick chimneys, which are a big source of leaks (see "Chimney Flashing" later in this chapter). If the chimney is connected to a wood-burning stove or fireplace, it may bleed a disgusting, evil-smelling, flammable form of liquefied creosote. This may indicate a water leak, a serious chimney hazard, or both (see Chapter 26, "Santa Don't Like Your Chimney, and Other Ruminations on Chimney Fires").

In the final analysis, you don't have much choice about roof leaks. Like sponging relatives, they won't disappear. They will only get worse. So you've got to find them and fix them.

Patrolling Your Roof from Outside

If your roof is shallow (say 4–12 to 6–12 pitch), get a ladder and haul yourself up. If it's steeper, use binoculars from the ground, or climb a ladder to the eave. Look for broken, buckled, or missing shingles, and rusted or detached flashing. Pay special attention to any place the roof meets something else—a dormer, chimney, vent, skylight, or another section of roof: Trouble loves these junctions.

Quickie Shingle Fixes

When you think about it, the blights that afflict shingles sound suspiciously like the diseases of aging people: buckles, bald spots, blisters, and premature curling. Let's diagnose and treat these ills, recalling that a bit of attention now can save serious woes later on.

➤ If a corner of a shingle curls up, smear roof cement under the curled portion and nail it flat with a couple of roofing nails. Then tar the nail heads.

➤ If a shingle is cracked, smear roof cement under the crack and on top of it. Or, better, replace the shingle.

➤ If a shingle is torn, treat it as a crack, but nail down the loose parts and goop the nail heads.

> **Handy Hint**
> Dry roof tar is murder to remove from tools. (You can rub off fresh tar with a gasoline-soaked rag, but that's a poisonous and explosive solution.) For your next roof repair, use a paint stirrer (or a split piece of wood) as a tar paddle. Then just pitch it when you're finished.

Presto-Chango Shingle Replacement

If a few shingles on your roof have lost their mineral coating, are curled beyond repair, or are split, missing, or otherwise AWOL, you'll have to replace them with fresh recruits (but see "A Total Loss?" later in this chapter). When you buy shingles, note that a bundle usually covers 33$^1/_3$ square feet.

Roof repair cautions:

➤ Bend old shingles carefully, particularly in cold weather. They're brittle.

➤ Use care on the roof—wear non-slip shoes and rig up a safety line if needed.

➤ In hot weather, put a lawn sprinkler on the roof for an hour or so to cool the shingles so you won't damage them (you'll also be more comfortable).

➤ Use common sense. If you're not happy on the roof, get off.

To fix shingles, you'll need a ladder, hammer, prybar, trowel, utility knife, roofing nails, new shingles, and roof tar. Then follow these steps to make your repair:

1. Examine the area and figure out how many shingles need replacement. Seriously curled, bare, or broken shingles are all candidates.

2. Separate the uppermost damaged shingles from the good shingles above them with a trowel (a brick trowel is best). Slide the trowel back and forth to break the seal. Don't be in a hurry or you'll tear good shingles.

3. Work downward, releasing shingles as you go. Use the trowel, hammer, or prybar to pull nails.

4. Remove all bad shingles down to the bottom of the repair area. To remove part of a shingle, cut from the top (see the photo below).

5. Clean out loose nails and scrap shingles.

6. Starting from the bottom, nail in the replacement shingles, matching the old pattern. Cut new shingles from the back, then fold to separate the pieces. Use the side of the hammer to nail under old shingles, so you don't curl them too much.

Old shingles cut easily, even with a dull utility knife.

Treat old shingles with respect—do your nailing with minimum damage.

7. Continue nailing shingles all the way up. Don't allow seams between shingles to line up—stagger them 6".

8. Smear roof tar on exposed nail heads and under broken or split shingles. Don't worry if the new shingles take a while to lie down flat: The sun will soften them and bond them together.

Follow the old pattern when nailing the new shingles. Never allow the vertical joints between shingles to line up.

Flat Roofs and Other Sob Stories

I'm always sorry to hear someone has a flat, or "built-up," roof. To a homeowner, these tar-and-gravel roofs play a typical Dennis Hopper role—pure trouble. You can repair blisters and other small problems with a flat roof, but big repairs are a pro job (unless you know how to handle large amounts of gravel and molten tar, which means that you are already a professional roofer).

The relatively new plastic membranes have solved many flat-roof woes, but they must be applied by roofers. To make the limited number of repairs possible on a built-up roof, sweep away the gravel from the injury, and use techniques in the next section on roll roofing.

The 3 R's of Repairing Roll Roofing

Roll roofing is a cut-rate stand-in for shingles. It's generally 36 inches wide and laid in horizontal courses, or strips, with at least a 3-inch overlap at the top and bottom seams.

To repair a **blister** in roll roofing, cut it with a utility knife, smear roof tar under the edges, making good contact between the roofing and the substrate, then start at step 2 in the following procedure.

To patch a **hole** in roll roofing (up to about 12 inches square), you'll need a utility knife, hammer, roof cement, paint-stirring stick, new roll roofing, and roofing nails. Chalk would be handy, too. Follow these steps:

1. Cut out a rectangular piece of roofing around the hole with the utility knife.

2. Cut a piece of new roofing 6" larger (in each dimension) than the cut-out section. Center it over the hole and mark its position, preferably with chalk.

3. Remove the patch and smear the entire hole with roof tar, out to the marks from step 2. Sneak some tar under the edges of the good roofing.

4. Replace the patch and fasten it securely with a nail about every 3". Tar the nail heads.

A Total Loss?

How do you know when a shingle roof is a total loss? Maybe you're seeing lots of mineral granules in your gutters. Maybe you're seeing lots of tired, bald, cracked, or curled shingles. Maybe you, like me, are starting to see multiple leaks inside the house. (Remember—drywall does not get dark and damp by itself.)

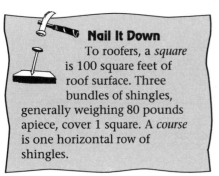

Nail It Down

To roofers, a *square* is 100 square feet of roof surface. Three bundles of shingles, generally weighing 80 pounds apiece, cover 1 square. A *course* is one horizontal row of shingles.

But whatever the reason, at a certain point, you just plain need a new roof. Small, simple, and shallow-pitched roofs are easy to replace, but that's beyond the scope of this book. If you are motivated, plenty of how-to books cover the subject. My advice is not to spend too much time repairing something that basically needs replacement.

Building codes, and common sense, both limit the buildup of shingles on a roof to two or three layers. Roofing material is heavy, and if it's too thick, it could collapse the framing. Furthermore, thick stacks of shingle wrinkle and collect water instead of shedding it. So at a certain point, it's better to tear off the shingles and start over on the decking.

You may be able to count layers from the rake edge. Or you can estimate, based on the age of the house, using twenty years as the average lifetime for asphalt shingles. (If the first layer contains wood shingles, figure it lasted thirty to forty years.) Thus a forty-year-old house that's approaching a reroofing job probably has two layers of asphalt shingles, and may need a tear-off. Unless you're a real masochist, or have lots of energetic friends, that's a pro job.

If you contemplate tearing off roofing, you should be aware that a small percentage of old shingles contain asbestos, a known cause of cancer. If you suspect that your shingles do contain asbestos, a firm that recycles roofing material may be able to test them for you.

Wood Shingles and Shakes

Shingles and shakes are high-class roofing, usually made of rot-resistant cedar. They are more attractive, durable, and expensive than the common asphalt-fiberglass shingles. Wood shingles are sawn and are about 18 inches long; shakes are usually split and about 24 inches long. Because wood swells when it gets damp and shrinks when it dries, in dry weather you may actually see sunlight through a working wood roof—the decking boards under wood shingles commonly are spaced a couple of inches apart.

The principle for replacing shingles and shakes is the same as for asphalt shingles (see the section titled "Presto-Chango Shingle Replacement" earlier in this chapter), except that you will need roofing nails designed for wood.

Wood roofs need protection from water, fungi, and ultraviolet light, particularly in damp climates. A buildup of leaves, pine needles, or moss will prevent water from running off, keep the wood wet, and promote wood-destroying fungi. Clean the roof with a hose or broom. If necessary, prune nearby trees to reduce organic buildup and allow sunlight to dry the roof. If it's still rotting, keep reading.

Treating a Wood Roof

If you've cleaned the roof and still see signs of dirt or decay (furry fungi, for example), a cleaning solution will kill the little rotters and remove stains. (Use appropriate hand and eye protection with all the following treatments.)

> **Cleaning solution for wood shingles:**
>
> 3 ounces trisodium phosphate (TSP or a non-phosphate equivalent, sold at paint stores)
>
> 1 ounce laundry detergent
>
> 1 quart 5% liquid laundry bleach
>
> 3 quarts warm water

Brush the solution onto the roof with a garage broom, then rinse it off. Rinse nearby plants if you spill any solution on them.

If stains persist, pour a stronger bleach solution directly on the stain, and wash it off within half an hour.

To control moss, use moss-killing chemicals sold at building material, roofing, or paint stores.

If, after all these measures, fungus is still alive on an otherwise solid roof, you'll need preservatives. Use a sprayer on a calm day. To get maximum retention of the preservative, use several light treatments, and let the end grain soak up as much as it wants.

Rotten Board Replacement

Let's say you've neglected your fiduciary duties to your roof, and discover that a venerable leak has rotted the roof boards or decking. My most intimate experience with a rotten roof occurred when Joe Lynch, a pure gentleman and old-time Wisconsin farmer, asked me to look over his roof while I was rebuilding his chimney. I promptly fell through, and wound up hip-deep in decay. When I stopped falling, I started laughing. Joe, a master of understatement, allowed that he hadn't used that wing of the house "for a while." From the look of it, he meant a decade or two.

It's not smart to let your roof take such a lengthy bath. If you find a persistent leak, or notice that a section of roof is feeling . . . er . . . spongy, you'll need to replace the decking and roofing. It's a dirty job, but on a shallow roof, not a difficult one. You'll need a pencil, level, cat's paw or prybar, circular saw, hammer, utility knife, trowel, tape measure, roof nails, replacement decking, shingles, roofing paper, and roof tar. Follow these steps:

1. Pull off all shingles from the rotten spot slightly past the rafters (the framing that supports the decking) at each end of the repair area.

2. Mark a rectangular area to be replaced with a level. Mark along the center of the rafters. With a cat's paw or prybar, remove any nails along the marks.

3. With the circular saw set to cut the thickness of the roof decking (to avoid cutting the rafters), saw out the bad spot. Remove all debris.

4. Saw the replacement board to fit, leaving about $1/8"$ at the ends to allow for expansion. It may be better to use the same type of wood, but the most important thing is to be sure it's as thick as the decking. Nail the patch with cement-coated 8d (8-penny) nails. Renail existing roof boards around the edges.

5. Tack roofing felt on the new section. If the house has several layers of shingles, lay new shingles flat to shim the patch flush with the roof. Finish according to suggestions in the "Presto-Chango Shingle Replacement" section earlier in this chapter.

Fixing Flashing in a Flash

Commonly, a roofing problem is not due to a shingle problem, but to a flashing problem. Flashing is rust-resistant, flexible metal (galvanized steel, aluminum, or copper) that joins roofs to other roofs and to dissimilar materials, like chimneys, vents, skylights, and walls. Flashing keeps the roof tight even if the various parts move due to expansion or contraction caused by changes in temperature.

Oops. If this fairy tale were universally true, you wouldn't be reading about flashing. The truth is that flashing can get sick—through rust, perforation, or simply separating from whatever it was supposed to join.

> **Don't Screw Up!**
> If you're like my seven-year-old son, Alex, you'll get a kick out of walking on a shallow roof. But keep your roof-hiking to a minimum, particularly in cold weather, when shingles are brittle, or in hot weather, when they're gooey.

Generally, the nails securing flashing are covered by shingles, but some, like those at the lower end of chimney flashing, are visible. If you see these nails coming loose, don't just hammer them down and smear them with roof tar—they'll just loosen up again in a year or so. They have lost their grip (sound familiar?), and must be replaced with galvanized screws, coated with roof tar. (If you've got copper flashing, you'll need copper nails—galvanized fasteners will cause rapid corrosion.)

Chimney Flashing

When I was in the masonry business, I learned how much chimney flashing loves to leak, partly because it's complicated and handmade, and partly because there's lots of movement between a chimney and a roof. You can try gooping chimney flashing with tar—this may work for a while, but an expert flashing job is much more likely to succeed. In many cases, the only cure is a complete chimney rebuild from just below the roof line (call 1-800-CHIMBLY or a local mason).

Ice and Your Roof

In colder regions, one of a roof's worst enemies is an ice buildup, or ice dam. The problem usually occurs near the eave, where snow that has melted from higher on the roof tends to freeze. Water trapped by the dam can build up and enter the roof, severely damaging the shingles and decking.

Try these solutions to ice dams:

➤ Increase ventilation through the attic and roof (see the section of Chapter 11 on "Roof Vents").

➤ Install de-icing tapes (sold at building suppliers or hardware stores) near the roof edge.

➤ Install roll roofing or special ice-dam membrane under shingles at the eave (this just about requires a reshingling job, since you'll need to rip out several courses of shingles).

Down in the Gutter: Repairing Eaves Troughs

Gutters, or eaves troughs, always look so—well—optional. All they do is collect water that's already run off your roof and dump it on the ground. Since the water would end up there anyway, why bother with eaves troughs? Because they save your siding from the stress of shedding all that water. Because they route water away from the foundation (see the section of Chapter 18 on "May We Talk about Your Soggy Basement?"). And most important, because they give you one more thing to fix.

Let's start with some gutter talk. Table 16.1 illustrates the different parts of a gutter system.

Table 16.1 Gutter parts

Item	Description
	Gutter section—sold in 10' and 20' lengths
	Downspout—sold in 10' lengths
	Inside corner—requires slip connector at each end
	Outside corner—requires slip connector at each end
	Slip connector—used to join gutter sections
	End cap—left and right are different

Item	Description
	Downspout elbow—comes in two styles—curving front to back, or side to side
	Downspout connector, or drop outlet—connects gutter to the downspout
	Gutter mounting strap—nailed to eave under shingles
	Gutter mounting bracket—nailed to fascia board
	Spike and ferrule (nail and spacer)—mounts gutter to the fascia board
	Downspout guard—keeps debris out of downspout

The best thing you can do for your gutters is, alas, to clean them regularly (use rubber gloves if you're squeamish). If you do this once or twice a year, organic litter won't have time to ferment, so the task will be far less disgusting than if you wait until Bonsai trees have sprouted along the eaves. Clean gutters are also less prone to overflowing, icing up, and falling off. And they carry water away from the house much more effectively.

Follow these hints for a healthier relationship with your gutters.

➤ Keep leaves out of gutters by installing protective screens.

➤ If the gutter is not draining, check for plugging at the downspout connector. Then check the slope by holding a level against the gutter at several places. The gutter should slope consistently toward the downspout, about 1 inch per 20 feet of run. You can remove and reattach gutter nails, straps, or connectors to get the right slope.

➤ If gutter straps are broken, repair them with sheet metal screws.

➤ If the gutter is leaking at connectors or through rusted holes, use gutter repair goop in a caulking gun.

➤ To refasten or repair gutters, use sheet-metal screws or a hand riveter. Use aluminum rivets on aluminum gutter.

➤ To saw a gutter or downspout section, mark square lines for an accurate cut. Turn gutter upside-down with a 2 × 4 or 2 × 6 inside, and cut with a fine-toothed hacksaw.

➤ Before making slip connections, fill the connector with gutter repair cement.

The Least You Need to Know

➤ Keeping an eye on your roof is one of the most effective and remunerative forms of preventive maintenance.

➤ Gutters are an essential part of your home's protection from the elements; gutter problems can damage the roofing, interiors, foundation, and basement.

➤ Most roof leaks occur where something like a chimney, vent, skylight or another roof meets a roof.

➤ Many roof problems are repairable, but don't bother fixing a roof if it really needs replacement.

➤ Wood shingles and shakes need protection from sunlight, dampness, fungus, and moss.

Chapter 17

Bricks and Stones . . . Doing Masonry and Concrete without Getting Stoned

In This Chapter

➤ Why masonry and concrete are different from all other building materials

➤ To work with mortar and concrete, you've got to keep time with it

➤ What the other do-it-yourself books won't tell you about masonry

➤ Sage suggestions for astonishing stonework

Let's face it: Masonry scares do-it-yourselfers—even gung-ho types who would routinely tackle a nasty roof leak or rotten floorboard. That's too bad, because stones are the most ancient form of construction, and masonry can be a satisfying—and economical—knack. It's not hard to learn. (If you're really lucky, you may even have a pleasant flashback to idle days in the sandbox with your childhood friends.)

How did masonry earn its reputation? Partly because the material sets the pace, in a way that's true of no other building material except plaster. And partly it's because every tool and material seems to have three obscure names. (This may be intentional: When I wrote my masonry book, a friend who is a mason and an architect explained: "We masons are an old guild, and we don't like to give away secrets.")

But you don't have to join the mason's guild (or the Freemasons, either) to learn to repair brick, block, stone, and concrete. As an ex-mason, I'm happy to reveal trade secrets, starting with the ABCs of masonry:

A. The materials are gritty, caustic, and heavy (think of this as the "nasty, brutish, and short" principle of masonry).

B. Mortar and concrete don't hold stuff together—they hold it apart.

C. Mortar and concrete harden according to an internal clock. You can't rush them, but you can't fall behind, either.

Because principle A is self-explanatory, let's talk about B and C. When we're done, you'll never again feel marooned at the thought of a simple masonry repair. Instead, you'll feel an itch to grab your trowel and start mixing mud. (I admit this might seem a bit peculiar, but keep things in perspective—some people actually *look forward* to plumbing repairs.)

> **Nail It Down**
>
> *Mortar* is a mixture of portland cement, lime, mason's sand, and water. (Old mortar, with no portland cement, is weaker and whiter than modern mortar.) *Concrete*, a mixture of portland cement, gravel, sand, and water, is used to build bridges, beams, roads and driveways. Concrete is often called "cement," but that's too confusing—I call it concrete, or 'crete.

The Foundation Principle of Masonry and Concrete

Mortar and concrete (masons call them both "mud," for obvious reasons) are roughly ten times as effective at holding things apart (this is called compressive strength) as at holding things together. Thus mortar is perfect for separating things that would otherwise fall in on each other, like the stones, blocks, and bricks in a foundation or chimney.

When concrete is pulled apart, as it is in bridge beams, the pulling, or "tensile," strength is supplied by hidden steel reinforcing rods. If you must use mortar to "glue" things together, you'll need special materials and techniques, which we'll discuss later. (Mortar will adhere to stone and brick if you set up the right conditions—I'll explain how—and learn not to expect too much from the bond.)

Mortar and concrete don't "dry," they "set." Setting results when the water and portland cement undergo a chemical reaction and the cement expands and hardens. You don't want mud to dry before it sets, since, without enough water for complete hardening, it will be weak. That's why you see sprinklers and tarps covering fresh concrete in summer—to help it set completely.

Oddly, concrete will not set while it's being mixed. The slower concrete sets, the stronger it eventually becomes. And the less mixing water you use (within reason), the stronger it sets. Finally, mortar and concrete are likely to shrink slightly when they set, which accounts for those hairline cracks around the edge of repairs.

Bricks come in essentially two flavors, depending on how hot they were fired during manufacture. Low-temperature bricks (including most antique bricks) are porous (as are concrete blocks). High-temperature bricks are smoother, glassier, and nonpourous. Why should you care? Because you must dampen porous bricks before repairing them—otherwise they will dry out the mortar and weaken it. But if you moisten high-fired brick, the mortar will drip from the joint like ice cream in the desert. To figure out the porosity of your bricks, simply splash water on a section away from the repair. If the brick quickly absorbs the water, it's porous. If water stays on the surface for half a minute or so, it's nonporous.

Builder's Trivia
Portland cement—the cement in concrete and mortar—was named for its resemblance to portland stone, a rock in Britain. Portland cement was patented by British bricklayer Joseph Aspin in 1824. It's made by cooking and pulverizing lime in a giant kiln at 2,800 degrees Fahrenheit, which makes an extremely fine powder. Why should you care how cement is made? For no reason—except that cement products are quite dusty, and you should use a dust mask when dry-mixing them. And while you're at it, make sure to use leather or rubber gloves while handling portland cement, concrete, and mortar. They're very hard on the hands.

Keeping Time

Unlike virtually every other building material, masonry and concrete have their own rhythm. Because the material changes as it sets, you'll need to use different tools and techniques as hardening takes place. So even though mortar and concrete are (literally) as dead as stone, they may seem alive in their response to temperature, humidity, and the condition of the bricks and stones (and, seemingly, your frustration level). In carpentry, you can nail boards at your own pace. But in masonry, sometimes you'll have to rush, and sometimes you'll have to twiddle your thumbs. If you tool (smooth) a mortar joint before the mud has set, the mud will squish out. But if you wait too long, the mortar will be as hard as . . . rock.

It may sound complicated, but working with these materials is mostly a matter of mindset. If you know to watch for changes as the mortar or concrete sets, that's half the battle. I'll take care of the other half in Chapter 18, where we jump from preparation to the actual repairs. Then, I'll explain, in each procedure, how the material changes as it sets, and when to perform each step of the repair.

Finally, I would avoid masonry if the temperature is likely to fall below about 40° F, because the mortar must set before it freezes. And besides, masonry is wretched winter work—take it from someone who's done it.

Special Tools and Materials

Most mason's tools—at least the trowels, chisels, and hammers a homeowner might need—look heavy, strong, and impossibly clumsy—until you watch a mason deftly build a wall with them. Masonry starts with trowels, and while catalogs list them in infinite variety, you will only need a couple. Incidentally, many masonry tools have multiple uses, which reduces the sting of their price. As usual, there's no need to buy everything at once; buy what you need, and let your tools accumulate along with your skills.

The first stage in masonry repairs is usually to destroy something (like old mortar or concrete). To do this, you'll need a 2- or 3-pound *hammer* (for this kind of walloping, nail hammers are flyweights). Don't spring for a fancy hammer unless you are in a mood for squandering—I found a great one at a rummage sale for a buck.

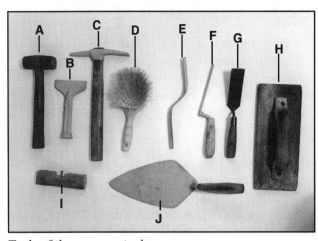

(A) 2-lb. hammer
(B) Brick chisel
(C) Mason's hammer
(D) Brush
(E) Brick jointer
(F) Tuckpointing trowel
(G) Margin trowel
(H) Concrete float
(I)   Homemade joint raker
(J) Brick trowel

Tools of the masonry trade

A hammer needs something to smash (aside from your wrist, that is), so you will want a 2- to 4-inch-wide *brick chisel* for breaking bricks, removing mortar for stone repairs, beating up on rotten concrete, and generally expressing yourself Neolithic-wise.

A *mason's hammer*, available in various sizes and styles, is essentially two flying chisels mounted on a handle. It's excellent for cleaning old stonemasonry before a repair; I'd get one that weighs about 24 ounces, but only if I had a lot of stone to fix.

Nail It Down

When masons say *pointing*, they're not talking about hunting dogs, but about replacing the mortar in a degraded joint. *Tuckpointing* is replacing mortar between bricks, because you must "tuck" the mortar into the joint.

Masonry being a grungy pursuit, you probably figured there'd be a *brush* here somewhere. The one I use is sold for cleaning dairy equipment (did I mention I'm from Wisconsin, America's Dairyland?). I use this cheap, durable, and effective brush for cleaning repairs after I chip out loose mortar. I use it for removing extra mortar after pointing, for cleaning wheelbarrows and tools, for repairing stucco, and even for cleaning up before painting.

Once you have replaced the mortar, you've got to press it into place, and then (and only then) will you need a *jointer*. Round and vee jointers come in several sizes, to match the kind of joint you are repairing (see this chapter's figure of joint varieties).

The *tuckpointing trowel* is a single-purpose item that will pay its freight in the first hours of tuckpointing. Use this long, skinny trowel to push mortar from a brick trowel into brick joints.

For versatility, my favorite is the *margin trowel*, the duck-billed platypus of masonry. This small rectangular trowel is first-rate for patching masonry and drywall, great for stirring and applying wood filler, and ideal for scouring the bottom of a goopy paint can, prying molding, scraping paint, even glazing windows. How many ten-dollar tools have that kind of portfolio?

The *brick trowel* may look awkward, but a good one (I'm not talking $3.95) is anything but. First of all, it can stir and deliver mortar quickly. Second, the corner, or heel, makes a great one-hand chisel for chipping mortar off old bricks or nubbins from oversize stones, and breaking the occasional brick. Finally, it's perfect for separating shingles during a roof repair, and it makes a tolerable paint scraper.

A *concrete float* settles the gravel and brings the sand-cement paste to the surface of a concrete repair. It's easy to make: Simply nail a 1 × 3 × 8" handle to the center of a 1 × 6 × 14" piece of scrap wood. If the larger piece is slightly warped, so much the better—nail the handle to the concave side.

Four Flavors of Masonry Joints

Look closely, and you'll notice that the mortar joints between bricks and stones are not created equal. Each of the common joint styles (see the illustration of joint varieties in this chapter) requires a different tool—which you must obtain before starting the repair.

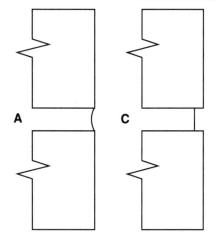

(A)   Concave joint, made with concave jointer (try to buy the correct size). You can substitute an 8" length of old garden hose to save money.

(B)   Vee joint, made with vee jointer (you may be able to simulate this jointer with a sharply sawn corner on a piece of wood).

(C)   Raked joint, made with an adjustable joint raker. For a handmade raker, see the previous figure in this chapter.

(D)   Struck joint, made by moving the edge of a brick or pointing trowel quickly along the joint.

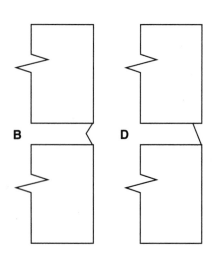

Mixing Mortar and Other Fun in the Mud

Now that we've met the tools and materials, it's time to get our hands dirty and actually mix some mud. One thing most handy-andy books ignore—if they even bother with masonry—is how to actually work with mortar. I won't fall into that trap; instead, I'll discuss the care, feeding, and mixing of mortar. (Incidentally, mortar is mortar, as far as quality is concerned. Most brickyards only sell one brand, although you may be able to find several colors.)

The key rule is not to mix up too much, particularly in hot weather. If the mud hardens too quickly, you'll either have to dump the stuff or rush your work. In summer, prepare only as much as you can use in half an hour. In cooler weather, it's probably okay to mix up an hour's worth. (You can safely add a little water to soften stiff mud at first, but be careful—a lot of water will weaken the batch. It's better to mix small amounts in the first place.)

For a small repair, buy premixed mortar, which is a blend of cement and sand. For larger repairs, you can save money by buying a bag of mason's cement and mixing it with clean (and very cheap) mason's sand. Start mixing after all your preparations are complete:

1. Add dry material to a wheelbarrow, or, for a small repair, a clean plastic bucket.

2. If you're using sand and cement, dry-mix three parts sand with one part cement until they are thoroughly blended.

3. Slowly add water while mixing with a trowel, shovel, or hoe. The idea is to layer the dry mix over the water, using the shovel or hoe.

4. After you've created sandwiches of dry and wet (yum-yum!), start stirring. Remember— you're not making soup du jour; mortar must be fairly stiff so it will stay where you put it. If it gets too soupy, add a bit of dry mix.

> **Handy Hint**
> Before you begin a visible repair, check the mortar color. Gray is the standard in premixed mortar and cement, but most brickyards also sell white and brown cement, and may have pigments for custom-tinting mortar (and concrete). Even if you don't hit the perfect shade, any effort to match the color will be repaid with a repair that's less noticeable.

5. Dump the mix onto a metal sheet or scrap of plywood, roughly 2 feet square.

6. As you use the mortar, stir it with your trowel, lifting and throwing the mud in against itself with a sweeping motion. This keeps the mortar flexible and ready to flow into the repair.

Making It Stay Stuck

Ideally, mortar and concrete will "key" (lock onto) a surface that's fairly deep and rough, so when you squish mortar into a gap between bricks or stones that's at least $3/4$ inch deep, it will get a good grip. But what if your repair falls outside this "rough and ready" category? For example, how can you apply a surface coat to improve the appearance of a pockmarked foundation? Or make a concrete patch that actually sticks to the edge of a stoop? By increasing the bond between the new mortar and the surface with a coat of cement paste or bonding agent.

Here's how:

1. Clean loose stuff from the surface with a chisel or mason's hammer and a brush. Clean the surface chemically with dilute muriatic acid (available at masonry suppliers). When handling acid, observe all cautions, particularly regarding eye and hand protection.

2. When the acid has finished foaming, wash away the remaining crud with plenty of water, then allow the surface to dry a bit.

149

3. Mix up a little dry portland or mason's cement (pure cement, without sand or gravel) with water. The mix should be pretty stiff. (If you bought a bonding agent from a brickyard, just follow the directions that came with it.)

4. Brush this goop on the surface and complete your repair before the bonding agent dries.

And Then There Were Stones

I get a kick out of homeowners who brag that their old stone house "was built of stones from the quarry just down the road." I love meeting somebody who's turned on by the most earthy and beautiful building material. But until recently, all stone was local, because stones tend to be . . . heavy. Nevertheless, there's a lesson here: The appearance, hardness, density, and handling ease of a stone are all influenced by its origin. So it's tougher to generalize about stonework than about other parts of masonry. Some stone is soft, some is hard, some splits easily (but only in one plane), while some is hard to saw even with a diamond blade. Some ages nicely, and some doesn't.

Furthermore, stone repair calls for more artistry than brick or block repair. First, if any stones are loose, they are more difficult to replace. Second, the joints are usually wider, meaning you must apply the mortar more slowly, allowing the first layer to set before you add more mud. In fact, stonework requires too much patience for people who like to finish jobs in a totally linear sequence. And third, it's more difficult to match the joint style in stonework than in brick and block work. Nevertheless, stonework is my favorite kind of masonry, because the rewards of ogling a deftly repaired stone wall greatly exceed the effort.

Hints for Working Stone

To make stonework more rewarding and less laborious, follow these suggestions:

➤ If you must pull loose stones out before replacing them, mark the location and top side on each with a light pencil.

➤ For a large repair, don't allow vertical joints to line up; this weakens the wall.

➤ To build up thick joints, use chips of concrete block to dry and stiffen the mortar (just make sure they won't show when you're done). Use wooden wedges to temporarily prop up stones while the mortar sets.

➤ Take your time—large mortar joints set slowly, and if you rush, mortar will be squeezed from the joint.

➤ If possible, find extra stones that match the original wall.

➤ To enliven old, moldy, discolored limestone, give it a light wash of muriatic acid. Make a mild mixture, don your goggles and rubber gloves, and sprinkle it on the wall. Then flush with clean water.

The Least You Need to Know

➤ Mortar holds things apart; it doesn't hold them together.

➤ Because mortar grips rather weakly, many surfaces need a careful cleaning before repair.

➤ Pay careful attention to mortar color—you won't get a second chance to choose the right one.

➤ Stir mortar repeatedly after you mix it; stiff, crumbly mortar is worthless.

Chapter 18

Bricks and Stones . . . Masonry and Concrete (the Sequel)

In This Chapter

➤ The fundamentals of masonry and concrete repair

➤ Tuckpointing for amateurs

➤ Curing water damage—before you get in over your head

Having read Chapter 17, you know the principles underlying the ancient sport of masonry and its modern cousin, concrete. Now that you're itching to grab a trowel, let's describe the general procedure for repairing masonry, then tailor it to specific circumstances.

But first I feel an urge to quote myself. In masonry, remember, the mud calls the shots, and you've got to go with the flow. Mortar and concrete harden at their own rates, depending on surface porosity, temperature, and other factors, and you can't finish the job until the mud has set to the right consistency. Be prepared to leave one part of a repair for a few minutes while the mud sets up, then return for further operations.

Repairing Masonry and Concrete for Keeps— The General Procedure

So gather your tools, and let's check out the general recipe for repairing masonry and concrete:

1. Masonry repairs are like dental repairs (although usually cheaper and less painful). Why? Because you can't build on decay. Start by removing decayed mortar with a mason's hammer, or a 2- to 3-pound hammer and a brick chisel. Although cleaner is usually better, use some judgment. Loose pieces of brick or stone must be removed and replaced, but a big hunk that shifts only slightly can probably remain in place because the new mortar will firm it up. If you try to remove every bit of old mortar, you'll just loosen stuff that's still solid.

2. When you've removed the rot, clean out the hole with a stiff brush (and a vacuum if you're the fastidious type, which I doubt—few fussy folks fiddle with masonry).

3. Test the surface you are repairing for porosity by splashing water on it. If the water seeps into the surface within a half minute or so, the surface will absorb water from the mortar and must be moistened—particularly where the mud will be thin—before mortaring. Dip a 3- or 4-inch paintbrush in water, and flick it at the repair, particularly where the mortar will be shallow. Get it wet, but not saturated.

4. Ladies and gentlemen! Start your—er—Mix your mortar! (See the section titled "Mixing Mortar and Other Fun in the Mud" in Chapter 17.)

Don't Screw Up!
As you start swinging your 3-pound hammer, remember three things:

1. That wall might be holding up something important, like your house.

2. If you hit your hand, you'll be sorry.

3. If you get crud in your eye, you'll be even sorrier. Wear safety goggles, silly.

5. Start by filling the deepest holes. Often the best way to do this—believe it or not—is to throw the mortar into place with a trowel (overhand and sidearm are both acceptable). Thrown mortar gets good contact with the surface, and thus better adhesion. A slightly more delicate approach is to feed the mortar into the joint by placing it on one trowel and using a smaller trowel as a pusher.

6. Avoid the temptation to fill large holes at once: Work several parts of the repair simultaneously. After the first coat has stiffened, add more.

7. As you finish the patch, let it set and tool it to match the surrounding masonry, using a trowel, a length of hose, or a jointer (see the figure illustrating joint varieties in Chapter 17). To use a jointer, simply rub it along the joint a couple of times, until the joint takes the proper shape, and the mud is pressed firmly into place. If you're working near a corner, always move the jointer from the corner toward the center of the work.

8. Finally, when the mortar is hard enough and bristle marks won't show, brush it with a stiff, plastic brush (don't use a steel brush, which could leave rust marks). Brush diagonally across the joints, to remove trowel marks and smeared mortar from stones or bricks.

Tuckpointing

Tuckpointing—repairing mortar in brickwork—is a simple, tedious, glamorless, and necessary (to owners of brick homes, anyway) skill that almost anyone can master. Doing your own tuckpointing has two advantages: It can save you money, and you can subdivide a large job, repairing smaller sections as time (or boredom) permits. Here are the steps you'll follow to handle your tuckpointing jobs:

> **Don't Screw Up!**
> Masons leave small holes in brickwork, called "weep holes," to allow water that gathers behind the wall to exit without causing damage. You'll find weep holes above windows, doors, and foundations. If they are plugged with debris, they may need cleaning, but don't be tempted to fill them with mortar—they have a job to do.

1. Clean out the old mortar to at least $^1/_2$ inch deep ($^3/_4$ is better) with a chisel or a rented grinder with a diamond blade. Wear eye goggles. Take care not to damage the brick—and don't get too aggressive. You may have to leave some soft mortar in place, or else you'll chisel out the whole wall.

2. Brush or vacuum debris from the joint. Don't use a water hose, unless you can let the repair dry for at least a day before continuing.

3. Test the brick for porosity (see step 3 in the general procedure presented in the preceding section).

4. Mix a small amount of mortar and push it into the deepest joints, using a two-trowel technique to minimize spillage. Hold the mortar on a brick trowel and push it in with a tuckpointing trowel (if you have one, a margin or pointing trowel will also work). Fill deep cracks in two or three steps.

5. When joints are "thumb-hard," tool them by running a jointer back and forth a couple of times. Press hard to compress the mud and make the joint stronger, cleaner looking, and more watertight.

6. Finally, let the mud set for a while, then brush diagonally to remove extra mortar and smooth irregularities.

Busting Blocks and Breaking Bricks— Not Just for Lifers

If you have a few bricks or concrete blocks to shape (to make an odd size or a corner), you should be able to cut them with hammer and chisel. Lay the brick or block on sand or something else that will support it uniformly (good support is crucial to this technique). Then gradually start tapping at the line where you want the break. Continue tapping on the line (turn the brick to hit the opposite side too), gradually increasing your force. When the noise starts to sound a bit hollow, indicating that the brick or block is about to fracture, hit it harder. Although you may need practice, this technique is far more effective than it sounds. The big mistakes are not obtaining enough support, and striking too hard at first. You also can saw most bricks with a circular saw and a fiberglass masonry blade—a noisy, dusty solution that usually works. A more sophisticated approach is to rent a diamond-blade tile saw (if the rental company permits you to saw brick with it). These saws are more accurate, quieter, and, because they are water-cooled, virtually dust-free. However, some bricks are too hard for either of these saws, so use them gingerly while you get the hang of it. And wear goggles.

A Word on Foundation Repair

Can you fix a crack in a concrete, concrete block, or stone foundation?

Yes.

Will it stay fixed?

That depends. Is the crack still moving?

Enough Socratic dialog—home-repair manuals should be light on philosophical blather. What I'm trying to say is this: Don't expect a little line of mortar to hold a foundation together if the foundation's got moving on its mind.

Some new foundations crack a bit when the soil settles, and then stay put. Look closely at the crack—if you see dirt, insect cocoons, or other crud inside, you may be lucky enough to have an old, inactive crack. Then go ahead and fix it, using the general repair procedure outlined earlier in this chapter.

If the crack is fresh and clean inside, then it's probably new and may still be shifting due to unstable soil or frost heaving. If you think water is running under the foundation and freezing, see "May We Talk about Your Soggy Basement?" later in this chapter. If that doesn't work, and you're worried that the shifting will damage plaster, doors, or windows upstairs, you're in pro territory—consult a mason or foundation repairer.

Stucco Repair—The Jackson Pollock Solution

Stucco is a decorative mortar coating with an irregular surface that can be finished in various ways. Although the repair procedure is simple, few homeowners know it, and judging by the average stucco repair, a lot of masons don't either. All you need are the instructions in this section, the usual tools, a big, coarse-fibered brush, and a bit of patience. Patience? Yes, you'll need to let the mortar set awhile between operations. Here are the steps:

1. Clean out all the loose, crumbly stuff from the hole with hammer, chisel, and brush. For a small repair, go directly to step 3.

    For a large repair, you've got to make sure the new stucco adheres. Choose 2a or 2b.

2a. *If the hole is backed up by masonry or concrete*: Clean the backup wall by brushing with diluted muriatic acid (it's sold at brickyards—be sure to protect your eyes and hands). When the acid stops foaming, wash it off with water, then allow the surface to partially dry.

2b. *If the damaged area is backed by anything else*: Buy some wire lath from a plaster or masonry supplier to anchor the new stucco (some people use chicken wire or $1/4$-inch screening, but wire lath is stronger). Cut the lath to fit inside the damaged area, and nail it to the studs with roofing nails. Make sure the lath stays tight, or it will protrude from the wall. Cut it with tin snips, and wear gloves—wire lath is sharp, and has a nasty temper.

3. Moisten the edges of intact stucco so it won't dry out the new mortar. (If you washed the backing with muriatic acid previously, you can probably skip this step.)

4. Mix a batch of mortar and trowel it into the deepest areas first. If you nailed up wire lath, press the mortar into it. Gradually work up to the surface level. If the mortar sags, you're adding it too quickly. If it dries out, you're adding too slowly. For a swirled stucco finish, go to step 11. For the common, nubbly finish of stucco, continue here.

5. When the whole repair is almost up to the level of the existing stucco, stop and allow the mortar to set up for a while—maybe twenty minutes in warm weather.

6. Soften the mortar still in your wheelbarrow with water. It should be medium-soupy—about the consistency of half-melted soft-serve ice cream.

7. Now for the Jackson Pollock routine. (Remember the paint-throwing abstract expressionist from the 1950s?) When the mortar on the wall is stiff, but you can still press your thumb into it, you're ready to begin throwing mortar. Take your stiff cleaning brush, smoosh it directly into the softened mud in the wheelbarrow, and throw this mud at the mud already on the wall.

157

8. If the thrown mud penetrates too deeply, wait a few minutes so the wall can harden a bit. Then resume throwing the soft mud, blending the patch to match the original.

9. If the original stucco was flattened on top, wait a few minutes longer, then trowel the high points flat to match that texture. Otherwise, you are done.

10. Moisten the patch repeatedly during the first week, so it can cure properly.

     For a *swirled finish*, follow the above through step 4, and continue here. You will also need a 4-inch paint brush and a soft rubber float (see the photo of plaster and drywall tools in Chapter 20).

11. Bring the mortar up to the surface level and allow it to set for a while.

12. When the mortar is fairly stiff, moisten the float and flick some water on the surface. Then start swirling the stucco, attempting to match the surroundings. If the float digs in too much, wait a while. If it does not dig in enough, add more water to the surface.

Taking the Bloom off Bloom

What do masonry walls have in common with angel food cakes? Not much—unless your house has a disease called "bloom," an ailment that shows up as a white "frosting" on the exterior. Bloom, aka efflorescence, is a deposit of white salts that originate in the mortar, bricks, blocks, or stones, and are carried to the surface by water. The problem requires moisture, which can come from the outside (rain or groundwater) or from the inside (condensation).

Efflorescence is not a pretty picture, and it's easier to prevent than cure. (Aren't warnings like this wonderfully helpful? Why would anyone bother preventing bloom unless they already had it? And by then, it's too late. However, you may be able to prevent the bloom from getting worse.) If the moisture is coming from outside, see "May We Talk about Your Soggy Basement?" later in this chapter. If the water is coming from inside, see the section of Chapter 11 entitled "Home Ventilation—Why and How."

To remove bloom, try a stiff brushing with water. If that doesn't work, brush on one part muriatic acid to twelve parts water (and don't forget to use caution, goggles, and rubber gloves). Then rinse with water—sparingly—because water can cause more bloom.

Some people suggest waterproofing the outside of a wall to prevent water from entering and causing bloom. But the Brick Institute of America, which presumably knows something about the subject, warns that a waterproof treatment can trap moisture inside the building and cause worse deterioration.

Concretely Speaking?

So much for masonry. What about its big gray sister, concrete? Chances are you have some of this handy, homely stuff around the house—in the driveway, the foundation, or the basement floor. What to do if concrete starts acting up? First, you figure out a plan of action, and second, you carry it out. We'll take things in that order.

Like all good doctors, a concrete doctor must start by diagnosing the trouble. If the stuff is heavily cracked or broken—usually as a result of poor ingredients or dumb pouring technique—the only solution may be to replace it. Unless you love jackhammering, or it's a tiny job, that's best left to the pros. Fortunately, usually the problem is more localized— a crack, chip, or break amidst an expanse of good 'crete.

Builder's Trivia

Concrete walks and driveways that have settled can be jacked back into position in one piece by specialists called *mudjackers* or *slabjackers*. Mudjackers drill holes in each slab, pump in soupy concrete to raise it, and allow the mud to set. Although it's not cheap, it beats replacing a slab.

As usual, the first step in repair is to "pound the pavement" and remove the damaged stuff with hammer, chisel, and brush. No matter what the shape, try to avoid thin, weak edges in the repair, which will crack immediately, by cutting the edges at a sharp angle (see the illustration below).

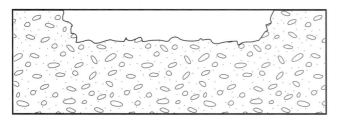

Cut the edges as square as possible, but don't get obsessive and try to make them perfect— it's impossible unless you rent a diamond saw made for cutting concrete. Strongly suggested: For better adhesion, clean the area, moisten it, and brush on a bonding agent or a paste of portland cement and water.

Preparing to patch concrete

Unless you're patching a hole on something flat, you'll have to set up temporary bracing, called *forms*, to hold the fresh concrete in place as it sets. If you're like me, you'll try to get away with the sleaziest, most entry-level form imaginable. And if your luck is like mine, you'll be repaid by a form that bulges, sags, or otherwise fails just when you need it most—when the 'crete is half-poured.

So do something slightly more impressive. Sharpen the point of a 1 × 3 or 2 × 4 with an ax or handsaw to make a stake. Then drive it into the ground with a sledgehammer, 3-pound hammer, or the back of an ax. Cut diagonal braces to fit; once they are long enough to wedge tight against the form, nail them in place. If there's no place to drive stakes, anchor the forms with concrete blocks or other weighty objects.

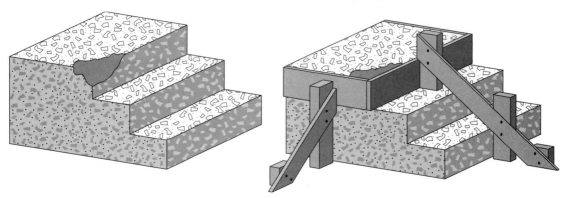

Remember—your repair will never be better than your form. Note secure diagonal bracing nailed to stakes.

Finishing Concrete—From Stone Soup to Smooth as Glass

Before I explain the steps for a concrete repair, you must understand how to finish concrete—how to convert fresh concrete into a smooth concrete driveway—in other words, how to smooth stone soup. Most people don't seem to think about finishing until they are midway through a concrete job—at least that's my style. Unfortunately, that's a bit late—without finishing, you'll wind up with a lumpy surface that's appallingly close to a gun-metal-gray version of kidney-bean stew.

The trick in finishing, I learned after one disastrous encounter with stone soup, is to repeatedly work the surface as the concrete sets. This process pushes the stones down while pulling the sand, cement, and water to the surface. This stuff, called *paste*, fills the gaps between the gravel and makes that smooth, attractive (well, relatively, we're still talking concrete) surface.

> **Handy Hint**
> Don't let anyone convince you that you can hammer "masonry" nails (aka "cut nails") into old concrete—it just ain't so. These nails will penetrate fresh (1- to 2-day-old) concrete, which is still pretty soft, but to fasten to old concrete, you've got to drill and set an anchor, or use the gunpowder-driven anchors sold at lumber- or brickyards.

There are two steps to working: screeding and floating. You *screed*—or "strike off"—by drawing a 2 × 4 back and forth across the surface. Rest each end of the board on a form or the surrounding concrete and hold the forward edge up slightly so it does not dig into the soup. (For smaller repairs like potholes in a driveway, you can skip screeding.)

The tool for floating is called, amazingly enough, a *float,* and you can make one from scrap lumber in about ten minutes (counting time wasted looking for the wood). There are instructions for making a homemade float in Chapter 17, under "Special Tools and Materials." The actual process of floating is covered in step 4, below.

If you're trying to repair an acne-infested, pockmarked section of concrete driveway or on floor, your best bet is to buy a latex surface repair material from a masonry supplier.

For medium-size jobs, you'll want to buy concrete mix in bags. For large jobs, it's cheaper to buy sand, cement, and gravel. The general recipe is one part of cement to two parts sand and three parts gravel. For a medium-size or larger job, do yourself a favor and rent a mixer—this stuff defines heavy!

Concrete Repair—The General Procedure

Once the preparations are completed, you can get down to the dirty work—mixing and pouring the concrete. Try to choose a day that's warm but not hot—not only is the work sweaty, but the concrete sets up too quickly in temperatures above 85 degrees or so. Don't work in weather colder than 40 degrees, because it will set too slowly.

1. Mix the concrete according to the directions on the bag. Then add water—but don't make it too soupy, which will weaken the batch. Dry-mix the materials, then add water and mix some more.

2. In hot, dry weather, dampen the old concrete around the repair to prevent overdrying of the patch. Add a bonding agent if needed. Then shovel fresh concrete into the repair, making sure it gets into all gaps and corners.

3. On a large job, screed the top with a 2 × 4, using a sawing motion to level it.

4. Allow the patch to set for a while—perhaps fifteen or thirty minutes. Then start floating by drawing your float around in a circle. If you start too soon, the float will dig in to the surface. If you start too late, the surface won't move around because it's too hard. Use light pressure, and don't expect to get too much done at once—repetition is the key. If rocks come to the surface, throw them away or push them back in.

5. After one or two more floating operations, let the 'crete rest, and switch to a concrete-finishing trowel or a plastering trowel (both work equally well). Again, using a circular motion, pull the paste to the surface, using more downward pressure.

161

6. It's hard to predict how many times you'll need to trowel—the best advice is to watch the concrete and make sure it sets with the finish you want. But don't over-work it, since this can weaken the surface and make it prone to "spalling," or flaking off.

7. If you want a "broom finish"—a safer surface that has fine ridges and better traction—draw a garage broom across the surface as it sets. As usual, if the mud is too soft, the ridges will be too deep; if the mud is too stiff, the ridges won't be deep enough.

May We Talk about Your Soggy Basement?

Some of my favorite moments in the masonry business occurred when I was called to fix a wet basement. I usually started by explaining (to my customer's relief) that most of these problems did not require expensive waterproofing, trenching, or sump pumps. Instead, they required the low-tech solution—getting the water away from the foundation before it could sink into the ground and cause a problem. (If you don't hear this from the people who sell pumps or waterproofing, it may be because they know which side of their bread is buttered.)

So when someone asked me to dry out a waterlogged basement, my first response was to roll my eyes to the sky. I wasn't being rude; I was looking for the problem, which was usually traceable to balky gutters. What is the lesson for you, dear homeowner-plagued-by-a-soggy-basement? It is to forget about making your basement as tight as a boat, and follow this easy script for basement dryness:

1. Standing outside the house, near where the water is entering the basement, look at the gutter. Is it leaking or plugged? Then fix the problems you find (see the section of Chapter 16 entitled "Down in the Gutter: Repairing Eaves Troughs").

2. Next check the downspouts, which bring water from the gutters to the ground. If the spouts empty out near the problem area, then direct the water elsewhere. (You can buy gutter material or flexible plastic pipe at hardware stores or lumberyards.)

3. If your house has underground piping in place to take run-off away from the house, you'll have to decide whether it's easier to clean this piping out, to install new piping, or just bypass it entirely by running downspout piping on the surface. There's a tradeoff here: underground piping is less obtrusive—but more difficult to install.

4. Finally, look at the grading (slope) of ground near the wet spot. Is the water simply doing what comes naturally—running downhill toward your house? Then you may need to add topsoil around the house, and smooth it so the water runs away. In an

extreme case, you may need to build a low berm to divert water coming from elsewhere to a place where it won't cause harm.

This may sound like a lot of toil, but it's cheaper than a basement waterproofing job, and much more likely to work. There are no guarantees, and you can always install a sump pump or hire a waterproofer later on. But do start by getting the water away from the basement.

The Least You Need to Know

➤ Put your repairs on a sound footing—clean out all rot first.

➤ There's no excuse for an ugly stucco repair—if you know the Jackson Pollock solution.

➤ Smoothing concrete is easy—if you know *how* and *when* to do it.

➤ Water can be murder on foundations and basements. The first and cheapest solution is to keep water away from the building.

Part 4
An Inside Job

When I rented an apartment, I loved having shabby walls. Huh? That's because they screamed a silent but unmistakable "paint me!"—just the sort of assertiveness that was needed to catch the landlord's attention. Now that I'm a homeowner, that squalor seems like injustice squared—first I've got to endure the sight of those walls, and then I've got to smear some paint on them.

Granted, the forces of entropy are not as severe inside a house as they are on the outside, which must withstand the weather. Still, the interior is subject to the forces of decay—judging by the squeaky floors, rotting plaster, and peeling paint I've confronted in various houses.

But the picture is not all gloomy. The indoor home repairs described in this part of the book can be the most satisfying species of home fix-up, because you can savor the fruits of your labor from the easy chair. And remember: it never rains when you are working inside. (If you bought that lie, I bet you haven't tried any plumbing repairs recently. But we'll save plumbing for last.)

Chapter 19

Getting a Solid Footing on Floors

In This Chapter

➤ Finding and fixing talkative floors

➤ Replacing subfloors and floorboards

➤ A technique for invisible carpet patching

➤ Simple fixes for tile floors

Floors—if you got stomped on as much as they do, you'd probably be protesting too. Floors protest by talking back. In my house, that kind of insubordination is worst in the kitchen, where the human equivalent of Hannibal's elephant-mounted army trudges past each day. And there's nothing I can do about it, because I stupidly had a parquet floor laid over the squeak before I "got around" to fixing it.

At least I learned my lesson: don't cover up problems—fix them first. Before a new carpet was laid over old linoleum in my bedroom, I spent a couple of hours renailing the floor to the joists (support beams). I located the first joist by drilling through the floor until I hit solid wood. Then I marked out the other joists, which were parallel to the first and 16 inches away (in rare cases, joists are 12 inches apart). Finally, I pounded $2^1/2$-inch spiral flooring nails 6 inches apart into the joists. Now, I doubt that Hannibal's elephants could raise a squeak from that floor.

In this chapter, I will discuss cures for some of the most common flooring woes, starting with suggestions for annihilating squeaks. Then I will discuss some other flooring repairs that you can realistically hope to achieve—and warn you away from repairs that are truly outside idiot territory.

Squeakproofing

Squeaks are caused by wood rubbing against wood, or against nails, in a floor that has loosened due to structural settling, poor carpentry, or alternating wet and dry weather.

Squeaks are easiest to silence if you have *access from below*. From below, drill holes for a series of flathead wood screws that are fully $1/4$ inch shorter than the combined thickness of the finish floor and subfloor (that's the bottom layer of wood; in new houses, it's usually plywood, in older houses, it's $3/4$-inch lumber). Ask somebody to stand on the floor while you tighten the screws to bring the finish floor (the top layer) down tight to the subfloor (see the illustration below). Don't overtighten. Stop when the squeak does.

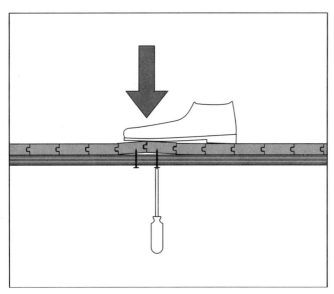

When repairing a squeaky floor from below, don't strip the screws. Be reasonable—the goal is silence, not punishment.

Glue and nail or screw a cleat (an extra piece of wood about the size of a 2 × 4) to the joist near the squeak (as shown in illustration). Because the cleat must hold the floor at the top of its movement, push up while fastening.

Tap a glue-coated shim into the gap between the joist and the floor. But take it easy—there's no point raising the board any further than it already is (see bottom illustration on facing page).

If you must *work from above,* find the joists by:

➤ Taking up some old floor covering and looking for nails.

➤ Looking inside a floor register for joists.

➤ Probing with a coat hanger, as shown in the figure on page 170.

➤ The other joists should be parallel to the first, and multiples of 16 inches away from it.

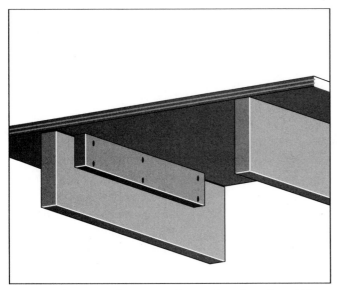

The cleat holds the floor up so the weight of people walking on it does not cause a squeak.

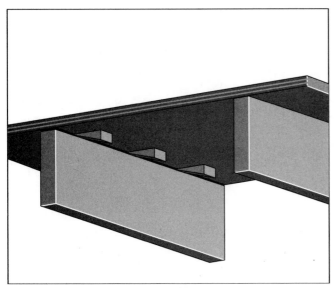

Shims underneath prevent the floor from moving—but use a light touch. Tap the shims into place.

To actually fix a squeak from above, try these suggestions: Drill diagonal pilot holes and hammer casing nails into a joist. Fill the nail holes with a wood filler afterward, and sand and finish as needed.

For a bad squeak, use several nails or wood screws—as long and large as you can hide with wood filler. Before fastening, pour in a puddle of wood glue. Make sure nails and screws hit a joist—reaching the subfloor is not strong enough. And remember that diagonal fasteners get a much better grip than vertical ones.

Stepping Stones to Silent Stairs

My in-laws never repaired the squeakiest stairs in the world, probably because they made a perfect alarm for signaling the after-hours return of the elegant teenager I later married. If you don't need to monitor errant youths, there are several ways to *silence squeaky stairs*.

But as usual, we need to start with a bit of lingo:

➤ Treads are the horizontal boards you walk (tread) on.

➤ Risers are the vertical boards between two treads. They're the boards you see as you walk upstairs.

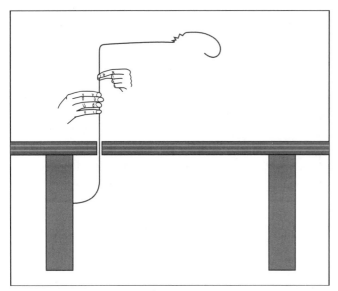

Find the joist by drilling and probing with a coat hanger.

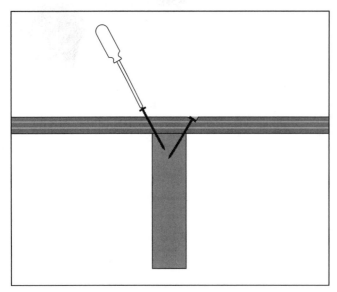

Wood screws, especially beefy ones, are stronger than nails, but you'll have more damage to hide with wood filler afterward.

➤ Stringers are the slanting framing lumber beneath the stairs. You will only see them if the underside of the stairway is not covered with drywall or plaster.

With the jargon under control, let's look at a few simple repairs:

➤ Drill pilot holes for long, thin screws to secure the treads to risers and stringers. The holes should be smaller in diameter than the screws, but should have a recess, or countersink, for the head.

➤ Drill pilot holes for long casing nails (thick versions of finishing nails). Nail at an angle for better grip.

➤ Pull out the molding between a tread and a riser (if there is one), then insert glue-coated wedges in the gaps. When the glue is dry, cut off the visible part of the wedges with a wood chisel or a utility knife and replace the molding.

➤ From below, coat two sides of a 2 × 2 with glue, and force it against the joint between a riser and the tread. Drill pilot holes and, with somebody standing on the tread, screw it into place. Make sure your screws are too short to pierce the tread.

Wood Subfloor Repair

The subfloor is the layer of rough flooring resting on the joists. If it's under a wood floor, it's usually ³/₄ of an inch thick—either plywood or another manufactured wood product (for relatively new houses) or individual boards (for older houses). If it's under a ceramic tile floor, the subfloor may be a sheet of material bonded with portland cement. If the house is built on a concrete slab, it may not have a subfloor, or it may have rigid insulation between the finish floor and the slab.

To repair a wood subfloor or patch a hole in it, you'll need a power screwdriver or variable-speed drill, circular saw or handsaw, plywood or boards as thick as the subfloor, 2 × 4 blocking, construction adhesive or wood glue, 16d (16-penny) sinker nails, and drywall screws. Once you've gathered the needed tools and materials, use these steps to make the repair:

1. Remove any finish flooring around the damaged area.

2. If the subfloor damage or hole is not already rectangular, mark out a rectangular cutout around the damage. Drill starter holes for the saw blade, if needed. If you can find the joists, saw alongside them, leaving adjacent subfloor nailed to them. Select step 3 or 4.

3. *If the floor joists are near the edge of the hole*

   A. Coat the side of at least two 2 × 4 blocks (to support the subfloor patch at either end) with construction adhesive or wood glue.

   B. Nail or screw the blocks to the joists, making sure they are tight to the bottom of the existing subfloor. Go to step 5.

4. *If the joists are not near the hole*

   A. Cut a pair of 2 × 4 blocks somewhat wider than the repair. Place the blocks on top of the floor and mark their location on the floor.

   B. Drill a few ¹/₈-inch pilot holes through the subfloor at each end of the marked area.

   C. Smear glue on each 2 × 4 block where it will contact the existing subfloor (see the next illustration). Clamp the block to the bottom of the subfloor if a C-clamp is handy.

D. Install drywall screws ($1^1/_4$ inches longer than the thickness of the subfloor) through the pilot holes, as shown. When all the screws are tight, allow the glue to dry.

5. Cut a piece of subfloor to size. Put glue on the top of the 2 × 4s, and screw the subfloor to them, pulling the screw heads down flush to the subfloor.

6. If the floor will be under a carpet, as in the illustrations in this chapter, or under tile or vinyl flooring, you may need to raise the surface further: cut a second piece of plywood to size and repeat step 5. Use pilot holes and drive plenty of screws down flush to the surface, as in the photo below, right.

7. If you have a noticeable gap around the edges of the repaired subfloor, carpet, asphalt tile, or linoleum may settle into it (this will not be a problem with wood finish flooring). Buy some floor filler and squish it into the groove, following directions on the package. But be warned—this stuff will have a hard time adhering to a floor that's loose and shifting.

The side and ends of the blocks are glued to bond to the bottom of the existing subfloor.

Make sure the block is tight to the subfloor as you start driving screws.

Carefully match the surface levels so the patch is exactly flush with the floor. Take the time for accuracy here—it's now or never!

To learn the right techniques to nail strip flooring to a subfloor patch, read on.

Replacing Strip Flooring

Let's say you want to replace floorboards because they are damaged or stained. First make sure you can find replacement floorboards. Strip flooring comes in standard sizes, but if you can't find what you need at a lumberyard, look for somebody who salvages old buildings. To be sure you get the right size, measure the flooring carefully and identify the wood species. The best bet is to bring a piece of flooring with you as you look around.

Wood flooring is made with square (flat) edges, or with tongue-and-groove (T&G) edges, which join to make a very strong floor. Hardwood (oak or maple) flooring is generally tongue-and-groove. T&G is "blind-nailed" through the tongue, meaning you don't see nails when the floor is finished.

On square-edge flooring, you can usually see the nails or screws (or the plugs or fillers concealing them). Square-edge is easy to repair, because you can find the fasteners, and you can lift boards out without disturbing adjacent ones.

T&G is difficult to repair, because the boards are keyed together on the sides and ends. Ideally, your patch will emulate the "staggered joints" you see in your floor (this means the joints between the ends of the boards do not line up). Some authorities suggest matching the staggered joints by drilling and chiseling out the old boards. You also can cut the boards with a saber saw and a fine-tooth blade (break the blade so it reaches only as deep as the finish floor [the top layer]). But because it's very difficult to stagger joints

Don't Screw Up!
The "strip flooring" in new houses is actually plywood with a hardwood veneer. You can spot this material by the unnaturally narrow and regular joints between the "floorboards." You can also pull off a floor heat register and examine the edge of the flooring. If you're unsure about your flooring, I'd suggest calling a carpenter or flooring outfit. I would not try to repair these floorboards, since the whole floor is knit together.

neatly, I suggest sawing out a rectangular portion. Granted, the patch will be visible, since the ends will not be staggered. But a staggered patch is also likely to be visible—and the repair will gobble up much more of your Saturday.

To replace a rectangular section of strip flooring, start by letting the replacement boards dry indoors for at least twenty-four hours. Don't work in humid weather, because when dry weather arrives, the boards will shrink, and gaps will appear. You'll need a circular saw, aluminum and/or carpenter's square, prybar, wood chisel, hammer, nail set, drill, nails, and replacement flooring. I strongly recommend renting a flooring nailer, since it brings the boards perfectly tight while it blind nails them. You might also want to use construction glue if the subfloor seems rickety. Then follow these steps to make the repair:

1. Mark out a rectangular patch on the floor for the repair. Using a square, nail wood strips to the damaged section of floor to guide the circular saw and *crosscut* the boards (cut across the grain—across the short dimension). Cut two sides of the rectangle at this point. Take your time and work patiently—this must be as close to a perfect rectangle as you can get.

2. Saw down the middle of one damaged board. It should be nailed only at the edges (through the tongue), so you won't destroy the saw blade. Pound a prybar or big screwdriver into this saw cut and pry out the board.

3. Remove the rest of the damaged floor, and pull all nails. If there are short (say 1 foot long at maximum) stubs of existing flooring at the edge of the patch, pull them out so you can slide new flooring into place. You may have to repeat step 2 to loosen these boards.

4. Trim one end of the new flooring square (at a right angle) using a miter box or a circular saw, and lay it in place so its groove fits over the tongue of the existing flooring. Carefully mark the other end and saw it.

5. For a stronger patch, squeeze a few lines of construction adhesive on the subfloor. Then, matching the existing floor, blind or face nail the piece into position. To blind-nail with a flooring nailer, simply follow the directions for the unit. To blind nail by hand, drill each tongue diagonally with a drill bit that's slightly smaller than

the nail. Hammer the nail most of the way into place, and complete the job with a nail set. Keep the boards tight against each other as you nail, using a rubber mallet or a hammer pounded against a scrap block of wood.

6. Cut or chisel the bottom of the groove from the last board, slip it into place, and face-nail it. Fill and stain the nail holes.

7. Sand the entire floor (this is a pro job, particularly if you have perfectionist tendencies).

Dealing with Wooden Floors

What ails thee, O wooden floor? Is it stains, gouges, or the ancient destruction of a persistent leak? Does thy varnish show gouges? Or art thou merely dull and scratched? Let's stop waxing poetical and look at a few repairs, small and large, for wood floors.

To make these repairs, you've got to know whether the floor has an oil finish (made with a blend of mineral spirits and turpentine, or the commercial equivalent), a wax finish (either paste or liquid), or polyurethane varnish. How to tell one from the other? Oil finish gives the wood a luster, but does not fill in the pores at all. You should know if you've been waxing the floor. And polyurethane varnish presents a clear, solid surface—you may be able to see pores in the wood, but you won't be able to feel them.

Fix It Before It's Really Broke

If you act soon, you may be able to fix problems before they get too extreme.

➤ A dull waxed floor may be restored with a rented buffer. Follow directions for the wax you'll be using.

➤ For a minor burn or defect in a waxed, oiled, or varnished floor, hand-sand the area with increasingly fine sandpaper. Scrape a deep burn with a sharp wood chisel held perpendicular to the floor. If the injury is noticeably hollow, use a wood filler. Then color the repair to match the surroudings, using stain, or a stain stick or scratch concealer. Then oil, wax, or varnish the repair area. For a waxed or oiled floor, treat the whole floor to new wax or oil.

➤ Stains: Depending on the source and the floor finish, you may be able to remove a stain by rubbing with fine steel wool and mineral spirits. Deep stains, or water damage that has separated the grain of the wood, call for either a complete floor sanding and filling, or floorboard replacement.

The Problem with Polyurethane

Polyurethane varnish is great stuff—easy to apply, good-looking, and pretty durable. But when it gets scratched, gouged, or worn out, you've got problems. It's extremely difficult to make invisible repairs on polyurethane, and a complete sanding job may be the best option (but first see "Don't Screw Up" on sanding, at left).

Don't Screw Up!
Plenty of rental outfits are happy to rent you floor sanders. My advice: Don't. Every time you set the sander down wrong, you'll leave an indelible mark. Unless you can tolerate the sight of these inevitable beginner's mistakes, I'd hire this job out. (If it's any consolation, the pros can't do a good job with this equipment either.)

The problem with patching polyurethane is that you've got to roughen the finish—usually with sandpaper—so the new stuff can adhere. But this sandpapering is a lot of work if you do it by hand, and dangerous if you do it by machine (as it's likely to gouge the wood).

In any case, sanding will lighten the bare spots, so you'll have to stain them to match the surrounding floor. Then you'll have to paint sanding sealer on the bare spots so the varnish does not sink in too deeply there. After the sealer dries, you can varnish the floor, and hope everything blends in (did I mention that this would sound like an advertisement for floor sanding?).

Carpet Repair

Oceans of carpet—you'll see them in ads, but in my house, the carpet looks more like the Caribbean Sea. It's a beautiful expanse of color marked by—may I call them islands? Sometimes, these stains—mementos of Maggie, the family beagle, or the house plant I watered too enthusiastically—can be cleaned. Otherwise, you can try to replace the sections of carpet. If you can't find spare carpet squirreled away in the attic or basement, steal a scrap from a closet or under a permanent piece of furniture. You'll need a utility knife with a new blade, carpenter's square, staple gun or tacks, double-sided carpet tape, foam padding (same thickness as the original), and that replacement piece of carpet. Then follow these steps:

1. Place the replacement piece over the damaged area, matching the pattern if there is one.

2. Match the backing fibers in the replacement and the original carpet (to ensure that the grain of the original carpet and the patch match), and cut the patch rectangular and slightly larger than the damaged area.

3. Position the replacement piece over the area to be patched, and cut through the existing carpet along one side of the replacement piece to make the first side to the cutout.

4. Cut the other three sides, using the patch as a template. Make sure the patch does not shift, and try to "crowd" it so the cutout is slightly smaller than the patch.

5. Remove the patch and trim up the cuts.

6. Cut the foam to the same size, and staple or tack it in place (see the photo below, left).

7. Lay out carpet tape per instructions. I used a double line of tape, using one piece of tape to hold the old carpet in place, and one for the new carpet. Install the patch and press firmly (see the photo below, right).

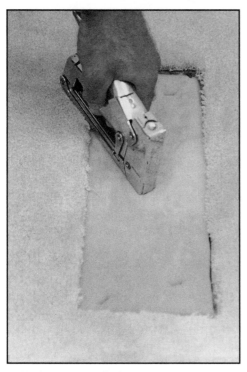

Tack the foam into place, making sure it's the same thickness and density as the original.

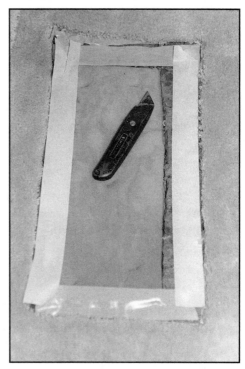

Lay out double-sided carpet tape along all four sides of the repair.

The Other Stuff—Tile, Vinyl, and Ceramic

Finally, let's take a look at some quick repairs for tile, vinyl, and ceramic floors. The first step is to understand the cause of problems. If you see regular ridges, they're probably caused by uneven subfloor. If you see tiles coming unglued, the problem is probably moisture—from a plumbing leak, groundwater, or condensation. Remember the rule— don't bury your problems. Fix them.

For most repairs, you'll need a source of replacement flooring—either something stashed away in the basement, or new material that's as similar as possible to your floor.

Repairing Curling Vinyl Tile

Using a propane torch with a flame-spreading attachment, or a heat gun, or a warm iron, loosen the glue holding the problem tile in place. (Don't get the tile too hot to touch.) Then remove the tile, scrape out old adhesive, and repaste it, using a notched trowel to apply an even coat of adhesive. (Consult the can for exact directions on applying the sticky stuff.) Clean up extra glue with the solvent specified. Then weight the patch securely until the glue is dry.

Fixing Roll Flooring

Sheet flooring—linoleum and its successor, vinyl—can be repaired with this "double-cutting" technique, but you'll always be able to see the fixup. Here's how: Take a scrap of new material, larger than the repair area, and place it over the damage, matching the pattern. Hold the new piece firmly underneath a carpenter's square and cut through the new material into the roll flooring. When you've cut through all four sides, remove the new piece and scrape or use heat to remove the damaged flooring. Clean out all excess adhesive, and glue the new piece into place, following the directions on the can. Weight the patch until it's dry.

Ceramic Tiles

If they didn't freeze your feet, ceramic tiles would be one of the nicest floors around. Independent, flinty, they exemplify durability. But ceramic tiles can break, and the grout between them can fall out. Let's look at some first aid for tiles.

Warning: Ceramic tiles are inflexible, and if you see much cracking, it's probably caused by flimsy support under them. This must be fixed before you repair the tiles. If the underside is accessible, you may be able to nail a second joist to each joist; otherwise, it's time to call the carpenter.

1. To replace broken tiles: Carefully chip out the remains of the tiles, using a hammer and a metal or stone-cutting chisel. If the tile is tightly adhered, score an "X" across it with a glass cutter, then break the tile with a hammer and chisel. Work slowly, or you'll loosen more tiles, and curse the day you ever read these instructions.

2. Clean out grout along the edges of the repair, never pulling up on the grout, which will loosen adjacent tiles. Work carefully.

3. When all the old grout and glue are removed, and the new tile will sit a little below the floor level, use the ceramic tile glue per instuctions and embed the replacement tiles.

4. When that's dry, regrout (read on for the goods on grout).

Great Grout!

If the grout between your ceramic tiles is eroded, you'll need to remove as much loose material as possible, without loosening the tiles. Vacuum or brush all debris out, then apply grout per instructions on the can. It's easiest to wipe the grout into place with a rubber squeegee sold for the purpose, or with a damp sponge.

Slick, highly polished tiles are unlikely to absorb much grout, but absorbent tiles will. For an extremely small area, you can use masking tape to mask absorbent tiles from grout. In any case, wipe off the grout immediately after work with a damp sponge. You may need to use a grout remover afterwards to clean up any grout haze on the tiles.

To brighten up stained grout, you may have luck with products sold for that purpose. Otherwise, you're facing the unenviable task of removing a lot of grout, without loosening tiles, and regrouting.

The Least You Need to Know

➤ Floor squeaks should be easy to control, if you can get under the floor. Realistically, if you must work from above, you may have to leave visible evidence of your repair.

➤ Don't be afraid of patching subfloor—it's fast and easy.

➤ For most idiots, the dream of a seamless replacement of tongue-and-groove flooring is just a dream. Still, you can make a very effective patch.

➤ You should be able to make inconspicuous repairs in carpets and vinyl and tile floors—if repair material is available.

Chapter 20

Cosmetology 101: Drywall, Plaster, and Molding Repair

In This Chapter

➤ Knowing your materials is half the battle in making an invisible wall repair

➤ How to cut moldings, tiles, and carpets to meet irregular surfaces

➤ Finding a stud—that elusive framing in your walls—can be easy if you know the techniques

---

I am a recovering plasterer, and it's been a long time since I felt the overwhelming urge to grab a plastering trowel and start smearing a heavy, abrasive glop on the walls—in fact, the very thought sends a twinge through my shoulder. No wonder they invented drywall—it's faster, easier, and cheaper, and if it isn't as hard or durable as plaster, nobody seems to mind—except the plasterers who have gone out of business.

In the course of making innumerable repairs to plaster and drywall, I learned many tricks of the trade, and I'm eager to pass them along to you in this chapter (that way, you won't even think about calling *me* to repair your walls!). The good news is that almost any flaw in plaster or drywall is fixable. The bad news is that it takes a bit of practice, and you've got to understand how the patching material changes as it hardens.

Meet Your Walls: Plaster, Lath, and Drywall

Plaster and drywall, the two common interior wall materials, are made of gypsum rock containing various additives. Plaster is applied as a stiff liquid that sets into an extremely hard material. Drywall is a relative of plaster that's sandwiched between heavy paper and sold in sheets which can be cut to size and nailed into place. Drywall is much softer than plaster, so it dents and scratches rather easily.

Plaster is rarely used in new construction because its application takes so much skill and effort. Most drywall is $1/2$ inch thick; the $5/8$-inch sheets used in high-class construction are stronger and better at deadening noise. The sheets are 4-feet wide and 8-, 10-, or 12-feet long.

Lath is a backing material nailed to the studs to hold wet plaster as it hardens. Originally, lath was made of wood strips; nowadays, it is a thin ($3/8$-inch) version of drywall.

> **Don't Screw Up!**
> Old wood lath and plaster are extremely brittle. If you ever need to cut them, do so with caution. Use a fine-tooth blade and cut next to a stud, where the lath has more support. If the lath vibrates, large sections of plaster can crack loose. (See "Cutting Back to the Studs and Starting Over," later in this chapter.)

A Note on Sand Finish

The surface on most old plaster is *sand finish*, a finishing plaster that—amazing but true—contains fine sand. You can recognize sand finish by its gritty texture. If you're repairing this stuff, remember these tips:

➤ Scrape off all sand around the repair area with a trowel. Otherwise, your trowel or drywall knife will ride up on the sand and leave a disgusting corrugated effect.

➤ Buy sand finish from a paint store and add it to the patching or primer. Then, if the surface is not sandy enough, you can always add more to the paint.

Meet the Fixer-Upper Materials

To appreciate how many blights, blues, and blisters can afflict plaster and drywall, just glance at the wall-repair shelf of a building supplier. Table 20.1 explains how to make sense of what you'll see.

Table 20.1 The wall fix-it materials

Name	Description	Advantages	Disadvantages
Patching plaster (plaster of Paris)	A gypsum-based material for filling cracks and holes; sets by a chemical reaction, not drying.	Sets quickly and very hard.	May set before you finish tooling it; very tough to sand; leaves a smooth surface that does not match sand-finish plaster.
Drywall compound	Glue-based patching compound; sets by drying.	Cheap, easy to find, easy to work, easy to sand.	Soft, does not match sand-finish plaster.
Durabond	Portland-cement patching compound; sold to set at various rates.	Easy to control, excellent for large, deep cracks and holes.	Very hard, tough to sand (best used as backing under another finish material).
Sand	A fine-grained, uniform sand sold at paint stores.	It's the only way to match sand-finish.	None—may be mixed with finish material, primer, or even paint.
Crack repair tape (drywall tape)	Fiberglass or paper tape applied over cracks, then covered by patching material.	Fiberglass sticks to the wall during the repair and won't bubble. Fiberglass tape is thicker than paper, and is somewhat harder to hide under subsequent coats of patching.	Paper must be applied over a thin coat of patching compound and may bubble.

The Tools

The tools for repairing plaster and drywall are pretty basic, and you may be able to substitute mason's tools, if you have them). See the illustration of wall-repair tools in this chapter.

A mud tray (mud box) holds the patching material; ideal for loading the drywall knife without spillage.

A corner knife is essential for mudding corners, but it's more useful in new work than repairs.

A drywall knife (available up to 10" wide; buy a 6" or 8" model to start) is used for patching walls and applying drywall compound.

A plaster trowel is used to cover large areas (it's also handy for plastering and for finishing concrete).

A float creates a sand-finish texture; it can also put a smooth texture on mortar.

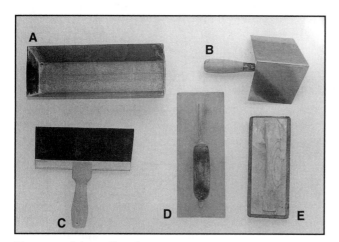

(A)   Mud tray
(B)   Corner knife
(C)   Drywall knife
(D)   Plaster trowel
(E)   Float

Plaster and drywall tools

Repairing Holes and Cracks in Plaster and Drywall

Let's start by dispensing with some idiotic conventional "wisdom" about patching walls. Most home-repair books tell you to "undercut" the edges when you clean out a damaged area, so the wound is wider at the back than the front. The idea is to allow the patch to "key" into the crack and hold tight. Let's undercut this business of undercutting right now. Problem number 1: If you can figure out how to undercut brittle plaster without pulling off half the wall, you should be writing books about home repair, not reading them.

Problem number 2: It's not necessary. Patching material bonds chemically to plaster and drywall, and mechanically to any rough surfaces, so long as you treat the patching right.

Before we give the step-by-step instructions for actually making repairs, let's talk about the first commandment of patching walls: Thou shalt not allow thy patching material to build up above the surrounding surface.

And don't forget the other commandments:

➤ Remove all crumbling or rotted material, without wrecking the solid stuff around the repair.

➤ Scrape or sandpaper any ridges or burrs that rise above the surface (otherwise, the patching material will build up and you'll have jumped from the frying pan of broken plaster to the fire of a globby, messy patch).

➤ If you're matching sand finish (see "A Note on Sand Finish," earlier in this chapter) you've got to use sand in the top coat of patching, or in the primer or paint.

➤ Moisten the edges of the damaged area before applying water-based patching materials that harden by setting. This prevents the patching from drying before it sets, which weakens it. Don't moisten for drywall compound or other materials that harden by drying.

➤ Fill deep holes with several layers of fast-setting material.

➤ Thick consistency is good for deep holes; soupier stuff is better for finish coatings.

➤ Stir the patching thoroughly, and keep crumbs, grit, or other crud out of it. These will all appear in the final surface.

➤ Always use compatible materials (if in doubt, make a small test first).

Repairing Nicks and Gouges

With the preceding precepts in mind, let's check out a few ways to easily, effectively, and invisibly patch plaster and drywall.

If your wall suffers from a series of little defects, repair is simple. You'll need patching compound, sandpaper, and a drywall knife or trowel. Follow these steps to fill in the holes:

1. Clean out anything loose or raised above the surface. If the drywall paper is sticking above the surface, cut it away with a utility knife.

2. If you're using patching plaster or another hardening material, dampen (don't flood) the repair area, emphasizing the shallow spots. This helps prevent bubbling and loss of adhesion. Allow the water to sink in for a few minutes while you mix your mud.

3. Apply a patching material with a trowel or drywall knife.

4. Clean off the surrounding areas with the trowel, and let the patching cure a bit. Then scrape the area with a trowel held perpendicular to the surface. A few minutes later, wipe the area with a damp rag. The more smeared patching material you remove now, the less you'll have to sand off later—a tedious and damaging job.

5. Prime and paint.

Covering with Fiberglass Tape

You can cover a small hole with several layers of fiberglass drywall tape and joint compound. (Fiberglass—and paper—tape are also used for patching across joints in drywall, where they supposedly can compensate for a bit of movement.) The technique is fast and easy, and will reduce the need to build up layers underneath the patch, but it may leave a visible mound on the surface.

Patching a small wound with fiberglass tape. Keep the tape thin and smooth as you cover the gap. The first coat of mud covers the tape and starts to taper the sides.

You'll need fiberglass drywall tape, joint compound, and a drywall knife. (Fiberglass tape is easier to use than paper tape, since it sticks by itself and does not trap air bubbles beneath it.) Use these steps to repair a hole using drywall tape:

1. Clean off all loose and ragged material.

2. Cut several strips of drywall tape and stick them across the wound, extending about 4 to 6 inches in each direction. Fiberglass tape has an adhesive backing, so you needn't put mud under it.

3. Cover the strips with a layer of compound as thin as possible (see the photo).

4. When dry, add a second coat of drywall compound and feather the edges. You may need a third coat as well. Don't worry if you end up covering an area much larger than the damage; each coat must spread beyond the previous one.

5. When the last coat is dry, sand it thoroughly to blend with the surroundings.

Cutting Back to the Studs and Starting Over

Let's say the damage is more like a disaster—the plaster is rotten, the drywall is crumbling, or the wall looks like it was used for artillery practice. What to do? Cut the whole thing out, that's what. You'll need something to cut drywall or plaster (see step 2 of the following procedure), replacement drywall, shims (possibly), power screwdriver and drywall screws (or hammer and drywall nails), drywall compound, and fiberglass drywall tape. These steps will help you make an invisible repair:

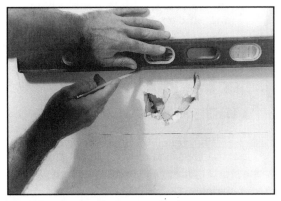

Use a level to mark out a perfectly rectangular cutout—your patch will be much easier to cut.

1. Mark the damaged area back to the center line of the nearby studs (see "Six Ways to Find a Stud," later in this chapter). Use a level to mark a perfect rectangle (as illustrated here).

2. Cut the drywall with a drywall saw, keyhole saw, saber saw, or utility knife. Plaster is difficult to cut without wrecking the nearby plaster. It's best to use a circular saw, but this will destroy the saw blade and create a dust storm reminiscent of the Dust Bowl in the 1930s. If you use a saber saw, press hard against the wall to minimize vibration, but in old plaster, you can expect some cracking unless you use a circular saw. It's your choice.

3. If you cut along the edge of the studs, screw a nailer to them using the technique shown in the section of Chapter 14 entitled "All Hands on Deck—Prepare to be Boarded! (How to Replace Rotten Deck Boards)."

4. Nail or screw the existing drywall around the edges of your cutout. If the wall is plaster, screw it to prevent cracking. Drill a pilot hole that cuts a countersink for the screw head, and don't overtighten the screw.

5. Cut a piece of drywall about $^1/_4$ inch smaller than the repair in each dimension. If necessary, shim under the drywall with strips of wood or asphalt shingle so the patch will sit flush with the surface.

6. Nail or screw the drywall into place. I prefer screws—hammering has a tendency to loosen the existing wall.

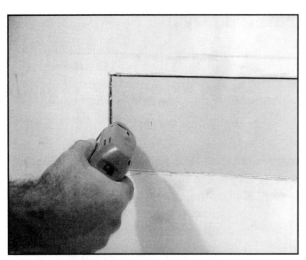

Screws cause much less damage than nails, but nails will work if you're a traditionalist.

7. Stick fiberglass drywall tape to the edges and cover it with mud.

8. When the compound is dry, scrape ridges and high spots off with the drywall knife.

9. Apply another coat of compound, and feather it to meet the wall surface. Sand, apply a third coat if needed, and sand again. Prime and paint when dry.

Six Ways to Find a Stud

In fixing walls, hanging stuff on walls, or making electrical repairs, you'll run up against the homeowner's nightmare: Where's the stud? (*Studs*, you'll recall, are the 2 × 4 or 2 × 6 framing lumber that hold walls up). You have plenty of alternatives for finding these elusive characters, and sometimes you'll want to use more than one technique.

Tapping with a Hammer

This was my father's favorite technique. If you tap carefully, and your ear is good, you'll hear the noise change from a hollow sound between studs to a tighter sound on top of the stud. This trick is not much good with thick, plaster walls.

Drilling

You can find a stud by drilling (use a $1/16$-inch bit) through the wall; the resistance increases greatly when you enter a stud. Because this technique requires holes, I use it only when I really need to check the accuracy of a less intrusive method.

Measuring

Studs are usually located 16 inches (or, rarely, 24 inches) apart. Once you've found one stud (perhaps by noticing that an electric outlet was secured to it) you should be able to measure to find the others—if the carpenter wasn't drinking too much brandy, and if you haven't found an oddly located stud, and if . . .

Baseboard

The baseboard—the trim along the floor—should be nailed to the studs. Look closely for nails (they should be visible, even if the holes were filled) and use a level to follow the stud up the wall.

Magnetic Studfinder

These gizmos contain a magnet that moves (theoretically, at least) when it is attracted by the nails that fasten baseboard, drywall, or lath to studs. These studfinders work better in drywall, where the nails are near the surface, than they do in plaster, where the nails are deeper.

Electronic Studfinder

The electronic solution, sadly, is not a surefire answer to the stud-seeking snafu. Success takes a bit of a knack, and depends on the wall construction. In my limited experience, I've found this electronic "wonder" is no panacea.

A Word on Molding

Molding is trim used to join windows, doors, and floors to walls. If you need to fiddle with molding while you're painting, or working on windows, doors, or floors, try the tricks described next.

Cutting Molding

To cut molding for an outside corner, simply (but accurately) measure the pieces and cut them at 45 degrees with a miter box (see sawing techniques in chapter 10).

To cut molding at an inside corner—say, where two baseboards meet in a corner of the room—don't repeat my mistake. Don't cut each piece at 45 degrees, even if that seems the obvious solution. Instead, leave piece "A" with a 90 degree end. Now mark the contour of piece "A" on the *back* of piece "B." Cut along the line on piece "B" at 90 degrees using a coping saw—a kind of hand jigsaw. (Fortunately this is much easier than it sounds.) Then quickly sand the rough edges from piece "B." Now, when you nail the molding into place, it won't pull away and leave an ugly gap where you wanted a tight joint.

Yanking Up Molding with Scarcely a Split

Let's say your repair requires you to remove the baseboard and quarter-round (the rounded molding that seals the gap between the baseboard and the floor). Let's say you don't want to buy, cut, and stain new molding. How can you pull the darned molding off without injuring it? By slowly and carefully prying off the top piece, working with two slender, low-impact tools.

Always remove one piece at a time—there's no future in trying to pull quarter-round and baseboard in one operation. You'll need a wood chisel, flat prybar, hammer, locking pliers, and wood scraps (optional: big flat screwdriver, and margin or pointing trowel). Don't feel terrible if you break one or two pieces—this is inevitable with brittle wood, or wood with a crooked grain, and if you're careful, you can probably glue them back together. To remove the molding:

The correct way to pull molding. The trick is to work gradually, with two prying tools, and to pry directly under the nails.

1. Starting at the end of a molding, insert the wood chisel under the molding to loosen it. As soon as possible, insert the flat blade of the prybar under the molding, protecting the floor with a trowel or wood scraps. Gradually pull the piece up. When there's room for another prying tool—a hammer, prybar, chisel, or trowel— insert it and pry with two tools at once.

2. If a nail head comes up, pull it, protecting the wood from the hammer with a scrap of wood.

3. Work your way slowly along the molding.

4. If, after you've gotten the molding off, it still contains some finishing nails, *do not pull them* the usual way (by hammering from behind so they come out the front). This will split the wood. Instead, grab the nail from behind with a locking pliers and swing the pliers down, pulling the head through the wood. You'll need to drill new holes to renail the molding, but the overall damage will be much milder.

Caulking Trick

You've got gaps where the molding supposedly meets the wall. You tried to pound the molding back into place, but naturally that failed—in home repair, anything so obvious and simple is almost certain to flop. But in this case, there's an even simpler solution that actually works: filling the gap with a paintable caulking compound (or white caulking if the walls are white). Smooth the stuff into place with a moistened finger or solvent-soaked rag. Paint when dry if you want. Done.

A Quick Trick for Matching Irregular Molding, Tiles, and So On

I cut my teeth in home repair on a farmhouse built in 1854, a place whose peculiar geometry became painfully obvious if I dared to use a level or a square in my fixes. Among the many tricks I wish I'd known then was this superb method of working with irregular surfaces. This trick is handy for marking the edge of linoleum so it will match an unsquare wall, for fitting baseboard along a sagging floor, and countless other finishing touches where straight lines and right angles are conspicuous by their absence.

In this example, assume you are cutting a floor tile to fit against a wall that is not parallel to the last line of tiles (as you'd find in an unsquare room, for example). The trick is to cut the irregular side (which meets the wall or obstruction) first, then set the tile back into place to mark the straight side that meets the existing tile pattern. You'll need a compass (AKA divider—you used one to draw circles in high school), and whatever will cut the material in question.

1. Push the tile face-up against the wall, as far as it can go without twisting (in other words, the body of the tile must not be rotated, compared to the other tiles in the floor). Set the divider to the largest gap between the tile and the wall.

2. Without moving the tile, scribe a line on it. Do this by holding the point of the compass against the baseboard, and the pencil on the tile. Keep holding the compass perpendicular to the wall as you mark across the whole tile.

3. Cut along this line. Now the wall side of your tile should match the angle (or other irregularity) of the wall.

4. Slide the tile against the wall and mark the opposite end straight across so it will fit the existing tile pattern. Allow about $1/8$ inch for clearance. (If you try to cut it to the perfect size, chances are you'll have to recut it smaller.)

5. Cut the straight line and set the tile in place.

The Least You Need to Know

➤ When you make wall repairs, never allow the patching material to build up on the surrounding surface.

➤ There's no need to undercut plaster or drywall before a repair; this only causes more damage. But you do need to ensure that the patching adheres well to the wall.

➤ The technique for repairing drywall or plaster depends on the construction, and the scale of the damage.

➤ Plaster cracks quite easily, so you need to use extreme caution when cutting it, particularly when it's supported by wood lath.

➤ By working carefully, you can remove molding intact, without damaging it or the surroundings.

➤ With a compass (divider) you can easily match repair pieces to irregular surfaces; the trick is useful in tiling, molding, and other trim jobs.

Chapter 21

Paperhanger for a Day

In This Chapter

➤ The tools and materials for wallpaper repairs

➤ Curing curling wallpaper

➤ The double-cut repair—simple to do, invisible to see, it's a patch made in heaven

➤ Starting from scratch: The fundamental steps in repapering

Wallpaper may be high-class stuff, but that doesn't insulate it from the slings and arrows (and stains and tears) of outrageous fortune. Maybe the wallpaper is intact, but the stairway wall, which your 4-year-old once used for balance before hurling herself down the stairs, shows a hundred grimy handprints.

Fortunately, wallpaper—a category that includes cloth, plastic, vinyl, even silk—can be repaired rather easily, if you understand your material, know a few tricks of the trade, and can find some spare material.

In this chapter, I'll show you how to repair curling edges, fix holes and tears, and cover your tracks. And if you can't stand the taste of the people who once lived in your place (or if you've outgrown your own passion for black-and-silver, '70s electrotech wallpaper), I'll discuss how to rip it all off and start over.

Tools and Supplies You Will Need

For occasional wallpaper repair, you can do as I do and get by with an extremely limited tool kit (see the next figure). Here are the basic tools you'll need:

Brush: For applying paste to large areas and smoothing paper after pasting (you can substitute a 3- to 4-inch paintbrush).

Paste: Must be compatible with your wallcovering (vinyl requires special paste).

Seam roller: Squeezes paste from seams so they will stick.

Razor blade: For all cutting jobs (it's got to be sharp, so use a new one). Hint: Save your fingers and use a sharp utility knife. The ones with snap-off blades are particularly handy, since you can get a new edge almost instantly.

Masking tape: Holds patches in position for a double-cut repair.

Straightedge: Or substitute a clean carpenter's square or a T-square.

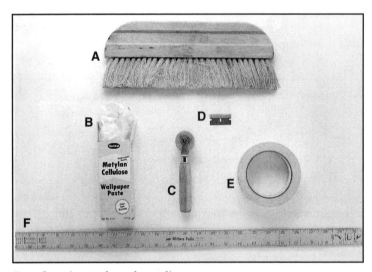

(A) Brush
(B) Paste
(C) Seam roller
(D) Razor blade
(E) Masking tape
(F) Straightedge

Paperhanging tools and supplies

Making Invisible Repairs

Wallcovering can be damaged by improper application, dirt, or physical injury. If the plaster or drywall is damaged, repair it first, following the suggestions in Chapter 20.

Patching tears, rips, and curling seams should be relatively easy, given the instructions that follow. (To replace stained and damaged areas, you'll also need wallcovering material—if you're lucky, the paperhangers stashed scraps in your house.)

To fix a *blister*, make one or more cuts on an inconspicuous part of the pattern with a razor blade. Usually, a bit of water on the surface will soften the paper and allow it to stick back to the wall—but test first, as water can damage some coverings. Apply white cement (good ol' Elmers Glue or its equivalent) behind the paper with an artist's brush, then press the covering into place. With a damp rag, wipe away extra cement.

Repair *small tears* by applying white cement to the substrate and pressing the covering into place. Wipe away any cement from the surface.

> **Don't Screw Up!**
> Dry paste goes a lot further than novices expect. Although paste is cheap, there's no point wasting it, so mix small amounts at first.

Sticking Curling Wallpaper so It Stays Stuck

One of the most common wallpaper problems—curled edges at seams—can be tough to fix, because the curls become stiff with age. To fix curled seams, try dampening the paper to increase its flexibility without slobbering on so much water that the paper will come loose or be otherwise damaged (it's a good idea to test the water on a small, inconspicuous area first). You'll need a sponge, wallpaper paste or white cement, and a seam roller. Follow these steps to remove the curl:

1. Soften the curling edges by sponging them several times over the course of a half hour. Don't stop until they flatten out easily.

2. Mix the wallpaper paste and let it rest for a few minutes.

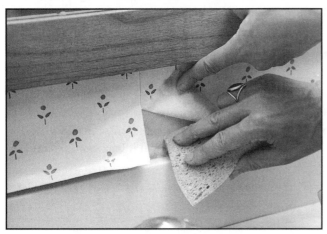

After you've let the repair area dry a bit, apply the glue across the entire loosened section.

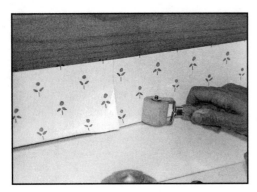

Don't roll hard enough to squeeze all the paste from the repair.

3. Dry off the repair area as well as possible, then get the paste between the wallpaper and the wall (as shown in the following figure).

4. Press or roll the wallpaper to the wall. If you can figure a way to press something against the patch to hold it flat for a few minutes, so much the better. (Try leaning a bookcase against a piece of wood, for example.)

5. Finally, clean any paste from the surface with a damp sponge.

Patching Holes and Other Devastation

To patch small areas of wallcovering, you can choose between the rip-and-cover and double-cutting methods. The first method leaves edges that may be harder to see, but double cutting is easier, and still hard to detect.

A *rip-and-cover* patch is most suitable to paper, as vinyl and cloth wallcoverings probably won't tear the way you want them to. You'll need sandpaper, a scrap of new wallpaper, paste, and a brush. Use these steps:

1. Feather jagged parts of the damaged area lightly with fine or extrafine sandpaper.

2. Tear out a piece of wallpaper that contains the correct pattern and is big enough to cover the damage. Tear so only the surface (not the backing) is visible.

3. Apply paste to the rear of the patch with a small artist's brush and place it over the wound. The patch must exactly match the existing pattern.

4. Carefully smooth the patch with your brush and sponge away excess adhesive.

To patch with the *double-cutting method*, you'll need a new razor blade, sponge, brush, spare wallpaper, paste, masking tape, and possibly a straightedge. Before starting, unroll the new paper and flatten it for an hour or so. If it's really stiff, roll it backwards (counter-roll it) to flatten it.

1. Tape a piece of wallpaper slightly larger than the injury over the repair area, matching the pattern (see left-hand photo on facing page).

Position the patch perfectly against the surrounding pattern and tape it into place with masking tape.

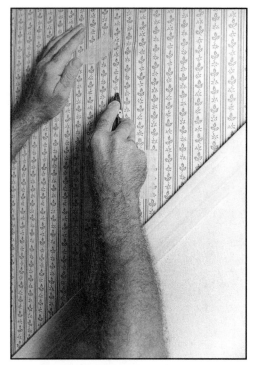

Cut deep enough to get through both layers at once; use a sharp knife so you don't need to push like a gorilla.

2. Cut through both layers of wallpaper around the damaged area with the razor blade (see the figure in this chapter illustrating such a cut). Use a straightedge if your hand is not steady. (Sometimes it's better to cut curves rather than straight lines, so you can cut through the background instead of the pattern.) Try not to cut deep into the drywall, and make sure the patch does not wander while you cut.

3. Mark the top of the patch (if it's not obvious), then take the piece down.

4. Remove damaged wallpaper within the cuts by a combination of:

   Cutting it into strips with a knife or razor blade (don't cut the drywall)

   Dampening to soften the paste

   Scraping

   Wallpaper remover

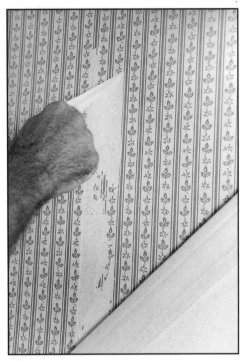

Remove the old paper by soaking, scraping, and/or pulling.

5. Allow the wall to dry.

6. Paste the back of the patch and slide it into place.

7. Roll the edges lightly and sponge off excess adhesive. Wipe with a damp rag. Return in a few minutes and press the patch down again.

The Rip-Off Solution—How to Repaper a Room

Sometimes, what you need is not repair but repapering. Say the damage is too great, or you can't find matching paper, or you've done some remodeling, or you simply can't stand the zebras and elephants that once seemed so hip. In these cases, the solution is to rip the wallpaper out and replace it. It's going to be a fair hunk of work, but if the room is not too big, or too irregular (and if you're not too much of a perfectionist), it's a reasonable homeowner job. (To paper a wall that doesn't have paper on it now, start with the following section, "Preparing for Papering.")

If your existing paper is well-hung . . . er . . . perfectly stuck and in good condition, you can take a chance by pasting new paper over it. But it's usually best to pull off all the old paper and start anew. If you're extremely lucky, the old paper is a tough, self-stick material that pulls down in large sheets. (Self-stick paper has dry glue on the back. To activate the glue, you soak the paper before application.)

If the paper does not come down easily, you'll have to soften it with wallpaper stripper (or a rented wallpaper steamer) and scrape it off. This may not be a pretty process, but when you're done, you'll have clean walls.

Preparing for Papering

Bring the room dimensions when you shop for new paper, and ask the store clerk to estimate how much you'll need (this can be more complicated than it seems). Buy a little extra to allow for mistakes and to ensure you have enough to finish the job without making another trip to the store.

When choosing patterns, remember that a pattern with vertical stripes will show every error or irregularity. Broad pattern elements, or tiny ones, are more likely to hide your little problems. If you're new at wallpapering, make sure to buy paper that's easy to handle, and avoid foil and other fragile papers—these are for pros. In the following instructions, I assume you've been sensible and bought pre-pasted paper, which saves time, equipment, and hassle. If you don't use pre-pasted paper, be sure to get the right paste.

Clean the walls with trisodium phosphate (sold at paint stores) or the equivalent. Then examine them for dents, gouges, or holes, and patch according to the instructions in "Repairing Holes and Cracks in Plaster and Drywall," in Chapter 20. If the wall has sand-finish plaster, you'll have to scrape off all the sand—an ugly prospect.

Once the surface is flat and solid, you'll have to apply something to regulate the absorption of the new wallpaper paste. Check with the manufacturer of the new paper and use either sizing or a primer-sealer. Apply this stuff and let it dry.

Pasto-Chango—Time to Hang Paper

Now comes the moment of truth—time for paper-hanging. No, I'm not talking about selling bonds on Wall St., which goes by the same name, but about sticking up a new layer of wallpaper. Here, in brief, is what you need to know to hang paper. For complicated situations, I'd encourage you to consult a more thorough treatment.

In the interests of keeping things simple, these instructions assume you are sensible enough to use pre-pasted paper. You will need a pan long enough to soak the paper, a brush to smooth the paper once it's on the wall, a long level, a pencil, a seam roller, and some new single-edge razor blades or a utility knife with blades. If you need to paste the paper, you'll need a paste bucket, a brush to apply the paste, and probably a table to work on.

1. Start your work in the most prominent part of the room. Using a level, lighty mark a vertical line in the center of the room. This will be your guideline for one side of the first strip. Work in both directions from here, so your last strips meet in the most inconspicuous part of the room—such as behind a door or piece of furniture. That's because the patterns will not match at the end.

2. Fill your pan with water. Cut some strips a few inches longer than you need (if you are using a big pattern, lay the strips on the floor to figure out exactly how long they must be to match). Roll the strips backwards to take out the curvature.

3. Following the manufacturer's directions, dunk the strips in water, then remove and fold each end back to meet at the center ("book them"). The pasted sides will be together when the strip is properly "booked."

4. Leave the strip booked for a few minutes so it can expand slightly. Otherwise, it will wrinkle on the wall.

5. Bring the booked paper to the wall and open the top fold (leave the bottom half booked). Now hang the top of the paper to the line, trying to put it in the right place to start with—lots of adjustment can cause wrinkles and tears.

6. Brush the paper, starting at the center, to remove air bubbles and improve adhesion.

7. When the top is in place, unbook the bottom and repeat. Trim the top and bottom with a razor blade forced into the corners.

8. Continue hanging paper around the room. After each seam is in place, roll it with the roller to press some paste out and improve adhesion. (But don't press too hard—that squeezes out too much paste).

Notes:

➤ Don't use your eye to get things right—use a ruler, a straightedge, and a level.

➤ Use sharp razor blades—there's no point in ruining a strip by ripping it after you've gone to all the trouble of pasting it into place.

➤ Outside corners should be wrapped (one strip goes 3 inches past the corner, and the next strip covers its edge). This allows you to make the second piece vertical, even if the pattern has gone out of plumb due to irregularies in the building.

➤ If your strips get out of vertical somewhere else, simply hang a new strip vertical, and make it overlap the existing strip. For the perfectionist, you can double-cut the seam to return the seams to vertical: (1) hang the second strip overlapping the first. Make the overlap wide enough so you cut a vertical line through both strips. (2) Hold a level vertically on top of the seam, and use it as a straightedge to cut through both layers of paper. (3) Remove the narrow strips you just cut, and roll the seam to flatten it.

➤ Wipe up extra paste with a damp cloth. Don't get the seams so wet that they come apart.

The Least You Need to Know

➤ Curling wallpaper has an attitude problem—which you can generally solve by dampening the paper before repasting it.

➤ With a deft hand, you can rip wallpaper and make a very subtle repair.

➤ Double-cutting is a foolproof and almost invisible trick for patching wallpaper.

➤ When attempting your first wallpapering job, stick to materials that are designed for homeowners and are inherently easy to apply.

Chapter 22

Putting a Good Face On—Choosing Paint and Painting Tools

In This Chapter

➤ Paint for practically anything—from Australian arbors to antique xylophones

➤ Why new wood loves paintable, water-repellent preservative

➤ Read problems in the existing paint, and avoid similar woes next time around

Boy, has paint changed since I first dunked a brush into a can of evil-smelling, lead-based oil paint. By the time the paint finally dried, it was slathered with an army of insects that had mistaken my house for a bright blue sheet of oversize flypaper. And who can forget the brush-cleaning ceremony—with those buckets of nauseating, flammable turpentine? Or hands tattooed for weeks afterward with paint spatters?

All told, it was a nerve-wracking one-two punch. And I mean this literally: Both the solvent and the lead pigment in that paint were toxic to the nervous system.

Today, lead is gone from paint (but see the section of Chapter 6 entitled "Nervous about Leaded Paint"), and water is rapidly replacing the volatile organic solvents. Furthermore, you can buy a range of specialty coatings for outdoor wood, ceilings, masonry, and wrought iron, which have solved some of the traditional pitfalls of home painting.

Although almost any paint will look good at first, I'd suggest paying extra for paint with a high solids content (since solids are what remains on the wall) and lower "vehicle," or solvent, content. Even if you're not interested in Sistine Chapel–type longevity, you need high-quality paint to justify the effort of good surface preparation and paint application.

Meet the Coating Family

The bucketfuls of wall coatings fall into three major categories:

➤ *Surface preparers* (primers, sealers, and fillers) get the surface ready for whatever coating will follow.

➤ *Film formers*, including paint and varnish, sit on the surface and protect from above. They last only as long as the film lasts.

➤ *Penetrating coatings*, including stain, water repellents, and preservatives, seep into the surface and protect from within. (The best wood preservative is factory-applied in pressurized tanks; see the section of Chapter 10 called "The Enemies of Wood.")

These coatings are often combined, and you'll probably end up using penetrating coatings and film formers, particularly to protect the exterior skin of your house from sun, rain, and fungus.

Our trip through the paint department will start with the surface preparers, move to the film formers, and conclude with penetrating finishes. Table 22.1 explains what kinds of primers and finish coats you should choose when painting particular surfaces.

Table 22.1 Primers and finish coats for almost any purpose

Note: (2) indicates 2 coats needed. Due to changes in formulation and terminology problems, always read the label and follow manufacturer's instructions when choosing and using paint.

Surface	Primer	Finish coat
Interior		
Drywall	Latex, acrylic latex, or vinyl latex primer	Latex or alkyd wall paint
Plaster	Alkyd or latex primer	(2) Latex or alkyd wall paint or enamel
Masonry: concrete, concrete block, unglazed brick, cement board	Latex wall primer, epoxy primer	(2) Alkyd enamel, (2) latex wall paint or enamel, (2) epoxy
Aluminum	Zinc chromate	(2) Latex or alkyd wall paint or enamel, or (2) aluminum paint

Surface	Primer	Finish coat
Galvanized steel	Acrylic metal primer or as specified by manufacturer	(2) Latex or alkyd wall paint or enamel
Structural steel and ornamental iron	Lead-free alkyd metal primer with rust inhibitors	(2) Latex or alkyd wall paint or enamel
Wood walls, ceilings, trim, cabinet work, hardboard, etc.	Alkyd undercoater	(2) Latex or alkyd wall paint or enamel
Painted wood floors	Industrial enamel or epoxy	Same as primer
Wood floors	Stain	Polyurethane varnish, oil finish, or wax
Exterior		
Masonry: asbestos siding, shingles, stucco, common brick, concrete walls	Fill rough surfaces first, then use self-priming latex house paint	Latex house paint
Aluminum	Self-priming house and trim (acrylic or latex)	Self-priming house and trim (acrylic or latex)
Galvanized steel	Alkyd metal primer	(2) Alkyd enamel or alkyd house and trim paint
Ornamental and structural steel	Rust-inhibiting alkyd primer	(2) Aluminum paint or alkyd
Prefinished metal siding and panels	Latex or alkyd house paint	Latex or alkyd house paint
Wood floors and platforms	Self-priming industrial enamel	Self-priming industrial enamel
Plywood	Semi-transparent preservative stain, or opaque exterior stain	Semitransparent preservative stain, or opaque exterior stain
"	Pigmented acrylic emulsion	(2) Latex exterior solid color stain; or (2) latex house and trim

continues

Table 22.1   Continued

Surface	Primer	Finish coat
Shingles, shakes, rough-sawn lumber	Alkyd exterior primer	(2) Latex or alkyd house paint
"	Semi-transparent preservative stain, or opaque stain	Semi-transparent preservative stain, or opaque stain
Siding, trim, doors, hard-board (bare or primed)	Alkyd exterior primer	(2) Alkyd or latex house and trim, or alkyd house paint; or (2) latex exterior solid-color stain
"	Semi-transparent preservative stain opaque stain	Semi-transparent preservative stain; opaque stain
"	Exterior varnish	(2) Exterior varnish

Surface Preparers

Surface preparers—primer, filler, and sealer—make a surface chemically and physically ready for later coats. Preparers look inward, toward the substrate (the coated material), while topcoats (the final coats) look outward, toward your admiring eyes, and the sun, rain, dirt, and ultraviolet light waiting to destroy the coating and substrate.

Primer is designed to penetrate the substrate and create a paint-friendly surface on top (and sometimes to kill mildew or prevent rust as well). A primed surface allows some paint to penetrate and get a foothold, but forces most of the paint to stay on the surface. Primer should not be left to weather for long, since it can be harmed by rain and ultraviolet light.

You'll need primer on unpainted drywall, plaster, wood, and metal. You don't need primer over a sound coat of paint, unless it's necessary for the specific new paint you've chosen. If you are priming a few areas in a repair job, you will "spot-prime" them. But if the repairs are extensive, you're better off priming the whole surface. In any event, if more than 50% of the surface needs primer, prime the whole thing.

The ultimate authority on primer is the can of the new paint you're going to use. Read the label, and follow it.

Filler is used on materials like rough masonry, concrete, and some open-pored woods to fill pores and make a good surface for the paint. You may be able to find a primer-filler to do two steps at once.

Sealer is used to cover nasty stains—including crayons, oily crud, and pitchy knots—that would otherwise bleed through the topcoat. Cedar and redwood, which contain water-soluble stains, both need sealing before painting.

Rust-inhibitive primer is needed before painting iron and steel. Talk about self-sacrificing! This stuff is designed to decay before the metal starts to rust; when the primer eventually gives out, it must be replaced.

Builder's Trivia

Exterior wood primer is quite similar to diluted, solvent-based exterior paint (commonly called "oil" paint, you'll find it labelled "alkyd" paint in the store. So if you're short of primer (or just need a bit), thin some alkyd exterior paint with mineral spirits.

Film Formers

Good paint, say people who claim to have expertise in this field, is no thicker than a sheet of newspaper. Nevertheless, this thin film faces many demands: Paint may be designed to be washable, breathable, or water-repellent; to shed water and dirt, resist air pollution, stay where you put it, and look smooth and suave in whatever color you have chosen.

Let's take a tour of the paint aisle and see how the various materials stack up. As we do this, remember that paint comes in various grades. Generally, the more you pay for paint, the higher proportion of pigment (solids) it will contain, and the better coverage it will give. Pigment proportions are found on the side of the can. Good quality is especially important if you want long-lasting coverage, or you are depending on one coat to cover.

Alkyd paint: Alkyd has replaced oil paint as the heavy-duty option for house trim and exteriors. Although alkyd produces a more washable, durable surface than latex, you'll need to thin it with mineral spirits (the modern version of turpentine). Contrary to what you may have heard, you may paint latex over alkyd, and vice versa, as long as the old surface is rough enough to allow good adhesion.

Don't Screw Up!

Don't dump old paint into the gutter, toilet, or backyard. Leave a can of latex paint open until it's dry, then put it in the trash. Give solvent-based paint to someone who has a need for it, or save it for a "clean sweep" hazardous-waste collection.

Latex paint: Latex paints are the water-thinned workhorses of interior painting, and increasingly for exterior painting as well. They produce hardly any fumes, and you can even use them on damp surfaces. Latexes are permeable to moisture, making them ideal for use on masonry, where moisture causes other paints to peel. They are not easy to wash, however.

Acrylic paint: Acrylic paints are generally water-soluble. They are a step up from latex in terms of ability to cover a surface, color retention, and glossiness. Just for the sake of maximum confusion, you may see acrylic latex, which is an improved version of plain latex paint.

Don't Screw Up!
Unless you like getting loopy on solvents, use good ventilation and wear a respirator when you use solvent-based paint.

Enamel paint: Enamels, made of various formulations, are glossy, durable paints used for high-stress areas, like kitchens, bathrooms, and outdoor metal. Industrial enamel is best for tough jobs, like repainting cabinets for a bargain-basement kitchen remodeling.

Epoxy paint: Epoxy is two-part paint for heavy-duty uses, like floors, appliances, and countertops. I've used this evil-smelling stuff—where nothing else would work. Use a respirator, keep the windows open, and work fast—epoxy paint dries quickly into a very hard surface.

Can You Put a Clear Finish on Outdoor Wood? (The Decline and Fall of the Varnish Empire)

When it comes to showing off the grain of wood, nothing comes close to the clear finishes—varnish and lacquer. For interior wood floors, polyurethane varnish is the finish of choice, since it is hard, clear, nonyellowing, and easy to apply. This varnish is sold in matte, semigloss, and gloss finishes. Like everything else, polyurethane can suffer from time, tide, and foot traffic. For more information, see the section on "Dealing with Wooden Floors" in Chapter 19.

Outside, however, the best reason for varnishing wood is to demonstrate your prowess with a paint scraper. Huh? Because clear varnish contains no pigment, there's nothing to stop ultraviolet light from wrecking it (and the wood it is "protecting"). So the decline and fall of outdoor varnish is inevitable; a year after you brush it on, the stuff will be flaking, and you will be (or should be) scraping.

If you're possessed with the urge to show off your glorious wood front door, give it some shade by planting a tree or building an overhang. Better yet, use a semi-transparent stain, which will show some of the wood grain while still protecting from ultraviolet light.

Bonus: Semi-transparent stain is a penetrating finish, meaning you won't have to perform scraping duty next time around.

Penetrating Finishes

So much for the stuff that sits on top. Let's talk about penetrating finishes—those invisible helpers which protect from below. Although stains and water-repellents are thin and splattery to apply, their many advantages over paint are gaining them increasing popularity:

> **Don't Screw Up!**
> Paint is almost never waterproof—at best, it resists water for a while. That's why experts recommend slathering on paintable, water-repellent preservative before priming or staining new wood.

➤ They can't peel, because they become part of the top layer of wood.

➤ They're durable, since they don't crack from swelling and shrinkage caused by changes in humidity.

➤ They are easy to apply because you don't need primer.

➤ Best of all, you won't need to scrape next time around—just wash and restain.

To get these advantages, you'll need to observe the cardinal principle of penetrating finishes: They've got to penetrate. Translated, that means that the surface must be porous enough. To test for porosity, just throw a few drops of water on the surface. If it sinks in, the wood is ready for a penetrating finish. If not, the wood is either too new for sealing and must weather for a while, or a previous coat of penetrating finish is still working. Don't renew a penetrating finish until water can sink into the surface.

Stain

Stain—either opaque or semi-transparent—has been edging out paint as an exterior coating on wood for many years (opaque stain will even cover many kinds of paint, although a light-colored stain may not cover dark paint). For rough-textured wood, stain is the clear choice, since the wood absorbs enough stain to obtain an excellent level of protection. On the other hand, smooth plywood absorbs little stain, so it receives little protection.

Interior stain is sold in many hues, which supposedly simulate various species of wood. When choosing these stains, remember that the wood you are working on may not resemble the sample in the store. It's best to bring an actual sample to the store—use the back of some molding, if you can't find anything else.

When applying stain, observe label directions. You may need to apply the second coat within a certain time period. Otherwise, the first coat may harden too much for the second to penetrate it.

Water Repellent

Water repellent is dissolved wax that sinks into wood and dries to make the wood shed water. Some water repellents contain preservative, to make life miserable for the fungi waiting to eat your house. Paintable, water-repellent preservative, as noted above, is your ace in the hole for preparing new, exterior wood for finishing.

How Much Paint Do You Need?

Have you ever been bamboozled by those authoritative estimates on paint cans, promising that the paint "covers 400 square feet per gallon"? I certainly have—usually to find myself running short of paint when I'm just about done. You can make better estimates if, when calculating the number of square feet, you consider these factors:

➤ Surface roughness and coat thickness both influence how far a coating will go. A rough surface can easily require twice as much paint as a smooth one.

➤ If you're buying an untinted paint (or a standard color), you may be able to return extra cans. If so, buy more than you expect to need.

➤ Second coats go further than first coats, because less sinks in.

➤ If you need three quarts, buy a gallon—it's cheaper.

➤ End grain is extremely thirsty; if you have much of it, you'll need more penetrating finish or primer.

➤ In general, thin coats are better than thick ones, but don't try to stretch the paint too far— it just won't work.

Doing the Coroner's Job—A Post-Mortem on Paint Problems

Does your house look like the showplaces in paint advertisements? Neither does mine. Between the fungus among us, the smudges, and the peeling, my house—like most—is a virtual encyclopedia of paint problems. That's the bad news. The good news is that these problems offer guidance for painting tactics that will prevent their recurrence (see Table 22.2).

Table 22.2 A rogue's gallery of paint problems

Example	Problem description	Likely causes	Solution
	Checking (hairline cracks)	Swelling and contraction caused by moisture changes are loosening the paint—most common on plywood.	Scrape loose paint. Ventilate the wall. Clean thoroughly, prime the surface, and paint. Consider switching to penetrating stain.
	Chalking (whitish film on the surface)	May be natural aging of "self-cleaning" paint. Excess moisture coming through the wall, or, on masonry, wrong paint choice.	Ventilate wall if necessary. Remove all loose paint, then scrub with stiff brush and detergent. Prime severe cases with oil- or alkyd-base material. For severe chalking on masonry, prime with a masonry conditioner.
	Alligatoring, a crazed surface that drives homeowners berserk	Second coat was applied before first coat dried; surface was too glossy; or paint was too thick.	Scrape or sand paint, clean surface, dull any glossy surface, prime, and paint.
	Chipped paint on gutters, downspouts and other metal	Poor adhesion between metal and primer.	Scrape or wire brush loose paint and feather-sand edges. Rinse metal with solvent to remove grease, then prime with the correct metal primer. Topcoat with enamel.

Painter's Tools

Just because painter's tools are basic doesn't mean you should buy them in the bargain bin. When I finally sprang for a super-expensive professional paintbrush, I was surprised to notice that it held more paint, laid the paint down more quickly, spattered less, and gave me a better job. On top of that, it'll outlast the cheapies I used to buy.

Here are the basic painting tools you need (we'll describe the tools and materials you'll need for preparation in the next chapter):

Roller tray: Holds paint for the roller.

9-inch roller: The basic tool for covering walls. Use a smooth roller for a smooth surface and a thicker roller for a rougher surface.

Roller extension: An adjustable pole, useful for painting ceilings without ladders and walls without bending. Also easier on the wrists.

1-inch trim brush: For fine trim. Use natural bristle for oil-based materials and synthetic bristle for water-based materials.

2¹/₂-inch brush: For cutting in before rolling. The angled bristles help you get into tight spots.

Drop cloth: For protecting walls, floors, windows, and so on. Note: A canvas drop cloth is less slippery than plastic, but more expensive. An old bedsheet on top of plastic is a cheaper alternative that gives much better traction, and contains drips and small spills better than plastic alone.

Stirring stick: Do you insist on an explanation?

Paint can opener: There's no shame in using a screwdriver, but this is quicker and surer.

You may also need scrapers, ladders, hammer and nail, masking tape, newspaper, a fan for ventilation, and a screwdriver for removing and replacing electrical cover plates.

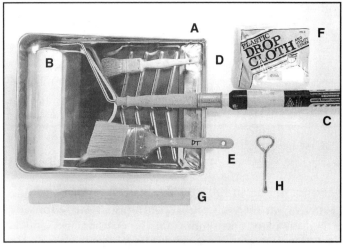

(A) Roller tray
(B) 9" roller
(C) Roller extension
(D) 1" trim brush
(E) 2¹/₂" brush
(F) Drop cloth
(G) Stirring stick
(H) Paint can opener

Brushes and rollers are the painter's best friend.

The Least You Need to Know

➤ Painting has become a lot more painless over the years, with the advent of fast-drying, water-based products for many new purposes.

➤ Primer looks inward; paint looks outward—so you'll usually need both. Fortunately, some "self-priming" products (like stain) serve double duty. (If you're painting over a sound surface, skip the primer.)

➤ Heard the old saw about learning from your mistakes? That's advice that can save a lot of aggravation in the painting department. Understanding why things went wrong last time can prevent screw-ups this time.

Chapter 23

Lay It On—But Not Too Thick

In This Chapter

➤ The whys and wherefores of paint preparation

➤ The ins and outs of paint-can etiquette

➤ Rolling, brushing, and spraying—the best ways to move paint from a can to a wall

I don't care if you're painting a single closet or a whole house—painting requires obsessive preparation. The bad news is that good prep takes time. But the good news is that it makes the painting itself a breeze, even a delight. In fact, slipshod prep wastes so much painting time that you might as well prep it right. Not only will the paint job look infinitely better, but repainting, when that gruesome necessity finally arrives, will be far less labor-intensive.

Painting is much more straightforward than, say, plumbing or even rocketry. Still, some of the tricks of the trade revealed in this chapter can make painting a smoother, briefer, and more satisfying experience.

Preparation—The Key to Success

Paint prep involves removing crud from the surface, fixing flaws, and putting on primer or sealer (see Table 22.2). Depending on the condition of the room or exterior surface you'll be painting, you may have to:

➤ Scrape peeling paint.

➤ Sand alligatored paint.

➤ Attack rust with a wire brush or steel wool.

➤ Sand glossy surfaces. (Most paint adheres poorly to slick surfaces; you'll need to dull them first with sandpaper or a chemical dulling agent.)

➤ Kill fungus with diluted household bleach.

➤ Wash the surface.

➤ Repair trim, siding, gutters, windows, and so on.

➤ Patch plaster or drywall.

➤ Repair and refasten siding.

➤ Prime nail heads.

➤ Mask and otherwise protect the surroundings.

The first step in prep work is to solve any problems in the substrate or previous coating. Then you'll need to protect nearby property. These are the common tools and supplies for paint prep:

Paint scraper: The number-one enemy of peeling paint.

Steel wool: Removes rust from metal, and smoothes interior surfaces between coats.

Window scraper: A razor for cleaning paint from windows, saves endless masking.

Sandpaper: Removes or roughens old paint, smoothes wood or filler, and smoothes between coats.

Sanding belt: For quick paint removal in a belt sander.

Hand wire brush: For removing peeling paint and rust.

Drill-mounted wire brush: For faster removal of paint and rust.

Masking tape: Keeps paint off light switches, outlets, and baseboard; attaches other masking, such as newspaper.

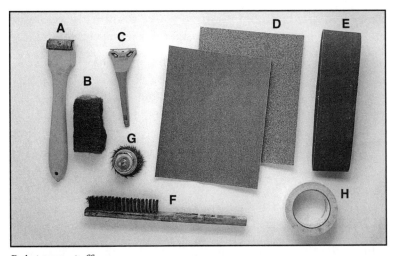

(A)   Paint scraper
(B)   Steel wool
(C)   Window scraper
(D)   Sandpaper
(E)   Sanding belt
(F)   Hand wire brush
(G)   Wire brush for an electric drill
(H)   Masking tape

Paint prep stuff

Preparing for an Inside Job

Prep often takes more time than the actual painting. The goal is to get the room so paint-proof that you can do an aerobic paint job without hassle or stumbling over tools. In general, when you paint inside, you should start with the ceiling, then move to the walls, trim, baseboard, and floor. Here are several suggestions for interior preparation:

➤ Remove everything portable. Pile heavy furniture in the center and cover with a plastic dropcloth—then with a cloth or a second plastic dropcloth. (I don't trust plastic enough to use one layer.)

➤ Assemble your ladders, tools, lights, and paint.

➤ Scan the surfaces for defects. Then repair them, using suggestions in the section of Chapter 10 entitled "Filling Holes in Wood," and the part of Chapter 20 called "Repairing Holes and Cracks in Plaster and Drywall." Prime all patches.

➤ Clean all surfaces with trisodium phosphate or similar material (sold at paint stores), then rinse and dry. Keep the solution out of electrical boxes.

➤ Remove outlet covers, switch plates, and light fixtures. Put masking tape across outlets and switches, and anything else you don't want to paint.

➤ Cover the floor with plastic and/or cloth dropcloths. If you're painting the ceiling, cover the entire floor. For walls only, cover out at least 3 to 4 feet from each wall.

➤ Rip newspaper into 6- to 8-inch strips, and tape them on top of the baseboard molding, so the newspaper extends above the floor masking. If you're painting the ceiling, it's a good idea to mask door frames and windows (but leave a slit for ventilation).

➤ If you can't be bothered masking every pane on a window, return after the paint dries and scrape the glass with a single-edge razor blade or window scraper.

➤ Set up lights and open some windows.

Preparing for an Outside Job

Preparing for exterior painting and staining is complicated, and I can only offer suggestions here. Again, the general sequence is stripping, patching, cleaning, masking, and painting. But outside, you've got to deal with more variables, and probably more scraping. If you need suggestions on repairing siding, consult Chapter 15, "Beauty's Only Skin Deep—Caring and Healing for Your Siding."

After you examine an exterior paint project, you may decide it's not for you (see "Are You Ready for This Job?" later on in this chapter). If you decide to go ahead, plot your strategy. Will you scrape and prep one side at a time, so you don't have to schlepp ladders so much? Will you scrape the whole house, then return for the repairs, so you won't need to keep so many tools in action at once?

A Word on Stripping

I hope you don't need to do a lot of stripping before the new coat goes on, but if you've got heavily alligatored, peeling, or flaking paint (see Table 22.2), you may need to.

The first step is to try a hand scraper. If that doesn't work, you can up the ante to a wire brush (if the one on your drill is not powerful enough, you can put a wire brush in a rented, portable grinder. Use eye protection with wire brushes.

From here on, the options get nastier: chemical stripper, a heat gun, or a propane torch. Each of these methods has disadvantages: the chemical stripper is toxic and expensive; the heat gun is slow, and the propane torch is dangerous. As we used to say as kids, "It's a free country." Translated: I'm not going to make this choice for you.

Application the Easy Way

Now that you've taken care of painting's dirty business—prep—it's time to buy some paint and start splashing. If you need advice on using ladders, see the section of Chapter 6 entitled "Basic Steps to Ladder Safety." With those final parts of preparation out of the way, it will be time to start painting like a pro.

Some Colorful Advice

Light-colored interior paint gets dirty with age, so the same tint fresh from the can will not match. To patch a small area without repainting the entire room, take some chips of the old paint to a paint store and ask them to match it. Or use this quick and dirty solution: Darken some of the original paint by decanting some into a yogurt container (you *have* been saving them, haven't you?), then blend in a few drops of a dark paint made with a compatible base (i.e., alkyd with alykd, or latex with latex). Even if you don't get a perfect match, the color will be much closer.

Don't Screw Up!
Scraping or stripping paint that was made before about 1980 can bring you face to face with lead, a nerve poison that's particularly dangerous to children. Unless a good laboratory or a reliable test kit tells you otherwise, assume that old paint does contain lead. Some municipalities restrict the scraping of lead paint; consult a building inspector.

For an entire re-painting job, examine paint chips in the light of the actual room or area you're going to paint. When you find a good combination, apply a quart of each color to see how they really work. If you don't like the choice, it will be much cheaper to change your mind before you buy ten custom-tinted gallons.

Paint Can Etiquette

Opening, using, and closing paint cans seems the most trivial part of painting. But if you want to do it cleanly and efficiently, follow these hints:

➤ When you first open a can, punch holes in the rim with a finishing nail. This allows the paint to drain from the rim (see the following figure).

➤ When pouring paint into a container or roller tray, immediately swipe up the drip with your brush, then clean the brush on the can rim.

➤ Before closing a can, wipe out the rim with a brush. Then hammer the lid closed. Don't pull a Neanderthal act—if the rim is clean, tapping is plenty of force.

217

Using a sharp nail, hammer half a dozen holes in the paint can rim—before it's full of paint. This will keep the rim clean so you can actually make an airtight seal when you finish.

The neatest paint can in history

➤ If you have more than one can of paint, mix ("box") them together so they all have the same color.

➤ For solvent-thinned paint: If the can is damaged, the rim contains dry paint, or the can has been open for a while, dump the mineral spirits you used in the brush-cleaning ceremony into the can, then stir and close the can. When some solvent evaporates in storage, there will still be enough in the paint to prevent a skin from forming.

Brushing

If you think I'm going to waste precious pages telling you how to brush paint, you're wrong. But I will paint a word picture of what I've learned in the course of painting dozens of houses.

➤ Tap the brush against the inside of the can to remove extra paint. Drawing it against the lid removes too much paint and harms the bristles.

➤ Use a paint bucket or another smaller container so you don't have to drag an entire gallon with you.

➤ To get paint into corners, press a loaded brush into the corner, give it a bit of a shimmy, and pull it off toward a flat area as the brush starts to dry out.

➤ On complex shapes and vertical sections, return for a quick brushing after a couple of minutes. This removes extra paint and prevents drips.

➤ Move the brush rapidly; don't start to smooth the paint until you have delivered enough to cover a relatively large area.

➤ Solvent-based paints thicken quickly in the can. If you don't thin them, the paint layer will get extremely thick. Besides, who wants to paint with molasses?

➤ On wood, stroke with the grain. Put plenty of coating on end grain, which soaks up paint and stain very quickly.

Handy Hint
To get a smooth surface with high-gloss paint, wait until the first coat is dry, and lightly polish it with ultrafine sandpaper or steel wool to remove bubbles and dust.

➤ To brush a broad area, quickly paint a pattern of stripes across the grain with a full brush. Then, without dipping the brush back in the can, stroke with the grain to merge the stripes and cover a large area.

Rolling

Rollers are the king of the interior painting hustle—it's hard to imagine painting walls with anything else. Even decks, siding, and floors can all be covered quickly with a roller. Nevertheless, rollers do have a few limitations:

➤ They spatter.

➤ They leave a stippled pattern (which you can smooth off with a light brushing afterwards).

➤ They stir up bubbles in some coatings, like polyurethane varnish.

➤ They are a real bear to clean.

For basic rolling, you'll need roller, pan, a trim brush, and a stepladder; I would strongly suggest a roller handle extension, which reduces wrist fatigue and eliminates stooping.

1. With a 1 $^1/_2$ - to 2 $^1/_2$ - inch brush, "cut in" the edges and corners of the section you will roll first.

2. Evenly load the roller in the pan. (If you leave the roller drenched in the pan, one side will be all gooped up, and the other side dry. So rest the roller in the shallow end of the roller pan, not the diving end, when you are not working.)

Nail It Down
Cutting in is not about lines or queues but about painting corners, where a roller can't reach. Cut in with a 1 $^1/_2$ - to 2 $^1/_2$ - inch brush, then immediately roll the area.

3. With your first strokes, make a long *W,* gradually increasing the pressure. Distribute the paint across a wide area—don't concentrate on one spot. Roll perpendicular to the "W" pattern, across a larger area. Use lighter strokes so the edge of the roller does not leave ridges.

Spraying

Even if you're not a gang-tagger or graffiti artist, spray paint in a can can be handy stuff, particularly for small jobs, intricate surfaces, and for metal, where brush strokes always show up. You don't need a Ph.D. to spray paint, but here are some suggestions:

➤ Shake the can thoroughly before starting, and occasionally while painting.

➤ Start the spray before the can starts to pass over the surface, and do not let up the spray until it has passed beyond the surface.

➤ Move your hand parallel to the surface; don't swing in an arc, which causes unevenness and sags.

➤ Keep the can moving, spraying light, sag-proof coats. Cover the whole surface, and give each part a few seconds to dry.

➤ When done, hold the can upside-down and spray until the stream is clear. Then wipe the spray nozzle with a rag, and cap the can. Then the nozzle will actually work when you want to use it again.

Test Your Mettle Painting Metal

As the old advertisement said, rust never sleeps, and while prep is important for any kind of painting, it's crucial for painting iron and steel. The better you clean iron and steel with scraping and wire-brushing, the longer you can defer the next paint job. Unfortunately, with iron and steel, it's usually not a matter of *if* the rust is going to reappear—it's a matter of *when.*

Suggestions:

➤ A wire brush mounted on a drill is the best tool for removing rust. Wear goggles, and run the drill at top speed. If you're really obsessed, rent a high-speed grinder with a wire brush, but use this brawny tool gingerly until you get the hang of it.

➤ For small amounts of rust, use a rust-removing compound called naval jelly.

➤ Paint on a warm, dry day. Consider using a hair dryer or heat gun to warm the metal and drive out moisture (water retained in metal is the major cause of paint failure in iron and steel).

➤ After all this work, don't scrimp on the quality of the primer and paint. Always use a rust-inhibitive primer.

➤ Many metal enamels take a few weeks to harden, so give your new paint job a chance to mature before you abuse it.

Clean Them Brushes and Rollers

I bet cleaning brushes is not your favorite part of painting, and that's good—I'm not crazy about giving advice to cleanliness freaks. I hate cleaning brushes too, particularly after a sweaty day on the ladder. But there's one thing worse than cleaning brushes —and that's wasting money to buy new brushes because I forgot to clean them last time around. Here are some hints for keeping brushes and rollers clean:

➤ Don't let the tools get caked and dry—clean them immediately after painting (if they do get caked, use brush cleaner).

➤ Add a bit of dish soap to water when you clean latex paint from brushes.

➤ Flick the brush against a log or board to remove the last bit of paint. (Or buy a brush spinner, which does about the same thing, but with considerably more style and expense.)

➤ If you're planning to paint again tomorrow, freeze the brushes, or add some water or thinner and wrap them securely in plastic bags. Likewise, you can seal a roller and pan in a couple of plastic bags to prevent a lot of cleaning (a roller cover will disintegrate after a few days of immersion, but you can just heave it at that point).

➤ When you're done, wrap brushes in folded newspaper so their bristles stay straight. Store brushes flat, or hang them from a nail.

Are You Ready for This Job?

Painting can be an enjoyable diversion for a weekend or two, or it can be a miserable waste of a summer, an endless drudge that drags you away from the inner essence of summer—novels, sports, and canoeing. By the time you buy the paint and prep materials, rent the ladders, and devote several weekends to a project, you may find you've "spent" more in time and money than a pro would have cost you. These pointers may help you decide whether you really want to tackle a painting project:

➤ Preparation is the wild card. Badly deteriorated surfaces are a pain to prepare, and if you can't face that chore, you'll have to pay somebody else to do it.

➤ How much heavy-duty repair (rotten soffets or window frames, moth-eaten trim) is required? Do you have the tools, skills, and time to handle this phase of the job?

➤ Renting a power washer can save a lot of time and aggravation, but be sure to allow time for drying.

➤ Renting or borrowing an airless sprayer can take a lot of the sting out of painting.

➤ A big paint job may call for a lot of ladders, which you'll have to buy, beg, borrow, or rent. Warning: Scrimping on ladders can be dangerous if it causes you to over-reach or to use ladders that are in poor condition.

➤ Exterior painting is mostly a spring and fall sport. Except in the warmest climates, winter is out, and except in the coolest climates, midsummer is out. And since you can't work on rainy or muggy days, either, you'll have to plan your schedule carefully.

The Least You Need to Know

➤ Just as possession is nine-tenths of the law, preparation is nine-tenths of painting. Don't open the paint can until you have everything clean, exposed, patched, primed, or covered.

➤ Although brushing and rolling look like real idiot work, it's goal-oriented stuff. A few basic techniques can save significant time, and perhaps make the new paint job last many years longer.

➤ Iron and steel are the biggest challenge in home painting. Although rust may win in the end, the cleaner the surface, the slower its victory will be.

Part 5
Mechanicals for Non-Mechanics

Time was, houses were built of lumber, nails, and hardware—and not much else. Nowadays, that simple list has been joined by the "mechanical" components. Think of these as your home's nervous and circulatory systems: the wiring, plumbing, and heating equipment.

I'm not going to pretend that reading a few chapters will make you into a mechanical repair whiz—mechanical problems are a lot more subtle and confusing than a leaking roof. But there's still room for savings in the mechanical department, as you'll learn in this last part of the book. Electrical repairs, for example, are much simpler than their reputation implies. And even in plumbing and heating, you can save big money with small repairs and avoid the humiliation that comes from paying that miserable "job charge" for a technician to inform you, after a 30 second inspection, that your problem is a blown breaker or closed valve.

Chapter 24

Breaker, Breaker on the Wall . . . Electric Fundamentals

Like masonry and plumbing, electric repair has a sinister reputation. First of all, it's confusing, because everything happens behind the scenes (or the walls, at any rate). And electricity is generally invisible until it's put to use (or it should be invisible—seeing electricity in action means sparks at best and fires or shocks at worst).

But a little understanding goes a long way in an electric repair. If you follow the instructions in this chapter, and don't do things that confuse you (see "When Do You Need Electrical Help?" in Chapter 25), you should be able to handle most basic repairs. Fact is, wiring repairs are much simpler than most people think; in many cases, the major challenge is distinguishing black and white (wires, that is). Granted, things get confusing if you start digging up buried mistakes, but that's one reason you bought this book, right?

Basic Stuff You Must Know

A book for complete idiots shouldn't be freighted with irrelevant theory—after all, who wants to read about Michael Faraday's dazzling insights into electricity when the light in the kitchen is flickering? But you've got to know a few things before you start working with whizzing electrons.

First of all, the control panel for your electrical system is the fuse box, or the circuit-breaker box. These boxes use slightly different means to serve the same functions:

➤ Route incoming electricity to the various circuits in your home

➤ Give you a way to shut off individual circuits

➤ Control how much current (how many amps) can flow on each circuit

Fuses are one-time protectors that must be replaced when they "blow" after carrying excess current. Circuit breakers are handier because they can be switched back on after they trip. A fuse box or breaker box is rated by the maximum number of amperes (amps) it can handle; 100 amps is the minimum on new construction. Some states require that the service be upgraded to 100 amps upon the sale of a home.

Going Around in Circles with Circuits

Electricity can only travel in a circuit. This is a loop of conductor (mostly wire) that connects a source of electricity (in other words, the fuse or breaker box) to a load (say a lamp, toaster, or motor) and then back to the source. Although circuits get hideously complicated in computers and space-shuttle control rooms, in houses they are essentially a loop from the hot side of the breaker box to a load and back to the neutral side of the breaker box, as you'll see in the first illustration in this chapter.

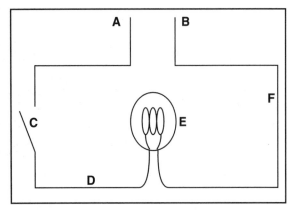

(A)   Source (hot side)

(B)   Source (neutral side)

(C)   Switch (shown open)

(D)   Hot wire (black)

(E)   Load (a light is shown, but it can be a motor, heater, etc.)

(F)   Neutral wire (white)

Parts of a circuit. A circuit must connect a source to a load and back to a source.

Two principles govern the behavior of electricity in circuits:

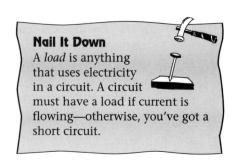

➤ Electricity must return to its source. That's why you need a circuit—you can't just connect a hot wire to a light and figure you've satisfied the National Electric Code. Not only won't the light light, but the electricity will try to improvise a way back to the source. Danger!

➤ Each circuit needs a load, such as a motor, light, or heating element. Otherwise, you have a short circuit—a connection between hot and neutral without the resistance of a load. That's another recipe for disaster.

And Now for Some Lingo: Amps, Watts, and Volts

You can't talk about electricity without some jargon, which, fortunately, is less fearsome than the average scientific mumbo-jumbo. You need to know only a few basic terms, and most are already familiar (even if you may not be able to rattle off their definitions on command).

Alternating current (AC) is used throughout your home wiring. This current changes polarity 60 times per second (60 hertz). *Direct current (DC)* is used only in cars and battery-operated stuff, and we won't worry about it. Phew.

Amps, or amperes, are a measure of how much current is flowing. Technically, one amp is a number of electrons flowing per second that would vastly outnumber the national debt, measured in pennies. (Didn't you want to know? If you need to know more than this, you're way beyond idiot territory.) Seriously, amps are important, because they tell you how much current a wire can carry. Try to squeeze too many amps through a wire, and the circuit breaker will open, the fuse will blow, or the building will burn down. Easy choice, eh?

Volts are units of pressure—of how hard the electrons are "trying" to get around the circuit. Most home circuits carry 120 volts. Heavy-duty heating appliances, like stoves, dryers, and water heaters, use 240 volts, because a wire can carry more power at this higher voltage.

Watts, units of power, are used to rate things that consume electricity, like lamps, appliances, and tools. Watts = amps × volts, so a 120-volt circuit carrying 5 amps supplies 600 watts ($120 \times 5 = 600$).

Wattage ratings, carried on most electrical appliances, allow you to tell if a particular circuit has adequate capacity for the job. Watts ÷ volts = amps. How many amps does a 1500-watt saw draw? 1500 watts ÷ 120 volts = 12 amps (which is near the 15-amp capacity of the typical home circuit). To find out how many amps are flowing on a circuit, simply add the number of amps on each appliance plugged into that circuit.

Incidentally, a *kilowatt hour*, the unit by which your electric utility enriches itself, is the flow of 1000 watts (1 kilowatt) for one hour—or the equivalent. Thus, a 100-watt bulb burning for 10 hours consumes 1 kilowatt hour.

Wire Size (Gauge) (Are We Confused Yet?)

Wire is sized by an ancient and bass-ackwards system called *gauge*. Gauge tells you how much current (how many amps) a wire can carry (wires can carry the same number of amps at either 120 or 240 volts). Most home wiring is 12 or 14 gauge, although heavy-duty, 240-volt circuits usually use 10-gauge wire. (Why are lower-gauge wires bigger than wires with higher gauges? Because I promised this would be backwards, and I keep my promises.)

Why should you care about wire size? Because it determines how much juice a circuit can carry, and also what size breaker or fuse you need to protect that circuit. Overloaded wires can get hot enough to burn. Note: Most outlets and switches are made for 15-amp circuits; you'll need to buy special devices for 20-amp circuits.

Table 24.1 lists the capacity of common wire gauges.

Table 24.1 Wire gauges, capacities, and uses

Gauge	Capacity in amps (equals breaker or fuse rating)	Typical uses
10	30	240-volt circuits: Clothes dryer, range, central air conditioning, and water heater
12	20	120-volt circuits: Kitchens, work-shops, and other heavy loads
14	15	120-volt general household circuits

Cable and Conduit

A *cable* is a group of several conductor wires inside one sheath. Modern cable, called *romex*, has a plastic sheath and usually contains one black wire, one white wire, and one bare copper ground wire.

Cable is designated by two numbers. The first is the gauge, and the second is the number of insulated wires (conductors) in the cable (the ground wire is not counted). Thus 12–2 cable has two 12-gauge conductors, and 14–2 has two 14-gauge conductors. 14–3, with black, white, and red 14-gauge conductors, is used for three-way switches. If you're wiring outdoors or underground, buy the special, ultraviolet resistant variety of cable made for outdoor use.

Conduit is a light steel pipe that carries insulated wires and is usually seen in basements and garages. You may also see a coiled steel sheath called *BX*, or flexible conduit. Conduit and BX need no ground wire, since the steel sheath itself supplies the ground connection. Although you'll need special tools to work on conduit, you can easily connect romex cable to boxes that are wired with conduit.

Some older houses have an outdated, ungrounded "knob and tube" wiring scheme. The insulated but unsheathed wires carrying each circuit are attached to insulated knobs mounted on the framing and passed inside ceramic tubes drilled into the framing. If I saw this stuff in my house (and trust me, I have), I'd seriously consider replacing it immediately to avoid the possibility of it shorting out. Replacing this stuff is a pro job, and an expensive one. But if you've got knob and tube, the ol' place probably needs rewiring anyway.

Electrical Tools and Materials

Electrical repair doesn't call for much in the way of tools, and the main ones are cheap. But don't try to skimp—at least get yourself a circuit tester and a wire stripper.

A *circuit tester*, aka electrical tester or circuit probe, is your safety net (see the photo of electrical tools in this chapter). It tells you when a circuit is dead, and thus safe to work on. It tells you if the ground is working. And it tells you when you've wired something correctly—all without requiring a Ph.D. on your part. The cheapest testers have short wires, or "leads;" I use one that's about 4 feet long. Occasionally that's very handy; usually it's just extra wire to tangle in something.

> **Don't Screw Up!**
> Don't use acid flux or acid-core solder in electrical work. These materials, used in plumbing, will cause corrosion and eventual destruction of an electrical joint. Instead, use resin flux and/or resin-core solder.

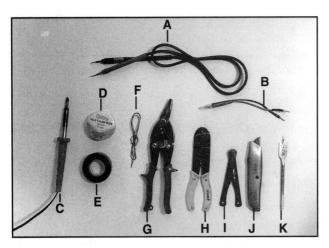

(A)   Circuit tester—with long leads
(B)   Circuit tester—with short leads
(C)   Soldering iron
(D)   Resin flux
(E)   Electrical tape
(F)   Solder
(G)   Tin snips
(H)   Stripper—with wire cutter and electrical bolt cutter
(I)   Stripper—with wire cutter
(J)   Utility knife
(K) $^1/_2$" to $^3/_4$" drill bit

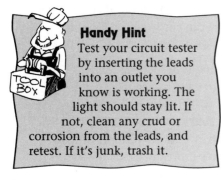

Handy Hint
Test your circuit tester by inserting the leads into an outlet you know is working. The light should stay lit. If not, clean any crud or corrosion from the leads, and retest. If it's junk, trash it.

With a *soldering iron, resin flux,* and *electrical solder*, you can solder wires, and permanently repair extension cords and splice phone cable. Soldering guns are handy—because they heat up immediately—but a 40-watt soldering iron is cheaper, and plenty adequate for occasional use (Chapter 25 explains how to make a solder joint).

You can cut romex cable with a cable shear, a pair of *tin snips*, or a big diagonal-cutting pliers. I would not buy a tool specifically for cutting cable unless I planned on doing a lot of wiring. For occasional use, use the blade of big wire strippers (it's designed to cut individual wires but will work on romex) or long-nose pliers.

I once knew a penny-pincher who tried to do electrical work without a *wire stripper*, and stripped insulation with a pair of cutting pliers. Half the time, after I'd worked myself into a lather fumbling with a Medusa's headful of wire, the wires broke where I'd nicked them with the pliers. When I finally came to my senses, I was flabbergasted at the efficacy of strippers. One flick of the wrist, and you've got a shiny, stripped, intact wire. Fancier strippers have shears for cutting electrical screws, which can be quite handy.

A *utility knife* is useful for stripping the outer sheath from cable (not the insulation on the conductors). Cut straight down the middle of the cable, so you don't injure the insulation on the wires. You can also do this with a vegetable peeler or a romex stripper, a tool made to remove the outer insulation. Don't try to remove the outer and inner insulation in one step.

You'll need $^1/_2$- to $^3/_4$-inch *drill bits* if you need to route romex cable through studs or joists.

Electrical Boxes and Paraphernalia

Electrical boxes are the skeleton of your wiring system—the bones that protect the cables, connectors, and devices that actually bring you Mr. Sparky's services. In repair work, you're generally stuck with whatever boxes you find, but you should be able to recognize the basic types for the occasional replacement of a corroded or undersize box, or for adding outlets and switches. Boxes come in various depths; unless the wall cavity is unusually shallow, choose the 2 $^1/_2$-inch depth, which has more room for wires and devices. Boxes with angled corners are much easier to place into a new hole in the wall, because the cables won't get in the way. The next illustration shows typical electrical boxes, which are listed here:

Plastic box: Easy to use because they need neither grounding nor cable clamps (but remember, the *devices* in these boxes must be grounded).

Shallow switch box: Used for switches and outlets in tight quarters.

4-inch square box: Can be used for a double-duplex outlet; it's usually nailed to a surface in a basement or garage and covered with a steel plate.

Round box: For a ceiling light fixture (or use an octagonal box).

Handy box: Gang several handy boxes side by side for multiple switches and outlets.

Switch box with tapered corners: Simplifies installation in an old wall, since the cables won't snag on the drywall.

(A) Plastic box

(B) Shallow switch box, with two romex connectors in place

(C) 4" square box

(D) Round box

(E) Handy box

(F) Switch box with tapered corners

Electrical boxes. Each style may come with a variety of mounting and cable-clamping devices.

You'll also be needing some stuff to go inside those boxes, like outlets and switches. Many of these things are cheap enough to keep around for an emergency repair.

Mounting straps: For attaching boxes to drywall or plaster. Once the box is in the wall, hold the strap by the two short ears and slip the long section behind the drywall. Holding the box at the proper depth in the wall, bend the ears over the edge of the box and fold them tight into the box, so they are bent 180-degrees.

Outlet with ground-fault interrupter (GFI): For outlets in kitchens, bathrooms, and garages.

Grounded duplex receptacle: The standard electrical outlet.

Two-way switch: One switch controls one or more lights. (Note: a pair of three-way switches, not shown, is used to control a single light fixture from two locations.)

Porcelain light fixture: The cheapest and handiest fixture for places where appearance is your lowest priority.

Protector plate: Shields romex cable running near the outside of a stud from nails.

Electrical staples: Attach cable in accessible locations.

Screw-on wire connectors: Connect wires with a simple twist; easy to remove.

Romex connectors: Secure romex cable in metal boxes.

Cover plates: Cover outlets and switches after the wiring is done.

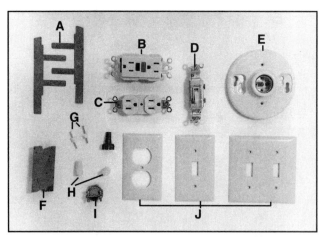

(A) Mounting straps
(B) Outlet with ground-fault interrupter (GFI)
(C) Grounded duplex receptacle
(D) Two-way switch
(E) Porcelain light fixture
(F) Protector plate
(G) Electrical staples
(H) Screw-on wire connectors
(I) Romex connectors
(J) Cover plates

Electrical paraphernalia

Safety

I had a physics teacher in high school who warned us to work on electricity with one hand behind our backs. This was a memorable way of reminding us that the most dangerous kind of shock is one that passes through your heart—as happens when a current passes in one arm and out the other.

But let's honor the memory of Mr. Singer by avoiding shocks altogether, whether we're working on an electrical system—or living with it. That takes a bit of understanding of the electricity's desires.

The nature of electricity is always to "want" to move from hot (or supply), to neutral, in the easiest and shortest path possible. This is why we use circuits—because electricity needs a path back "home" on the neutral wire. The neutral and ground wires are connected to the same place on the fuse or breaker box; the job of the ground is to give electricity an easy return path in case the neutral fails.

To get a shock, you must be touching a source of current—usually a defective tool, appliance, or device. You must also be grounded—either by touching something conductive that's connected to the ground, like a pipe or electric box, or by standing on damp soil. That's why electricians sometimes wear rubbers—to keep themselves from being grounded and shocked.

> **Nail It Down**
> A *cover plate* is what you see covering an outlet or a switch on the wall. Blank cover plates close boxes that contain wires but no switches or outlets. Steel cover plates are sturdy enough for use in basements or garages.

> **Don't Screw Up!**
> What's the big fuss about electrical fires? If you want to see how much heat an electric circuit can carry, remember those brighter-than-the-sun, burn-your-eyeballs sparks produced by an arc welder. Then you'll pay more attention to good wiring, and to selecting the right circuit breaker or fuse.

The Golden Rule of Electric Repair

Now it's time for the golden rule of electric repair: do unto a cold circuit, or a hot circuit may do something shocking unto you. *In other words, shut off the power, feverbrain, before you go poking around with the juice.*

Got that?

Now for the subtle rules. Make sure you switched off the right circuit breaker or fuse before you go poking into an electric circuit (see "Making Sure an Outlet Is Cold," later in this chapter).

And a few more guidelines:

➤ Use tools (screwdrivers, pliers, and strippers) with insulated plastic handles—just in case something goes wrong. To be extra safe, wrap electrical tape around the shaft of your screwdriver.

➤ Avoid being grounded (unruly teenagers will love this rule!). Keep your hands dry, and don't wade around in water when messing with electricity. Remember, you are grounded every time you touch a grounded electrical box or a metal pipe. Avoid damp floors, or insulate yourself with rubber boots if you must work on them.

➤ Don't do stuff you're not confident of.

➤ Get help when you need it.

Living with Electricity

A good electric system is pretty hardy, but there's no point in trying to see how far you can push it. Here are some ways to reduce your family's electrical worries:

➤ Locate your main disconnect—the switch or fuse that controls all power to your house. It's your last line of defense in an electrical emergency, when you can't stop to figure out which circuit is causing the difficulty.

➤ Don't overload circuits (see "Problems at the Circuit Breaker or Fuse Box" later in this chapter).

➤ Never, ever, solve your blown fuse or tripped breaker problems by installing a fuse or breaker with a rating higher than the circuit can handle.

Nail It Down

The *main disconnect* is the switch or fuse controlling all electricity entering your home. In a circuit-breaker box, it's marked "main," or "100," or "200" (or however many amperes your system supplies). In a fuse box, it's the big black fuseholder marked "main." To shut off power, flip the switch or pull out the fuse holder.

➤ Don't run extension cords under carpet, across doorways, or in damp areas. And keep a close eye on cheapo extension cords. They cause a lot of fires.

➤ Make sure your extension cord has enough capacity for the load. Cords are rated in amps (amps = watts ÷ volts).

➤ Outlets, switches, plugs, and electric cords should not get hot in use. If they do, investigate and fix or replace them. (However, some dimmer switches do warm up after operating for a while.)

➤ Ungrounded outlets (2-prong) are hazardous, particularly in damp locations. In bathrooms, kitchens, and outdoors, install ground-fault circuit interrupter (GFI) receptacles, which prevent shock by shutting off when they detect current leakage (see "Installing an Outlet—The Basics," in Chapter 25).

➤ If you have young kids, install plastic outlet protectors in any outlets they can reach. Keep an eye out for kids who think it's fun to stick keys in an outlet (they'll do this).

Builder's Trivia

The prongs of modern electrical plugs are not created equal. The smaller one carries the hot current, the larger one the neutral, and the round one (on a three-prong plug) the ground. Electronic devices "care" which wire carries which, so be sure to religiously connect black (hot) to the brass screws on a receptacle, and white (neutral) to the silver-colored screws.

Making Sure an Outlet Is Cold

This little test sounds harder than it is, but if you do it right, you'll be breathing easier (as will your life insurance agent). You'll need a circuit tester (see "Electrical Tools and Materials," earlier in this chapter) and a screwdriver. Follow these steps to test the outlet:

1. Go to a working outlet and stick one prong of your circuit tester in each slot (avoid the round, ground hole). If the tester lights, then the tester is okay (you only need to do this test once in a while).

2. If the outlet you want to test is controlled by a switch, turn it on.

3. Switch off the breaker or unscrew the fuse that (you think) controls the outlet.

4. Insert the tester in the outlet you want to test. If its light does not illuminate, test the other pair of slots (in rare cases, only half of an outlet is hot). If the tester stays lit, cut off another circuit and repeat this step.

5. When the tester does not light on either pair of slots, the outlet is truly dead, and you can work on it.

Growing up, one of my daddy's-helper tasks was helping shut off the fuse so he could do some electrical work. More precisely, my role was to bellow downstairs when the light or outlet went off when he had cut off the right breaker. When my son was still too young for this kind of hollering (apparently it seemed too productive for him), and I had to work alone, I used to plug a portable radio into the outlet. Then, with the radio going full blast, I'd go downstairs and flip circuit breakers until a sudden silence indicated that I'd got the right circuit. Surprisingly, this trick even helps to shut down circuits feeding ceiling lights. Just plug the radio into an outlet near the light, and when it goes silent, the light circuit is probably dead, because nearby fixtures are often on the same circuit. But test the light circuit anyway, as described next.

Making Sure a Light Switch Is Cold

If the light you want to work on is functioning, just turn it on, turn off the breaker (or pull the fuse), and check that the light is off.

If you're trying to fix a switch or light that's giving problems, gather your screwdriver and circuit tester for this slightly more elaborate check that the circuit is off.

For a two-way switch, start by placing the switch in the "off" position:

1. Shut off the circuit you think controls the light, and make sure nobody absent-mindedly turns it on while you're working on it.

2. Remove the switch plate (the cover on the switch). Carefully reach in with your circuit tester and touch one lead to a ground (bare) wire. (If no ground wire is present, touch the box, which may be grounded.)

3. Place the other lead on each switch terminal in turn. *If the tester lights*, go to 4a. If it *does not light,* go to 4b.

4a. Cut off a different breaker or fuse and repeat step 3.

4b. Stick one tester lead into the ground socket of a grounded outlet. Touch the other lead to each switch terminal in succession. If the tester does not light, the circuit is cold and ready for repair. Otherwise, shut off another breaker or fuse and retest.

For a *three-way switch*, test all terminals, flip the switch, and retest all terminals. (Three-way switches are easy to recognize because they have no "on" or "off" markings.)

On What Grounds Is It Grounded?

The ground system allows electricity to leave your house if there's a problem with neutral wire, which is the normal "escape route." The ground system requires a good connection to—believe it or not, Ripley—the ground! Typically this is a water pipe or a grounding stake, a long metal rod driven into the ground near your foundation.

A ground is a safety measure that only comes into play if something screws up. If, for example, the insulation on an electric tool fails while you're running it, or water gets inside a toaster you are touching, you want the electricity to "drain away" through the ground wire rather than your body.

In modern systems, every electric circuit has a ground, which connects to every outlet and metal electrical box. (Plastic boxes are not grounded, and many switches are only grounded through contact to a metal box.) The ground conductor in a cable is easy to recognize, because it's bare copper. In steel conduit and flexible conduit, the conduit itself provides the ground.

The ground system should take nothing for granted. The ground wire entering a box is connected to the greenish hex-head screw on the body of the outlet and to the box.

If a box is in the middle of a run (meaning it supplies power to another box), then all ground wires (from all cables, the device, and the box itself) should be joined by a screw-on wire connector.

Updating an Ungrounded Outlet

Although relatively new wiring systems should have floor-to-ceiling grounding, older systems are another story. You may find only ungrounded outlets (which have two slots, and no round grounding hole). But it's easy to install grounded (3-hole) outlets *if the boxes are grounded.* You'll find ungrounded outlets in grounded boxes if the old wires are conduit or BX cable, which are grounded by the steel sheath.

(Grounded outlets are safer for you and the electrical equipment, but that doesn't stop people from cutting the grounding prong of the plug on a new computer or phone answering machine so they can stick it into an ungrounded outlet. The next time you do this, heed the voice of your conscience—or your soon-to-be orphaned children—and do something slightly more intelligent, like installing a grounded outlet.)

To figure out if the box holding an outlet is grounded, touch the screw holding the cover plate with one prong of the circuit tester. Touch each slot of the outlet with the other prong. If you get a light from either slot, the box is grounded. If the box is not grounded, test nearby boxes. In older houses, the grounding pattern can be erratic, so make many tests and few assumptions. (If you can't find a grounded box, updating the outlets is a pro job.)

To install a grounded outlet in a grounded box, you'll need a circuit tester, screwdriver, a grounded receptacle, grounding screw, and bare wire lead (same gauge as the circuit wire; use 12-gauge if you're not sure). Use these steps to install the outlet:

1. Shut off the circuit and pull the box apart.

2. Start the grounding screw in the hole in the back of the box that is threaded for it.

3. Cut a 9-inch piece of bare grounding wire, make a hook in its end, and secure it under the grounding screw.

4. Attach the other end of the bare lead to the hexagonal-headed grounding screw on the new outlet.

5. Attach black and white wires to the appropriate terminals of the new outlet and screw it into place (see "Installing an Outlet—The Basics," in Chapter 25). Check that the new outlet is working (see "Testing a Receptacle," in Chapter 25).

Got Aluminum Wire?

Most homes are wired with solid copper wire, a soft, light-brown metal that's an excellent conductor. But in the 1960s and early 1970s, some houses were wired with pure aluminum wire, which was cheaper than copper. This cable is usually marked "aluminum" every few feet on the outside.

Aluminum wire conducts well, but it is not compatible with fixtures designed for good ol' copper wire. So if your house has all-aluminum wire, be sure to use fixtures marked "CO/ALR." If they are hard to find, try an electrical wholesaler. Copper-coated aluminum wire—aka "copper-clad"— requires "CU/AL" type fixtures, the same ones sold for pure copper wire.

Problems at the Circuit Breaker or Fuse Box

The heart of your electrical system, and its main safety feature, is the fuse box or the circuit-breaker box. These boxes (you'll have one or the other, but seldom both) control the maximum amount of current flowing in the circuits, and allow you to shut circuits off.

Although you want to know where the fuse or breaker box is, you don't want to be intimately familiar with it—since that's a sure sign of problems. Still, it's best that problems show up at the fuse box, since the alternatives are rather grim. So as you, gentle reader, stumble down the stairs with a new fuse in one hand, a flashlight in the other, and an oath on your lips, remember that the fuse that just blew may have prevented a fire. Overloaded circuits get hot fast (you could almost say lightning fast).

The rating of each circuit breaker or fuse depends on the size of the wires and fixtures on the circuit. Because 12-gauge wires can carry 20 amps, a circuit wired with 12-gauge wire and 20-amp devices would use a 20-amp fuse or circuit breaker. Similarly, because 14-gauge wire can carry 15 amps, the breaker or fuse would be rated at 15 amps.

Breakers or fuses blow when the circuit is asked to carry too much current—either because too many things are drawing current, or because some malfunction is allowing excess current to flow. So before you screw in another fuse, or switch the circuit breaker back on, try to figure out why it blew in the first place. Did you just plug in a vacuum cleaner to a circuit that was already carrying a heavy load? Then plug the vacuum into a different circuit before restoring the power.

If breakers or fuses blow once in a great while, and you know why, it's not something to get too excited about—that's their job. But if it happens repeatedly, or you don't understand the reason, sniff around. Really: You may sniff out the putrid burned-plastic stench of hot electrical insulation—a sure-fire sign of trouble. If this bloodhound imitation fails, try to isolate the problem by unplugging stuff from the circuit, and slowly adding things back until you trip the breaker or blow the fuse. Or call 1-800-BLU-FUSE and ask for an electrician.

> **Don't Screw Up!**
> If you feel compelled to remove the inside cover from your breaker or fuse box, get out your rubber gloves and rubber boots, and then, before you actually touch the thing, go to the phone and call your electrician. Unless you're in the middle of a city-wide blackout, some parts of the box may still be hot even after you throw the main disconnect.

Making a Circuit Map

If you're regularly blowing fuses or breakers, chances are that at least one circuit is undersized. (Sometimes, a "tired" circuit breaker merely needs replacement). If there's a motor on the circuit, you may need a "delay" (aka "slow-blow") fuse, which allows the short surge of heavy current motors need to start up. Pay special attention to electrical heating devices—heaters, toasters, and coffee pots. These gadgets can slurp more juice than a dozen light bulbs.

If these hints don't help, it's time to make a circuit map—a diagram or list of the outlets and lights on each circuit. Circuit maps are also handy for future electrical repairs, because they show you which circuit to shut down (although you will *test* the circuit anyway before you dig in, won't you?).

To make a circuit map, you'll need a circuit tester, clipboard, and pen. Turn off one breaker or unscrew one fuse, and walk through the house and list which outlets, lights, and appliances don't work. Repeat for the other circuits. Don't be surprised if circuits meander through the house—electricians often run cables so a room has several circuits. That way, a blown breaker or fuse will not darken the whole room.

Now add up the wattage of devices on the problem circuit, and divide by 120 (for a 120-volt circuit). The sum should be less than the amperage rating of the circuit (which is marked on the fuse or circuit-breaker handle). If it's higher than this rating, move some appliances to other circuits, put in another circuit to share the load, or hire an electrician.

The Least You Need to Know

➤ A wire stripper and a circuit tester are the bare minimum for electrical repairs.

➤ Before doing any electrical repair, shut the circuit off—and then test that it's really off.

➤ Grounded circuits are used in all modern construction; if the boxes are grounded, you can easily put in an ungrounded outlet.

➤ Choosing the best electrical box can simplify repairs.

➤ A circuit map can help you isolate overloaded circuits and simplify future wiring work.

Chapter 25

Getting Wired without Getting Zapped

In This Chapter

➤ Making connections—with solder, screw-on wire connectors, and screw terminals

➤ Deciphering wiring layouts

➤ Replacing bad outlets and switches

➤ Adding outlets where you need them—painlessly

➤ Phone phacts for phone phreaks—how you can have two phones in every room

What's wiring got in common with politics and espionage? Like politics, it's all about connections, about working the network, and finding the source of power. Like espionage, it involves deception, because the electrical system should blend in with the local landscape.

But let's not overwork the simile. While the occasional political shock keeps people reading the papers, shocks have an entirely different meaning in electrical work. Nevertheless, if you use your circuit tester and common sense, and don't do things you don't understand, you'll stay out of the headlines while keeping your electrical system in top shape.

Got Connections? You'll Need Them

Connections are the glue that knits an electrical system together, so you'll need to learn the simple but crucial tricks for making connections with solder, screw-on wire connectors, and screw terminals.

Soldering? Nothing to It!

Soldering is a technique for joining pieces of metal by melting another metal—called solder—on them. Clean copper wires are easy to solder, but dirty or corroded wires are impossible. To do it right, you'll need a wire stripper, soldering iron or gun, nonacidic flux, solder, sandpaper, and electrical tape. Put on your safety goggles, to protect your eyes from molten solder, and follow these steps:

1. Plug in your soldering iron and set it aside, with the tip safely in the air.

2. Strip about $^3/_4$ to 1 inch of insulation from each end of the wires you're joining.

3. Lightly sandpaper the bare ends, to remove corrosion.

4. Twist the wires tightly together, so the joint does not move while you solder it.

5. Apply some soldering flux to the joint.

6. Touch the iron tip to the solder to pick up a small puddle of solder, which conducts heat faster than a dry tip.

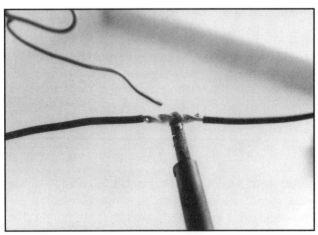

When you solder a joint, hold the iron on the joint a few seconds after the solder starts to melt, so it can really penetrate.

7. Hold the soldering iron to the joint until the flux begins to boil. A clean, well-fluxed joint will pull in the solder when the joint is hot enough. Then touch solder to the joint (*not* the iron) and let it run into the joint (see the photo showing how to solder a joint).

8. Heat for another few seconds, then remove the iron. Don't blow on the joint—it will be weak if it cools too quickly.

9. When the joint has cooled, clean the joint with rubbing alcohol and bind it with electrical tape.

Finito!

Connecting with Screw-On Wire Connectors

The easiest way to connect unstranded or solid, single-conductor wire (the kind you'll find in your walls) is with fast, cheap, and virtually foolproof screw-on wire connectors, often called by the trade name, wire nuts. These little plastic gizmos screw onto the ends of wires and solidly join them in a joint that can be taken apart later on. Each size screw-on wire connector works on a certain number of wires of various sizes; this information is listed on the package. I try to keep three sizes around—which is plenty for any wiring problem I'll face.

Screw-on wire connectors are a real no-brainer to use. You'll need wire strippers, the connectors, and possibly a pair of pliers. Use these steps to join wires with these handy connectors:

1. Strip all wires about ⁵/₈ inch (see the package for the exact length).

2. Hold the wires with the ends aligned and flush, and slip the nut over the top (see the following figure).

> **Don't Screw Up!**
> According to the National Electric Code, the only place that is safe and acceptable to join wires is in junction boxes. And all junction boxes must be accessible without taking walls apart. So don't join wires outside a box, or hide a box behind a wall. If you really need to make a connection where there's no box, install a box in a wall or ceiling and cover it with a blank cover plate so it's accessible from within the room.

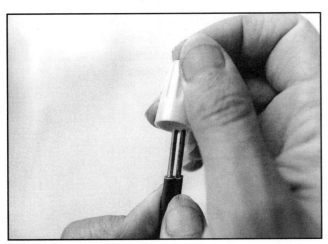

To connect wires with a screw-on wire connector, just slip the connector on top of the stripped ends of the wires, and twist it clockwise.

3. Twist the nut clockwise, as seen from the top. If you have a weak grip, tighten gently with pliers.

4. Tug to check that all wires are tight. You should not be able to see exposed bare wire (unless you're joining ground wires).

That's all there is to it—no goop, no heat, no solder.

You can also use screw-on wire connector on multistrand wire, but it's more difficult. Twist the wires together, screw on the nut, then tug securely to make sure all wires are joined. Multistrand wire, which is more flexible than single-strand wire, is used in extension and appliance cords, and dimmer switches.

Connecting to Switches and Outlets

Outlets love connections so much that they generally have four slip-in connectors and four screw terminals for connecting to incoming and outgoing wires. Switches always have screw terminals, and sometimes slip-in connectors as well.

Handy Hint
Having trouble reinstalling a fixture connected to a mess of wires? Make a U-shaped bend in the wires about $1/2$ inch away from the connector, then grab the connector with pliers and stuff the wires into the back of the box. That way, you won't stress the joint or damage the insulation.

Slip-in connectors are easy. A "strip gauge" on the back of the outlet shows how much insulation to remove—about $5/8$ inch. Then just stick the bare end of the wire into a round hole on the back of the receptacle (the white goes near the silver-colored screws, and the black near the brass screws). The connector grips the wire in place. Give a little tug to make sure the connection is solid, and you are done. To release the wire, stick a finishing nail (the circuit is off, isn't it?) into the slot near the wire and pull the wire out.

To connect a wire to a screw terminal, strip the end of the wire and form a loop that will stay on the terminal as you tighten the screw. If you make the loop backward, the screw's twisting will open the loop. I find it easier to make a hook, place it over the screw, and bend the wire around the screw before tightening. You'll need a wire stripper, screwdriver, long-nose pliers, and the switch or outlet. Use these steps to connect a wire to a screw terminal:

1. Strip about $3/4$ inch from the wire.

2. Make a hook with long-nose pliers.

3. Slip the hook over the screw in the direction shown, *never* the reverse.

4. Squeeze the hook tight (ape-man force not needed) with long-nose pliers (see the photo showing how to attach to a screw terminal).

5. Tighten the screw, making sure the wire stays under the screw head.

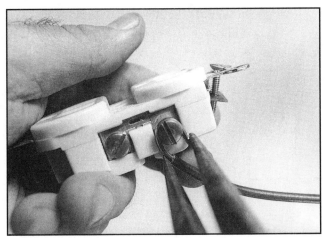

Long-nose pliers are perfect for closing a hook over the screw. Then simply tighten the screw for a secure connection.

Switches

Switches usually control built-in lights, but they also can control outlets, motors, fans, and other conveniences. Let's get acquainted.

One "single-pole" or "two-way" switch controls one or more lights. The switch has two terminals, and its toggle is marked "on" and "off." A two-way switch can be located either before or after the light it controls. Both configurations control current to the light; the wiring pattern is chosen for convenience at the time of wiring.

In a switch that's *before the light*, the power comes through the switch (see illustration). Because a white (neutral) wire is present in the switch box, you can wire an outlet to this switch box. (Note: Not all switches have a ground screw; many are grounded by contacting a grounded box.)

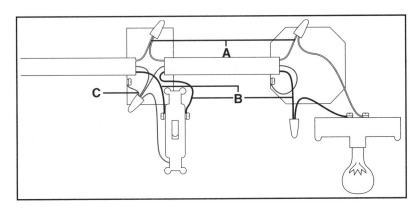

A 2-way switch *before the light* (current comes to the switch first). White wires are joined with a screw-on wire connector in the switch box.

(A) White (neutral) wire

(B) Black (hot) wire

(C) Bare (ground) wire

In a switch *"at the end of the run,"* power comes through the light box. The white wire leading to the switch terminals should be painted black, or flagged with black electrician's tape. Because there's no neutral at the switch box, you can't add an outlet to the switch.

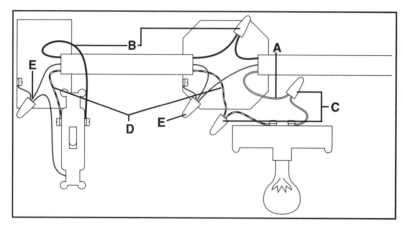

A 2-way switch *after the light*. Current comes to the light box first, then is diverted to the switch, which controls the current flows to the light.

(A)   White (neutral) wire

(B)   Black (hot) wire

(C)   If the light fixture does not have wire leads, omit these screw-on wire connectors.

(D)   The white wire should be painted or taped black, indicating that it is serving as a hot wire.

(E)   Bare (ground) wire

IMPORTANT: The neutral (or white) wire is never switched. (However, if a white wire is used as a hot wire, it is switched and flagged with black tape.) The neutral wire must always be continuous so current can return to the circuit breaker or fuse box. Switches control the supply of current *to* the light, not the current coming from it.

Don't Screw Up!
Some electrical boxes contain wires unrelated to the fixture in the box. These wires don't connect to the fixture, and you should try not to touch them. If they are controlled by a different circuit breaker, they might be hot even after you shut off power to the fixture in the box.

Two "three-way" switches are used to control one or more lights (they're commonly found at both ends of stairs or hallways). A three-way switch has three terminals, and the toggle *is not* marked "on" and "off" because you cannot tell from the toggle position whether the light is on or off. Three-way switches require a cable with three conductors (red, black, and white) plus a bare ground wire. Generally, you can replace them by simply matching up the wiring you find.

Three "four-way" switches can be used to control a light. They have four terminals, but they're rare, and are outside idiot territory.

Need More Outlets?

The need for outlets—aka plug-ins or receptacles—has mushroomed along with the invention of a million uses for electricity: dehumidifiers, heat guns, hair dryers, curling irons, bacon-fryers, seal-a-meals, electric can openers—the creation of these "electrical necessities" has been a triumph of the twentieth century. If you've lived in a house that was last wired fifty years ago, you know that nobody foresaw how much juice a home would eventually need. When you try to plug in all this junk—whether in a home office, kitchen, or a basement—you're going to suffer outlet inadequacy.

Don't Screw Up!
Treat old wires with respect. They're likely to be brittle, and if one breaks, you may end with a lead that's too short.

A simple solution to the shortage of outlets, if a grounded outlet is nearby, is to screw a 6-outlet expander to the face of it. Or you can double up an existing outlet by installing a pair of duplex receptacles in a new, double-size box. You'll have to remove the outlet and the box, and cut the drywall or plaster to hold a 4-inch box. (If the existing box is a handy box, you can screw a second to it, possibly without removing any wiring.) Cut short leads of black, white, and bare wire to connect two receptacles, side by side, so you have four outlets.

But if you don't have electricity where you need it, or can't abide the sight of a snarl of wires bulging from one spot on the wall, you'll need to install an outlet. Remember, as you think about putting in more "plug-ins," that each circuit has a capacity, in amps, that should never be exceeded. To figure out how many amps are already on a circuit, see the section on "Making a Circuit Map" in Chapter 24. A final note: The devices on a circuit can draw more total amps than the rating, BUT NOT AT ONE TIME.

Installing an Outlet—The Basics

When deciding where to place an outlet, the first step is figuring out where you want it. Then you'll have to figure out where it's easy to get power (running cable to a new outlet is the hardest part of installing outlets). The following places should be relatively easy:

➤ Near an existing outlet (see "Running Cable in the House: Your Options," later in this chapter).

➤ On the reverse (opposite) side of a wall with an existing outlet.

➤ Beneath a switch box that contains *a neutral wire* (see "Adding an Outlet to a Two-Way Light Switch," later).

➤ Near an accessible basement, attic, or attached garage (see "Using the Basement or Attic," later).

➤ Anywhere you can tolerate the sight of surface cable carriers on the wall or baseboard (see "Surface Wiring," later).

To install a new outlet, you will need a drill, saber saw or keyhole saw, screwdriver, circuit tester, wire stripper, new outlet, electrical box, screw-on wire connectors, and cover plate. Use these steps to install the outlet:

1. Plan how you will get power to the new outlet. You may be able to feed cable through one stud (stick a long drill through the box hole). You can also run cable along the baseboard, or through a ceiling or basement. If you can't get power to the outlet, stop right here and find a better location.

2. Measure the height from the floor of other outlets in the room. Locate the studs in the area (see "Six Ways to Find a Stud" in Chapter 20). It's easiest to screw the new electrical outlet box to a stud. You also can screw it to wood lath, or secure it to drywall with the sheet-metal thingamajiggies shown in the photo of electrical paraphernalia in the last chapter. Now, with the box located, mark a horizontal line at the outlet location with a level.

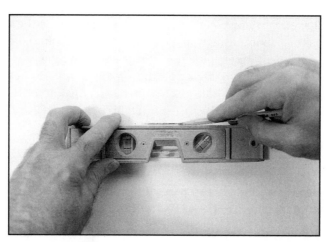

To place an outlet accurately, mark the first line with a level.

3. Shut off the circuit (see "Making Sure an Outlet Is Cold," in Chapter 24) and pull the faceplate off the existing outlet. Pull out the receptacle and make sure you have enough room in the box for a new cable. If not, you may have to install a larger box first.

4. Using the new box, trace the cutout on the wall, as shown on facing page.

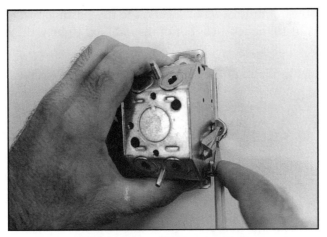

A box serves as its own template

5. Using a $^3/_8$-inch bit, drill holes to start the saw and to allow room for the screws.

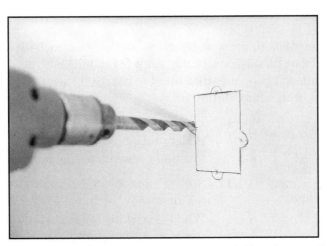

Drill holes to allow room for the saw blade. For the box shown, drill at the x marks to allow room for mounting screws and brackets, then saw from the drill holes.

6. Saw out the opening with a saber saw, keyhole saw, or drywall saw. Press the saber saw hard against the wall to prevent vibration. Make the hole slightly larger than the box, so the box can slip in, but smaller than the cover plate.

7. Disassemble the old box (the one supplying power to the new box). If the wiring seems complicated, mark the wires to simplify reassembly, but in general, everything should be black to black, white to white, and bare to bare. If the box does not have built-in cable connectors, loosen the box, remove a knock-out, and insert a connector and screw it tight.

8. Feed new cable from the new box location to the existing box, through the connector, until about 10 inches sticks out of the old box. Tighten the connector and remount the old box.

9. Strip the outer insulation from about 8 inches of the new cable (don't cut the inner insulation).

10. Strip wire ends and observe the cardinal rule of wiring: black to black and white to white. Using a screw-on wire connector, connect the old ground wire entering the old box to:

    A wire to the old box (unless it's plastic; plastic boxes need no grounding);

    A wire to the old receptacle; and

    The ground wire to the new box.

11. Reinstall the receptacle, but leave the cover plate off.

12. At the box you are installing, cut the new cable so about 10 inches will protrude from the box. Draw the cable into the new box (see step 8) and tighten the cable clamp.

13. Fasten the new box to the stud, using two or three 1¼-inch drywall screws. If no stud is available: (a) slip some handy strips behind the box, hold the box-front flush with the wall, and bend the strips into the box; or (b) screw the box to wood lath, or (c) use a box with self-mounting strips.

Handy Hint
A vegetable peeler is great for stripping the outer insulation from romex cable without harming the wires inside.

14. Wire up the outlet, referring to step 10. Screw the outlet to the box and turn the circuit on to test it (see "Testing a Receptacle," later in this chapter).

15. If there's a problem, examine both outlets to check for loose wires, or failure to keep colors separate. When everything tests okay, shut the circuit off, screw on the cover plates, and restore the power.

Adding an Outlet Near an Existing Outlet

Sometimes it's easier to add a nearby outlet (as you'll see in the following illustration) rather than expand a box to two duplex receptacles. If you're within one stud of the existing outlet, there's no need to do heavy construction to connect the cable from the old outlet to the new one—a big time-saver. The outlets can also be on the opposite sides of a wall.

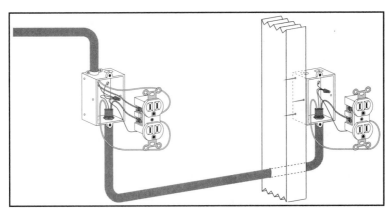

The easy way to double an outlet is to install another outlet nearby.

Adding an Outlet to a Two-Way Light Switch

Switches offer an easy place to connect outlets—if both hot (black) and neutral (white) wires are present. How can you tell? Shut off the circuit, remove the switch plate, remove two mounting screws holding the switch in place, and gently pull it from the wall.

If only one cable is entering the box, it has only hot wires (the white wire in the cable should be painted black or flagged with electrician's tape) and you can't wire an outlet (see the figures illustrating two-way switch wiring earlier in this chapter). However, if two cables are coming into the box, and the black wire from each cable is connected to one switch terminal, and the whites are connected to each other, and bare ground wires are also present, you're in luck, because you can wire an outlet to this box.

To attach an outlet to a two-way switch, you'll need a circuit tester, stripper, box, outlet, screw-on wire connectors, and a cover plate. Then follow these steps:

1. Turn the circuit off (see "Making Sure a Light Switch Is Cold," in Chapter 24). Figure out which black wire supplies the box: Turn the circuit back on, turn the switch to "off," and carefully hold one lead of the tester to ground, and the other to each switch terminal in succession. The hot terminal is connected to the black wire supplying the box. Flag that wire with tape.

2. Shut the circuit off again. Insert your new cable into the box, remove the outer insulation, and strip the ends about $3/4$ inch.

3. If you are afraid of getting confused, mark the wires with tape. Remove the black supply wire you flagged from the screw terminal.

4. Cut an 8-inch piece of black wire from a scrap of cable and strip both ends. Using a screw-on wire connector, connect this lead to the old black supply wire and to the new black wire feeding your new outlet. Push these wires into the back of the box.

5. Attach the 8-inch black lead to the screw terminal you loosened in step 3.

6. Loosen the connector holding the white wires, insert the white wire from the new cable, and retighten. Repeat for the ground wire. (You may need larger connectors to hold the extra wires.)

The connections at the switch box should now be as follows:

Black: One screw-on wire connector joins (a) the old supply wire, (b) the wire to the new outlet, and (c) the 8-inch lead supplying the switch.

White: One connector joins all three wires.

Bare: One screw-on wire connector joins the incoming ground wire to (a) a lead to the box, (b) the switch (if it has a ground screw), and (c) the new receptacle. (Many switches are grounded by contacting a grounded box, not by a ground wire.) Reassemble the switch and screw the switch plate back on.

7. Make the following connection in the new (outlet) box:

White and black go to their respective terminals on the receptacle.

Bare: A screw-on wire connector joins wires (a) from the old box, (b) the new box, and (c) the receptacle.

8. Restore power and test the new outlet.

Testing a Receptacle

When you're finished installing a receptacle, it's only sensible to check that it works. With the cover plate on and the power on, insert one prong of your electrical tester in the narrow (hot) slot of the outlet. Touch the other to the wider (neutral) slot. If the tester lights, test the hot and ground slots. If the tester lights again, the outlet is okay. If not, shut off the power and fix any loose or broken wires, and check that the black wire goes to the brass screw, and the white to the silver-colored screw.

When Not to Install an Outlet

Although you can add an extra outlet or two to most circuits, some circuits—like those feeding a refrigerator or a furnace—should be left alone. Why? So a problem with another device on the circuit, say a video game or a bacon-fryer, does not trip the breaker and shut down your furnace on a January night, while you are drinking margaritas and watching the sunset in Acapulco.

Likewise, all 240-volt circuits, used for water pumps, stoves, dryers, and water heaters, should feed only one appliance. These circuits are easy to recognize, because the circuit breaker is twice as big as normal, and the outlet is an unusual, three-prong monster.

Running Cable in the House: Your Options

Electricity can't take the plane, it can't take the train, and it can't take a tram from point A to point B. If you want to give electricity a ride from an old outlet or switch to a new one, you've got to run some cable. Make no mistake: This can be the most unpleasant part of updating an electric system, because it could require you to rip out drywall (that's fun, but then you'll have to repair it). Following are some relatively easy routes for running new cable.

Baseboard

A baseboard that is at least 3 inches high offers a decent location to run cable. You will need a utility knife, hammer, drywall nails or screws, scrap drywall, a drill with $1/2$ inch or larger wood-metal bit, and a carpenter's square or straight length of 1×3. After you've gathered your tools, use these steps to put the new cable in place:

1. Pull off the quarter-round and molding at least as far as the stud past the new cable run (see "Yanking Up Molding with Scarcely a Split," in Chapter 20).

2. Cut the drywall horizontally, at least 2 inches above the floor and $1/2$ inch below the top of the baseboard (measure the baseboard if it's not obvious where it reached on the wall). Cut the drywall vertically down the middle of each stud at each end of the cable run. Remove drywall from the cut down to the floor.

3. Using a $1/2$-inch bit, drill through the bottom of each stud to make a pathway for the cable. Drill close to the center of each stud, at about 90 degrees.

4. Put the cable into place and feed it into the old and new electrical boxes. Let 12 inches protrude from the box to allow enough wire for the connections.

5. Finish your electrical hookups and test.

6. Cut a new piece of drywall to fit, nail or screw it in place, and replace the baseboard. Don't bother taping the drywall—it will be covered by baseboard. Its role is to let the baseboard lie flat.

7. Renail the baseboard and molding, taking care not to nail through the cable. Fill the holes with wood filler and stain or paint.

Using the Basement or Attic

If you need a new outlet near the floor on the ground floor, you may be able to wire it through a basement or crawl space. Eighteen-inch drill bits are useful for this kind of work because they can go all the way from the new box into the basement. (Do some reconnoitering first so you don't drill into something awkward like wiring, a duct, or a pipe.)

You can also wire through the attic, using the same jumbo drill bit.

Surface Wiring

If all these discussions of sawing drywall or drilling floors are making you a bit queasy (and nobody said this would be a bucket of laughs), there's a homely but acceptable solution called surface-mounted wiring. You've seen this before, usually as an earth-tone blemish running along baseboards and walls. The stuff is flexible, adaptable, and easy to use, although the outlets look suspiciously like rectangular blobs stuck to the wall. You may be able to hide the stuff behind some furniture. Otherwise, hire an electrician to put in some new outlets or circuits.

When Do You Need Electrical Help?

The easy answer is when you're confused, and before sparks start flying. Wiring, like astrophysics, has a way of sounding simpler when someone else describes it, and there's no way two chapters can cover every circumstance you might encounter. For example, say you find an ugly knot of wires inside a box, many of which don't connect to the fixture in the box. Although this is normal—electricians route wires wherever it's most convenient—you've got to remember that these wires could be on several breakers or fuses. In this case, how will you make sure every wire is cold? You could open up screw-on wire connectors and test the wires, but they may be hot. If you're a truly determined do-it-yourselfer, you could pull the main disconnect to work on the circuit, but I'd consider calling the wire wizards in a case like this.

Three- and four-way switches are another potential problem area, since there are so many possible ways to wire the switches, supply, and load. (If you're just replacing a switch, you can probably get by wiring the new one exactly as the old one was wired—using masking tape to identify wires. But if you can't tell which switch is causing the problem, I'd suggest picking up the phone instead of the circuit tester.)

Handy Hint
Let your confusion be your guide. Electrical work is not difficult, and properly done, not dangerous, either. But an overwhelming level of confusion on your part is a sign worth heeding. Get advice, get help, or get both.

You also may run into wiring done by a blew-it-yourselfer—somebody who had yet to meet the first principles of wiring: grounding, matching wire colors, or observing circuit capacity. It may be hard—bordering on impossible—to correct that kind of work, and I wouldn't suggest it.

Plugged In—The Phone Story

Now that telephone companies are charging astronomical rates to install and repair phone wiring, homeowners have an incentive to understand their wiring. Fortunately, standardization and the modular, plug-and-play mentality have prevailed in phone wiring for many years; and phone wiring is extremely simple.

And because the voltage in a phone system is low, you don't even need to worry about shutting off circuits. However, the 90-volt dc ringing current can still give you a pretty decent jolt if the phone happens to ring when you're monkeying with the wiring. Thus if there's a quick-disconnect at the telephone company interface (where the house wiring meets the phone company's wiring), it's smart to disconnect it before working on the lines.

If you want to add jacks (phone outlets), just observe these pointers:

➤ Phone cable has three or four conductors. Four-conductor cable (black, red, green, and yellow) can carry two separate lines. The three-wire cable can carry one line.

➤ Modular jacks are used to attach the plug-in phone lines to the phone cables running through a house. They are marked "B," "R," "G," and "Y," to indicate which wire goes where.

➤ Modular plugs, and the cords attached to them, come in two sizes. The larger ones link phones to the wall wiring; the smaller ones link handsets to phones. The sizes are not interchangeable.

➤ Electronics supply stores stock a good range of gizmos for linking phone systems—wire, connectors, staples, and jacks. For example, they sell a "splitter" which allows a modular jack carrying two phone lines to feed two separate phones.

➤ When you're running phone cable in the house, an 18-inch drill bit can be handy for reaching between floors.

➤ To connect a new jack, either: (a) attach to the screw terminals on the metal block where the phone wire enters the house; (b) solder into a phone cable; or (c) attach to an existing phone jack.

The Least You Need to Know

➤ Electrical devices are made for easy connections; screw-on wire connectors can take care of most other connections.

➤ Switch wiring patterns vary according to whether the power feeds into the switch or into the light box.

➤ Replacing switches is usually just a matter of copying the existing wiring.

➤ Adding outlets can be easy, difficult, or impossible; the limiting factor is how easy it is to supply current to the new outlet.

➤ You can tap a new outlet off a two-way switch if power comes to the switch (neutral will be present in the switch box), but not if power is supplied through the light.

➤ Baseboards, attics, basements, crawl spaces, and outlets on the other side of the wall are all good sources of power for a new outlet.

➤ Phone wiring is as simple as matching wire colors.

Chapter 26

A Welcome Blast of Hot Air—Heating System Tips

In This Chapter

➤ Troubleshooting and maintaining your heating system

➤ Simple tune-ups and repairs you can make

➤ Chimney safety, inspection, maintenance, and repair

Heating systems can be temperamental. When my first son, Alex, was trying to get himself born, I pleaded with my heating repair guy, "I'm in the delivery room, and my wife is about to give birth, and my neighbor tells me it's 44 degrees in my house, and it's *winter* here in Wisconsin, and could you *pulleeze* get over to my house before the pipes turn to icicles?"

True, you could prevent this kind of humiliation (and countless other kinds) by not having children, but that's giving the furnace more power than it deserves. The lesson I took away is to pay more attention to sob stories from the furnace in the first place. You see, I already knew the clanky old thing had a cracked heat exchanger, and that's the one part that can't be replaced in most furnaces.

At least I earned a good story from the experience—as did the repair guy, who's probably still chuckling about that moron who thought the only way he could get immediate service was to lie that his wife was in labor!

Heating systems do two things: They create heat, and they distribute it. Heat usually comes from burning natural gas, propane, or fuel oil; it's usually distributed as hot air, hot water, or steam. With so many fuels and designs in service, there's no way this book can cover them all.

And while I had intended to talk about air conditioning as well, there is nothing user-serviceable in the average cooling system. Even though I've written a book on industrial and commercial air conditioning, I still hire an expert to work on my system, so you shouldn't feel bad if you do likewise. The same precaution applies to heat pumps, which use air-conditioning technology to heat and cool the house. However, the thermostat, filter, and duct information that follows does apply to air-conditioning and heat-pump systems.

Instead of discussing things that are best left to experts, in this chapter I'll concentrate on user-serviceable parts of the heating system, then conclude with some troubleshooting suggestions.

Understand Your Thermostat

A thermostat is a thermally operated switch that signals the furnace when to start and stop burning. The thermostat "calls for" heat by sending an electrical signal to open the gas valve (in a gas furnace) or start the burner motor (in an oil furnace). When the house warms up enough, the thermostat shuts the flame off. Thermostats don't directly control the heat distribution system—that's the job of the fan and limit control (see the figure illustrating the roles of the thermostat and fan-and-limit control during the heating season).

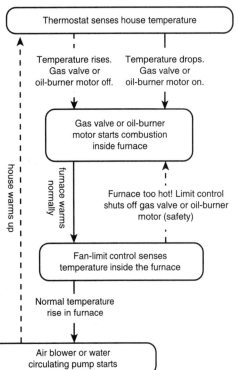

When house temperature drops below the set point, the thermostat sends an electric current to open the gas valve or fire up the oil-burner motor. When the furnace warms up, the fan control closes a switch, sending current to the air-circulating fan, or the water-circulating pump. If the furnace gets too hot, the limit control closes the gas valve or stops the oil-burner motor, shutting down the furnace for safety. In cooling mode, the thermostat starts the cooling system when the set point is exceeded. To reduce energy consumption, "set-back" thermostats can be set to a cooler temperature at night (and sometimes during the day, when

Roles of the thermostat and fan-and-limit control

the house is unoccupied). The idea is that you can stay warm when you're up and about, but sleep in cooler, more economical conditions. The thermostat package may give some indication of how much money you can expect to save (if any) with a set-back thermostat, compared to a conventional one.

Thermostats have an adjustable "anticipator" mechanism to prevent rapid on-off cycling of the furnace. The anticipator allows room temperature to cool a couple of degrees before the furnace restarts; otherwise, the furnace would continually cycle on and off, which is not just annoying, but harmful to the system. If your furnace is cycling too rapidly, increase the anticipator setting (consult the instructions for your thermostat). On the other hand, if the furnace is cycling too slowly, and the room cools too much before the furnace kicks in, reduce the anticipator setting.

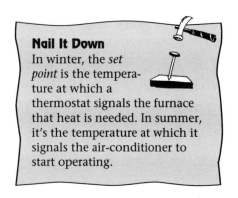

Nail It Down

In winter, the *set point* is the temperature at which a thermostat signals the furnace that heat is needed. In summer, it's the temperature at which it signals the air-conditioner to start operating.

Fan and Limit Control

The fan-and-limit control is a thermally operated switch that regulates the blower (in hot-air systems) or circulating pump (in hot-water systems). Please see the figure "Roles of the thermostat and fan-and-limit control," earlier in this chapter). Caution: This switch commonly wears out in older furnaces.

The fan portion of the switch signals the heat-circulating apparatus to start operating after the furnace has warmed up sufficiently—otherwise, the system would circulate cold water or air. (The lag between the burner start-up and the start of the circulating fan is called the *system delay*.)

The blower or water pump keeps running after the furnace shuts off. When the furnace temperature falls below a second, cooler set point, the fan or pump stops circulating, and the whole system idles until the thermostat calls for more heat. However, if the furnace gets too hot for any reason, the limit control shuts off the burner to prevent fire.

Pilot Lights, Thermocouples, and Gas Flames

A pilot light is a small flame that burns constantly in older gas furnaces and water heaters. Its job is to light the gas so the furnace can start operating. Just above the pilot light is a *thermocouple*, a thermally operated safety device. If the thermocouple does not sense heat, it "thinks" the pilot light is off and shuts down gas flow.

You won't see a pilot light on modern furnaces and water heaters, which use electric (spark) ignition instead. Electronic ignitions are highly reliable and economical, because they don't burn gas unless heat is needed, but they are not owner-maintainable.

To light a pilot, follow these steps:

1. Turn the main gas valve off.

2. Find a long match while you wait five minutes for any gas to dissipate.

3. Turn the gas valve to "pilot."

4. Now press the red button on the pilot valve down and light the pilot (the button overrides the thermocouple, allowing gas to flow even though the pilot is off).

5. Hold the red button down for a minute, while the pilot warms the thermocouple. The pilot should stay lit when you release the button. If it doesn't, wait five minutes for the gas to dissipate and repeat the process.

6. Turn the main gas valve to "on." If the thermostat is calling for heat, the furnace should ignite. In any case, the pilot should remain lit.

On a gas furnace, a blue flame with a few tips of yellow gives the highest efficiency and makes the least soot. You should be able to adjust the air intake to achieve this kind of flame, but see "Know When You Need Help," later in this chapter, first.

Furnace Wiring

As a safety measure, a furnace should always monopolize its electrical circuit. Otherwise, a short circuit in something less important, like a lava lamp, could blow a fuse and freeze your home in January. (How does the lava lamp know to malfunction in January, while you are out skiing the Rockies? Karma, that's why. But that's slightly beyond our scope here.)

If my furnace blew its breaker even once, I would go scurrying to my furnace guru—a good furnace should not draw anything near the 15 or 20 amps that would trip a breaker or blow a fuse.

Replacing Filters for Fun and Profit

Furnace filters—found in hot-air systems only—are generally quite easy to replace, and you can find the common sizes at anything from a supermarket to a hardware store. Your best guide to the frequency of replacement is the condition of the used filters. If only a little crud has accumulated, then you may be replacing them too often. But if the filter is a filthy gray, you've waited too long. It all depends on how dusty your house is, and on how much of that dust gets into your ducts.

Allergic? Then Meet These High-Performance Filters

Because simple filters don't catch enough flying crud for people with serious allergies, several companies have begun selling high-performance dust catchers. You'll have to get a furnace specialist to install these gadgets, because the ductwork must be changed, but the payoff is fewer allergic reactions and possibly a cleaner house. Some of these improved filters have an accordion-shaped paper filter that you can clean with a vacuum. Even more effective are electrostatic precipitators, which put an electric charge on the dust, then "pull" it to a disposal plate by electrical attraction.

Damper Adjustment

Forced-air heating systems generally have a damper (an adjustable shut-off plate) in each duct, to regulate airflow. You can see the simple crank handles that operate these dampers in ducts in the basement or crawl space. These handles follow the plumber's convention for valves: When the handle is oriented across the line of flow, the valve is closed, and when it's parallel to the flow, it's open.

You can use dampers to balance the airflow around the house. If a room is too hot, close the damper a bit; if it's too cold, open its damper (or close other dampers to force more hot air to the cold room). If you have trouble figuring out which duct goes where, ask someone to bang on the various registers while you listen in the basement. Then label the ducts with a marker.

Bleeding Radiators

Like politicians, radiators (which distribute heat in hot-water systems) are prone to filling with hot air. Unlike politicians, however, radiators are equipped with a valve for removing ("bleeding") this hot air. (Otherwise, the radiator can't fill with hot water, and the furnace can't distribute enough heat.) The bleeder valve is at the top of each radiator; some valves require a special, square wrench (hardware stores sell them); others turn with a screwdriver. Just open the valve until water comes out (catch the spill in a cup). Bleed the system every fall, then refill the system with water by opening a valve on the water inlet to the reservoir or boiler.

Draining the Boiler

Hot water systems have boilers—big tanks usually in the basement—and boilers collect sludge. Once a month during the heating season, it's a good idea to drain a couple of quarts of water from a boiler, which will remove most of the sediment. Look for a valve near the bottom, but use a bit of caution. If the valve has not been operated for a long time, it may not close securely, and may need repacking (see the section on faucet repair in Chapter 27).

Troubleshooting

Heating-system troubleshooting can grow into a murky, complex subject that is not idiot-proof. The following troubleshooting guide can cover only the most obvious problems (see Table 26.1).

Table 26.1 Troubleshooting heating systems

Problem	Cause	Cure
General problems		
No heat, no response from furnace	Blown breaker or fuse	Reset breaker or replace fuse
	Thermostat not calling for heat	Repair or replace thermostat
	Emergency safety switch off	Turn switch on
	Furnace door open	Close door
Gas burner not functioning	Pilot out	Relight pilot (see "Pilot Lights, Thermocouples, and Gas Flames," earlier in this chapter); clean pilot opening if gas is not coming out
	Pilot valve set in pilot mode	Set in "heat" mode
Pilot won't stay lit	Thermocouple (the heat sensor that allows gas to flow to the burner—see "Pilot Lights, Thermocouples, and Gas Flames," earlier in this chapter) is loose or broken, shutting the gas valve	Tighten thermocouple connection nut slightly, or replace thermocouple
	Pilot flame is not heating the thermocouple	If flame is misdirected, read pilot fixture or thermocouple; or turn pilot valve to enlarge pilot flame

Problem	Cause	Cure
Oil burner malfunctioning	Empty oil tank, oil filter plugged, or valve is shut	Add oil, turn valve, or replace filter
	Burner motor not starting	Check the master switch (if your home has two, one on the burner, and another at the top of the basement stairs, both must be "on")
		Push the reset button on the safety control on the furnace stack. Push the reset button on the burner motor.
Forced-air systems		
Inadequate flow of warm air	Dirty filter	Clean or replace filter
	Air registers dirty or blocked by furniture or drapes	Clean registers or move obstructions
	Air leaks in ducts with duct tape	Find leaks and cover them
	Dampers on ducts closed or maladjusted (can also cause large temperature differences between rooms)	See "Damper Adjustment," earlier in this chapter
Hot water systems		
Top of radiators or baseboard heaters are cold; inadequate heat	Air in the system	See "Bleeding Radiators," earlier in this chapter
Water coming out of safety valve on top of the expansion tank	The tank should contain air and water; if it's hot all over, it's waterlogged	Call heating technician to bleed the tank
Leaks at shut-off valve on radiator or baseboard heater	Valve packing is dry or worn	Try tightening nut around the valve stem. If that doesn't work, drain system until water level is below the valve, and repack (see "Faucet Repair [Dig it! Whatsa Trouble with the Spigot?]," in Chapter 27).

Know When You Need Help

Heating work, like other repairs, is not for everyone; as usual, the key sign that you need help is confusion. And because many of the repairs involve electrical controls, you must be comfortable working with simple control systems, and possibly with various electrical gauges, which is totally out of our league. And don't forget that many people recommend an annual service call on oil and gas furnaces, just to keep them in tune. My advice: Skim off the cream of the repairs and maintenance, and leave the heavy lifting for the pros.

Santa Don't Like Your Chimney, and Other Ruminations on Chimney Fires

If you burn wood in a fireplace or stove, you owe it to yourself to keep a close eye on your chimney. The hazard is simple: An accumulation of a black, stinky goo called creosote can catch fire and burn your house down. Creosote, the product of partial combustion of wood, condenses on the flue because the flue is relatively cool. This glop burns quite hot (above 1,500 degrees Fahrenheit). Chimney fires, which often burn unnoticed until it's too late, are a major cause of house fires in winter.

To contain chimney fires, chimneys must be lined with a metal or ceramic flue liner, which is supposedly able to withstand the high temperature created during these fires. Before using a chimney for burning wood, I'd ask a chimney expert or mason to inspect it.

Creosote condenses on the chimney most quickly if you:

➤ Burn green (uncured) wood)

➤ Set an airtight stove to burn slowly (with the air intakes almost closed)

➤ Have a cold chimney, with lots of exposure to the outside

➤ Have a long chimney

Removing a creosote accumulation is a pro job. But if the chimney is *in good condition* (as demonstrated by a recent inspection), you can burn out creosote before it accumulates by starting fires with a lot of paper and plenty of air. A big fire will briefly enter the chimney and flare off the creosote before it gets a chance to cause problems. *Do not try this* unless you are sure the chimney is clean and in good condition, as it could start a chimney fire.

(To repeat: If you're not sure the chimney is clean and sound, *don't operate* the stove or fireplace.)

The Least You Need to Know

➤ Many minor sources of heating-system trouble, including problems with the furnace and the heat-distribution system, should be within your grasp.

➤ A furnace should always occupy its own circuit—to prevent problems elsewhere from shutting off your heat.

➤ A variety of high-tech filters can ease life for allergy sufferers.

➤ If you're feeling that queasy "can I really do this?" feeling, back off. The heating system is no place to learn which way to turn a screw.

➤ Chimney fires are a leading cause of fire in northern states, but they are highly preventable.

Either It Leaks . . . (Plumbing, Part I)

So you've been putting off that little plumbing repair? Believe me, I understand the fear of plumbing—did you notice I left it for last in this book? I just finished installing a water softener—a "simple" project that consumed seven aggravating hours, three trips to the hardware store, and most of my stock of "marital goodwill."

I'm not the only do-it-yourselfer who finds plumbing extremely tough. A few years ago, trying to fix my kitchen sink, I installed a repair kit—and watched as a drip grew into a steady stream. Then I put in a "universal" replacement cartridge—and uncorked a geyser to rival Old Faithful. My friend Richie Salomon called to offer the kind of wisdom that can only come from a Sanskrit professor who spends his spare time fiddling with a '53 Studebaker. "You bought a 'universal' repair kit," he sneered. "That means it fits everyone's but yours."

So after a grateful nod to Professor Salomon for his timeless wisdom, in this chapter we'll plumb the mysterious depths of plumbing—the stuff you can't live with, and can't live without.

The Basic Principles of Plumbing

Everybody knows plumbing is devious and vindictive, a fountain of bafflement and consternation. It's something that can cause you to grab the phone more quickly than any other kind of repair. But plumbing also responds to some simple physical laws:

Water seeks its own level.

The more water pressure there is, the more likely something will leak.

Drain pipes get larger as they go downstream, because they must carry more water. Supply pipes get smaller as they go downstream, because they must carry less water.

Hot water is more corrosive than cold water.

Falling water must be replaced by air (from the venting system).

Don't put anything (like leaded solder or other contaminants) in your water supply that you don't want to drink.

Watch the sequence of parts during disassembly—lay them out, all facing the same way. You'll find that the most innocent-looking parts may be reassembled in a bewildering number of wrong sequences.

Plumbing is governed by plumbing codes (contact your city or township building inspector if you need more information).

Finally (and I mean it literally this time), don't get in over your head. If you're totally confused, get information or get help.

Water Quality

Because people tend to drink the water that comes from their pipes, it pays to pay attention to the condition of those pipes, as reflected in the quality of your water. If you're a city person, the city water system should be testing the supply—but it wouldn't hurt to check that they are doing their job. If you drink your own well water, it certainly seems logical to have the water tested occasionally—and, if it is contaminated, to install a filter or take other corrective measures.

A major cause of home water contamination is lead pipes, which were installed until about 1929. If your house was built before then, I would suggest testing for lead in the water. At the very least, look around for lead pipes—a soft, gray metal that's shiny when you scratch it. Tin solder, which was used to join copper pipes until recently, contained some lead, but it's a much smaller source of contamination. Nevertheless, you will solder copper pipes with lead-free solder, right?

If you have lead pipes, you can reduce your lead consumption by running the tap until it's cold before drinking or cooking with water, particularly in the morning. Don't drink hot water, which dissolves more lead. (If you have hard water, see "Hard Facts on Hard Water," next.)

Hard Facts on Hard Water

Hard water contains high levels of dissolved calcium and magnesium salts, which originate in rocks the groundwater flows through, and are usually called "lime" when they build up on something. If you have hard water, you may notice a white deposit on drinking glasses, and inside pipes and the toilet tank. Hard water is much less effective for cleaning clothes than soft water, because you need more additives, and soil tends to redeposit in the washer.

Lime does have one benefit—it accumulates inside pipes, coating lead pipes and leaded solder, and thus helping prevent water contamination. Nevertheless, lime is hard on the plumbing, because it clogs small openings and builds up inside the water heater (think of it as the cholesterol of a plumbing system). Here are some suggestions for controlling liming problems:

➤ Lime can clog the holes underneath the *toilet* rim (these hard-to-see holes feed water into the bowl to cleanse it during flushing). If they're clogged, ream them out with a bent coathanger, then flush the toilet and clean them again.

➤ Lime can clog holes in a *showerhead* (look for a blocked or dribbling stream). Remove the screws holding the face plate (you probably don't need to remove the shower head) and soak it in strong vinegar. (If there's no faceplate, unscrew the shower head and disassemble it.) After a couple of hours, poke a wire or nail through the holes, then reassemble the head.

➤ Lime can cause big problems in a *water heater* where it builds up and acts as an insulator, thus reducing efficiency. The best solution is to install a water softener in the hot water lines, to remove lime before it reaches the heater.

➤ If lime builds up on fixtures (around the spigot or faucets) you may be able to dissolve it with strong vinegar. If this doesn't work, try one of the commercial acids sold for this purpose—using goggles and rubber gloves, naturally.

Tools and Materials

Plumbing can call for a wretched number of special tools, but for most purposes, a few basic ones will serve (see the photo of plumber's tools). Here are the bare minimum items to have:

Plunger: You'll probably need two, a small one for sinks, and a big one for toilets.

Pipe wrench (12" shown): Smaller ones are handy for tight quarters, like under the sink; larger ones are great for rusty pipe joints.

Pipe cutter: Cuts copper pipe quickly and cleanly.

Joint compound: Lubricates, rustproofs and seals threads of steel pipe, making disassembly much easier (you can use pipe-thread tape, but it's more expensive). Don't confuse this stuff with the cement used to join plastic pipe.

Seat reamer: Smoothes seats in compression faucets.

Smooth-jawed wrench: Turns polished fittings without wrecking the finish (or substitute an open-end or adjustable wrench).

Seat remover: Unscrews seats in compression faucets. One end is square, the other hexagonal.

Propane torch: Solders copper pipe, thaws frozen *metal* pipes.

Lead-free solder: Makes a non-toxic joint in copper pipe.

Soldering flux: Prevents corrosion, helps solder flow and bond.

Packing (graphite variety shown): Seals the shaft in older faucets.

O-ring: Makes a seal in many plumbing fixtures, including faucets and toilet parts.

Washers: For compression faucets only.

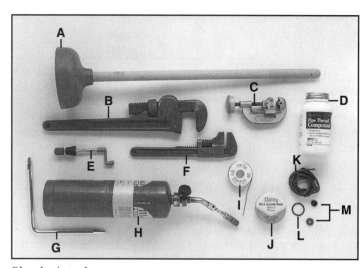

(A) Plunger
(B) Pipe wrench
(C) Pipe cutter
(D) Joint compound
(E) Seat reamer
(F) Smooth-jawed wrench
(G) Seat remover
(H) Propane torch
(I) Lead-free solder
(J) Soldering flux
(K) Packing
(L) O-ring
(M) Washers

Plumber's tools

Caution: depending on your plumbing project, you may also need a plumber's snake (used to unclog drains), cleaner and cement for PVC (polyvinyl chloride) pipe, buckets, a hacksaw, rag, level, a bountiful supply of patience and ingenuity, and almost anything else in your home toolbox.

A Little Terminology Goes a Long Way

When it comes to suggestive lingo, nobody can beat plumbers, who describe the mating surfaces (you listening, Dr. Freud?) of pipes and fittings as "male" or "female." The names of the common plumbing fittings are only slightly less self-explanatory, although they are significantly less titillating (see Table 27.1).

Table 27.1 Fitting identification

Fitting	Name	Description
	90° elbow	Turns a corner. A variation called the street elbow has one male and one female end. Another variation, the long-sweep 90° elbow, is used to connect to horizontal drain runs.
	45° elbow	You can also buy a $22^1/_2$° version.
	Reducer (bushing)	A male-to-female fitting that changes the size of piping—you can put one inside another to make a bigger change in size.
	Coupling (female thread or soldered fitting on both ends)	Joins two same or different diameter pipes.
	Union	Joins two pipes that cannot be turned because they are installed. Unscrew the large nut, and the union comes apart.
	Nipple (male thread on both ends)	A short section of pipe, available in various lengths; joins two fittings, like a valve and an elbow.
	Plug	Closes a female port on a fitting.
	Cap	Seals the end of a pipe.

continues

271

Table 27.1 Continued

Fitting	Name	Description
	Tee	Makes a three-way intersection of pipes with same or different sizes.
	Wye	Used for drain and waste lines, gives a better flow. The side outlet is angled, so water enters the drain without slowing down.

On the Virtue of a Main Water Shut-Off

The main shut-off is the valve that controls all water entering the house; it's usually located in some fiendishly inaccessible location next to the water meter, near the exterior wall at the front of the house. If you need to be convinced of the importance of main shut-offs, listen to the story of a Waterloo, Wisconsin, couple who had the good sense to flee south during the brutal winter of 1979 but didn't have enough sense to shut off the water. When a pipe froze in the basement, rising water snuffed out their furnace and formed a giant block of ice in the basement. By the time the unlucky couple returned from sunny Florida, their front steps were covered by a frozen cascade of water.

Handy Hint
Can't turn a plumbing joint? Join the club. Try banging on it with a hammer, drenching it in penetrating oil, or heating it with a propane torch. When it comes to breaking open a rusty joint, plumbing is like pro wrestling. The ends justify the means.

That flood is the best argument I can think of for shutting off your water when you leave town, particularly in winter. And because other plumbing emergencies can require quick action at the main shut-off, it wouldn't hurt to test the valve before you really need it. Unfortunately, because the shut-off is seldom used, it may not close completely. Repairing this valve is a pro job (because you've got to shut off the water outside the house), but if it's in working order, your plumbing repairs will be greatly simplified.

Nevertheless, you should be able to make some repairs with a drippy shut-off. Close the main valve off as much as you can, then open a faucet below the one you're fixing (or at the same level if necessary). This relieves the water pressure and should allow you to complete the repair without a flood.

Emergency Repairs

If you've got a leak that needs stopping now, first close the main shut-off (see the previous section). If that doesn't work, or you want water in the house for some other reason (like eating or drinking), try the following techniques to slow the leak enough to catch in a bucket while you plan a permanent repair or await the plumber.

➤ Stretch electrical tape around the leaking pipe. Dry the pipe as much as possible and wrap the tape tightly around it.

➤ Take a section of garden hose, slice it lengthwise, and clamp it in position with pipe clamps.

➤ A locking pliers (preferably with a curved jaw) should hold a pliable patch in position for a while. If you have several pairs, use them.

If a threaded joint is leaking, try to disassemble it, smear some joint compound on the threads, and screw it back tighter. Unfortunately, you can only do this if one end of the pipe can move. If you're working on the middle of a pipe with a union, loosen the union to detach the leaking joint. Similarly, if you need to splice in a new section of threaded pipe to repair a leak, but neither end can turn, you'll have to install a union in the line.

Faucet Repair (Dig it! Whatsa Trouble with the Spigot?)

Faucets shut off the water supply, theoretically, without leaking, grabbing, or requiring steroid-enhanced muscular force. The old compression faucets controlled hot or cold water, so they were used in pairs. Most newer faucets use one handle to control both flows, usually with a cartridge or a ball mechanism. As we look at these faucets in this involuntary introduction in plumbing, remember that you may meet variations on the general theme—yet another reason to bring the carcass of the faucet to the store when you buy parts.

Fixing Compression Faucets

Compression faucets close the flow of water by pushing a washer against a seat. The most common cause of failure is a worn-out washer, but because the root cause is often a rough seat that ripped up the washer, seats and washers may need to be replaced together. You'll need a screwdriver, wrench, and possibly a seat-dressing tool or a seat-removing tool, faucet grease, and pipe joint compound. Use these steps to repair the faucet:

1. Turn off the water, preferably at a shut-off valve just before the faucet, otherwise at the main valve.

2. Pull off the handles by loosening the handle screw (see the figure illustrating compression faucet repair). You may have to pry off a decorative cap on top of the handle first.

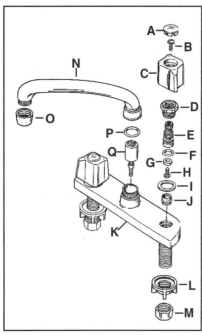

(A) Decorative cap
(B) Handle screw
(C) Handle
(D) Bonnet nut
(E) Stem
(F) Washer
(G) Seat washer
(H) Washer screw
(I) Washer
(J) Seat
(K) Faucet body
(L) Lock nut
(M) Supply nut
(N) Spout
(O) Aerator
(P) O-ring
(Q) Diverter (diverts water to spray hose)

Compression faucet repair. You'll see countless variations on this basic design for the compression faucet.

3. With a smooth-jawed wrench, loosen the bonnet nut. Then slip the handle back on and unscrew the stem.

4. Shine a flashlight on the seat, or poke it with your little finger. It should look and feel smooth. If the seat is rough or uneven, it won't seal against the new washer, and will damage it. If you see a square or hexagonal opening for a wrench inside the seat, your best bet is to replace the seat (step 5a). If the seat is fixed (laundry sinks, for example, often have nonreplaceable seats), you'll have to smooth it with a seat-dressing tool (step 5b).

5a. *Remove the seat* with a seat-removing tool (plumbing *can* be very logical!). Slip the tool into the seat, tap it into place, and unscrew. Take the seat to a plumbing supply or hardware store, buy a replacement for each faucet, and install them with the same tool, using pipe joint compound on the threads.

5b. To *smooth a fixed seat,* buy or rent a seat-dressing tool and insert it into the faucet so it sits squarely; then clean up the seat with the coarse blade. Once it's smooth, switch to the finer blade. Be sure to hold the tool perpendicular to the seat, and smooth both seats while you're at it.

6. To *replace the washers,* first decide whether to use a beveled or flat variety (each style comes in several sizes; flat washers are more common). Don't just replace what you

find—some bozo might have put in the wrong type. All washers are held in position with a retaining rim. If the rim is broken, replace it or get a new stem—replacements are usually pretty easy to find if you bring the old stem to the hardware store. The washer screw should come right out (despite years of immersion in water); simply screw a new one into place. Use brass screws, *not* steel ones, (they will rust).

7. For a good repair, apply faucet grease to the mating metal parts and inside the packing so they can operate smoothly.

8. Thread the stem into the bonnet nut and screw the nut into the faucet. Before the final tightening of the bonnet nut, back off on the stem so it does not bottom against the seat.

9. Restore the water pressure. If the faucet leaks around the stem, keep reading.

Packing; or, Does Your Stem Leak?

Many compression-faucet problems take place at the seal between the bonnet nut and the stem. This seal may come from an O-ring (a special washer) or a flexible material called *packing.*

You can recognize packing leaks because they occur only when the valve is open (when the valve is closed, there's no water pressure on the packing). If the packing is really loose, the stem may slop around a bit. Often, you can seal a packing leak by tightening the bonnet (use reasonable force—if you squeeze too tight, you won't be able to turn the handle). If this does not work, unscrew the bonnet nut and check out what type of packing material you have. If it's a glob of material pressed into place, add a few turns of packing around the stem and retighten, or replace all of the packing. If the seal is made by a solid packing washer or an O-ring (a narrow washer surrounding the stem), just replace the seal.

Cartridge Faucets

Cartridge faucets use a replaceable, cylindrical cartridge to mix and control the flow of hot and cold water. Although you might be tempted to buy cheap, replacement seals instead of the whole cartridge, you'll do better in the long run replacing the entire thing.

The cartridge for a Moen brand of faucet is fixed in place with a retainer clip (other types are held in place with a nut). To disassemble, turn off the water, pull the handle off, pull the stem nut or clip off, and pull out the cartridge (see the figure illustrating cartridge faucet repair). You may need to use a special cartridge tool to get the thing apart. To make sure you remove all the parts, compare what you remove to the contents of the replacement kit. Then simply slap the replacement cartridge back into place. If the faucet operation is stiff, try using faucet grease—cartridges can lime up.

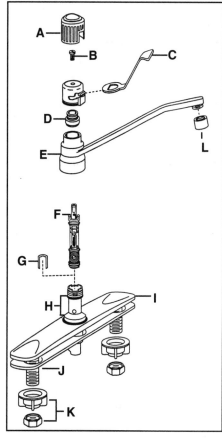

(A)   Handle cap
(B)   Handle screw
(C)   Lever handle
(D)   Retainer pivot nut
(E)   Spout assembly
(F)   Cartridge
(G)   Retainer clip
(H)   Spout O-rings
(I)   Escutcheon
(J)   Deck gasket
(K)   Lock nuts
(L)   Aerator

Cartridge faucet repair

Ball Faucets

Ball faucets are an alternative to cartridges, and they're considerably cheaper to repair. You'll need a repair kit, new O-rings for the spout (optional), an allen wrench (which may come with the kit), arc-joint pliers, and plumber's luck. Here's how:

1. Shut off the water and loosen the allen-set screw on the bottom of the handle (see the next figure, which illustrates ball faucet repair). Remove the handle.

2. The adjusting ring should be visible; tighten it slightly and test whether the faucet still drips (drips can be caused by inadequate pressure on the seals).

3. If the faucet still drips, remove the adjusting ring, and pull out the cap and the ball under it.

4. The seals are the two small disks under the ball (see the figure on following page). Note their location and remove them. Don't lose the springs!

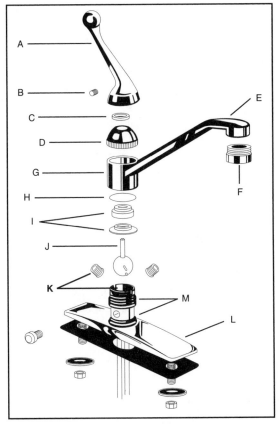

(A)   Handle
(B)   Set screw
(C)   Adjusting ring
(D)   Cap
(E)   Spout
(F)   Aerator
(G)   Spout sleeve
(H)   Slip ring
(I)   Cam and packing
(J)   Ball
(K)   Seat and spring
(L)   Faucet body
(M)   O-rings (spout seals)

Ball faucet repair. The set screw releases the handle so you can begin the disassembly. The springs push the seats against the ball to control flow.

5. With the faucet apart, you might as well replace the O-rings sealing the spout (unless you'd rather face another repair in a few months). Pull up on the spout and twist to remove it. Carefully dig the O-rings from their grooves. Clean lime out of the grooves and put the new O-rings in the grooves. Twist the spout back into place.

6. Put the new seals in place and press the ball and cam back into position, making sure the seals don't jump out.

7. Screw the adjusting ring back on and tighten firmly. Turn the water on and tighten some more if it's leaking. Then replace the handle.

8. While water is running, push down on the handle. If water leaks out under the handle, tighten the adjusting ring.

Builder's Trivia

Some valves, particularly those used in gas piping and main shut-offs, have a lever handle and only turn 90 degrees from open to closed. There's a simple trick to remember which position is open and which is closed. Pretend the handle is a gate inside the valve. When the gate is across the line, and the handle is at 90 degrees to the pipe, the valve is closed; otherwise, it's open.

What about Low Water Pressure?

If your faucets have lost their former oomph, it's likely the aerators are plugged (you should always be so lucky—this is the cheapest and quickest plumbing fix you'll ever meet). Aerators (see the following photo) are screens mounted on the end of faucets to conserve water and create a foamy stream. Simply unscrew the aerator body from the end of the spout with pliers (protect the chrome with adhesive tape), take it apart, and clean rust and crud from the screens. You may have to do this every few months, but it's amazingly effective.

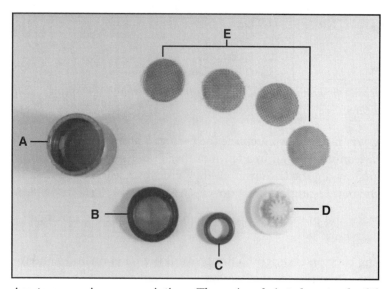

(A) Body
(B) Inlet screen
(C) O-ring
(D) Flow restrictor
(E) Screens

Aerators come in many variations. The main rule is to keep track of the parts as you remove them— so you don't replace them backward (counterclockwise from right).

For clogging caused by liming, see "Hard Facts on Hard Water," earlier in this chapter.

Note: if you have a private water system, low pressure could be caused by a faulty or water-logged air tank, or a problem with the water pump, both of which are beyond idiot territory.

To conserve water in dry regions, or to conserve the energy used to heat water, hardware stores sell (and some utilities give) low-flow aerators and showerheads. In addition, some older showerheads have an adjustment knob on the side to slow the flow.

Soldering Copper Pipe

I used to be so scared of soldering copper pipes that I used a baroque, overly exacting technique. Needless to say, it backfired; I botched the job by overheating the metal. Truth is, a clean, fluxed joint is almost impossible to solder badly, as long as you supply enough heat and don't overheat. That's because clean copper and hot solder have an irresistible attraction called capillary action, which "pulls" the solder evenly into a joint.

You'll need a propane torch, sandpaper, emery cloth or steel wool, flux, and lead-free plumbing solder. Use these steps:

1. Inspect the fittings and the pipe. They should be sound, round, and free of nicks and deformities. Check the joint—does the pipe enter straight, giving a tight fit? Correct any problems now, while the pipe is cold.

2. Clean the mating surfaces (the outside of the pipe, and the inside of the fitting) with fine sandpaper, emery cloth, or steel wool. Get them bright and clean.

> **Handy Hint**
> If you can't remember which way threads should turn, use this jingle: "Lefty loosey, righty tighty." This tells you how the top turns when you're looking at the fitting, valve, screw, or aerator.

3. Apply no-lead nonacidic flux to both mating surfaces, assemble the joint, and twist it a bit to distribute the flux. But don't eat the flux, or inhale more fumes than you must—the stuff isn't real healthy.

4. Light the torch and put the flame on the fitting. Do not concentrate the heat— move the torch and heat the pipe as well as the fitting. Concentrate your heat at the most massive part of the fitting.

5. A few seconds after the flux begins to bubble, remove the torch and touch the solder to the crack between the fitting and the pipe. A hot joint will pull the solder in.

6. When an even bead of solder forms around the whole joint between the fitting and the pipe, pull the solder away and let the joint cool for about a minute without disturbing it. Wrap a wet rag on the joint to cool it faster.

Plastic Pipe

If you're ancient enough, you may remember the immortal advice Dustin Hoffman received in the movie *The Graduate*. The future, he was told, was "plastic." In plumbing, certainly, copper and steel now face competiton from a growing number of plastic materials. In general, these plastics are easier to use and require few or no tools. They're also cheaper than metal, but they are not for everyone. Some plastic, for example, can handle only a limited amount of pressure, or cold water only. You can find fittings that will adapt plastic to copper, steel, or cast iron, so you can extend a metal plumbing system with plastic.

Consult your local building code to see what's allowed in your area; here's a brief run-down on some of the plastic pipe on the market.

➤ PVC (polyvinyl chloride): used for drains and vent lines.

➤ ABS (acrylonitrile butadiene styrene): used for drains and vent lines.

➤ CPVC (chlorinated polyvinyl chloride): allowed for water piping in some areas.

➤ Polybutylene: allowed for water piping in some areas.

➤ Polyethylene: used in well piping.

Joining Plastic Pipe

Some types of plastic pipe can be joined with special fittings that are tightened with a wrench. Others can be joined by pushing the pipe into a fitting. Many plastic pipes are welded together using a special solvent. Make sure you buy the solvent that's recommended for your pipe material. Here's the general procedure for welding plastic pipe together with solvent:

1. Cut the pipe square at the end with a hacksaw (use a miter box if you have one).

2. Using sandpaper, trim off burrs and roughen the outside to prepare it for solvent.

3. Line up the joint dry (you won't get a second chance, since plastic can bond in less than a minute).

4. Disassemble the joint. When everything is ready, wipe solvent on the pipe end and inside the fitting.

5. Press the pipe into the joint until it bottoms, then give it a quarter turn. Quickly make any adjustments to the position of the fitting, and let the joint set up.

Frozen Pipes—and How to Avoid Them

Frozen pipes sound so, er, boring. Nobody has them anymore, right? Well, according to one insurance company, 250,000 Americans have them each year. And, if you read the horror story in "On the Virtue of a Main Water Shut-Off" at the start of this chapter, you know frozen pipes can spell disaster.

The pipes most likely to freeze, amazingly enough, are those in cold locations like underheated crawl spaces, basements, and along outside walls. Here are suggestions for preventing the big chill:

At Hose Connections

Outside faucets (called sillcocks or hose bibbs) are a prime place for a freeze-up. Here are some suggestions to keep you out of trouble.

➤ Disconnect the garden hose.

➤ If you have a "frostproof" sillcock, that's all you need to do. These faucets shut off inside the wall and drip dry to prevent frost. You can recognize these faucets because some water drips out after you shut them off.

➤ Otherwise, close the valve inside the wall (if there is one) on the pipe supplying the hose connection. Then open the faucet to let it drip dry.

Other Anti-Frost Measures

➤ Warm up the foundation by caulking and insulating cracks.

➤ During the winter, keep the thermostat up (heat can—believe it or not—prevent freeze-ups). Open cabinet doors in the kitchen so warm air can reach pipes under the sink. If you go away in the winter, shut off the main water valve, and ask a neighbor to monitor the house.

➤ Put insulation between the pipes and the cold (pipe insulation will help for a while, but eventually, the pipe will reach ambient temperature unless water is flowing).

➤ As a last resort, if you can't warm pipes in any other way, install pipe tape. To prevent fire, follow all directions, and buy a UL-approved product.

> **Don't Screw Up!**
> Natural gas is supplied at low pressure, so it's less likely to leak than water. Use joint compound on good, clean threads, and avoid "Tarzan-style" tightening, which is a recipe for stripping threads and cracking fittings. Then restore the gas pressure and brush on some soap suds to test the joint. Bubbles indicate a leak. Do not use matches to test for leaks!

Four Thaws for Icy Pipes

Let's say you've got some frozen pipes. First, open a faucet at the end of the pipe, to give the water some place to go after it thaws. Then select among these warm-up options:

➤ Wrap the pipe with rags and pour boiling water over them.

➤ Warm the pipes with a heat gun or heat lamp.

➤ Wrap the pipe with a heating pad.

➤ As a last resort, if you are comfortable with it, use a propane torch with a flame spreader in place. Move the torch around, and be careful. Don't work near any wood or foam insulation.

Once you've thawed the pipes, it's time to figure out how to avoid a freeze next time. See "Frozen Pipes—and How to Avoid Them," earlier in this chapter.

Your Water Heater

Let's face it—life would be pretty squalid without a water heater. And while they don't need much maintenance, it won't hurt to make sure the safety valve is working, and to drain sludge from the bottom of the tank once in a while.

The *pressure-temperature relief valve* on top of a water heater is an essential safety feature—because an overheated water heater could cause a steam explosion and send shrapnel right through the roof. The valve has a small handle and is attached to the overflow pipe running down the side of the heater. Once a year, test the valve by lifting the handle and making sure water runs out the overflow tube, and the valve snaps shut afterward. If it doesn't, call a plumber—an inoperative valve is a hazard. (This valve will spill water into the overflow, so keep a bucket handy. Never attach a hose to the overflow, for safety reasons.)

Over time, sludge can build up inside water heaters. Remove sludge every few months by draining the tank through the valve at the bottom. Let the water run until it's clear.

To adjust the temperature in an electric water heater that has two elements, set the upper thermostat about 10 degrees warmer than the lower one. (This is because warm water rises, and the top of the tank will always be warmer than the bottom.) If you have small children, avoid burn hazards by limiting the temperature to about 125 degrees. (Note: electric water heaters can cost more than twice as much to operate as gas heaters, so I wouldn't spend much money repairing an electric heater.)

Putting the Kibosh on Water Hammer

Water hammer is the loud clanking you hear when you quickly close a faucet; it's caused by the sudden stopping of water in the pipes. Water hammer sounds obnoxious and can loosen the piping. If your house has this problem, you need to add support for the pipes, have a plumber install water hammer arrestors, or simply close the faucets more slowly.

Some houses have air chambers in the piping—dead-end fittings containing air designed to prevent water hammer. If you have these chambers, you may be able to restore the air in the air chambers and temporarily silence water hammer. You will need a working main water valve, and these instructions:

1. Shut off the main valve.

2. Open valves on every floor of the house, particularly the lowest valves, and wait about fifteen minutes so the entire plumbing system can drain. Air will replace the water in the pipes and the air chambers.

3. Shut the faucets and open the main valve. Your air chambers should be restored, and water hammer should be a noisome memory. But if this cure works, you'll have to repeat it periodically. And don't be surprised if some of your faucet aerators get plugged by grit that gets loosened by this little fix-up.

The Least You Need to Know

➤ Water systems can benefit from a surprising amount of preventive help, most of which will increase your convenience or comfort *and* reduce your maintenance bills.

➤ Faucet seats—the overlooked cause of many drippy faucets—can be repaired or replaced.

➤ Believe it or not, many faucets are built for repair. The hardest part is often figuring out how to take them apart; once you've done that, the rest should be easy.

➤ Hard water can cause a damaging lime buildup in many parts of a plumbing system.

Chapter 28

. . . Or It Doesn't Drain (Plumbing, Part II)

It's time to cut the crap. You didn't start this chapter from some abstract interest in the plumbing code, or a fascination with the flow of filthy water. You're reading in hopes of getting some action in the drains, right?

Right. So let's get right down to the dirty work—and get that drain back in business. We'll start with the least dramatic techniques, and move to increasingly invasive procedures (as the M.D.s put it) you might need if milder techniques don't work.

Feeling Trapped by Your Trap?

A trap is a U-shaped piece of drainpipe that's usually directly beneath the outlet of a plumbing fixture. Traps have two important purposes: to create a "water seal" so you can avoid intimate contact with the sicko world of sewer gas, and to give liquid crud a place to hang up so you can test your new plumbing skills (just kidding).

Traps look simple, and they are. But because the water seal is so important, plumbing codes strictly limit the design and construction of traps (see the figures illustrating traps).

For example, multiple traps are forbidden because they create too much resistance to the flow; thus you should not see a trap beneath a toilet, which has a built-in trap.

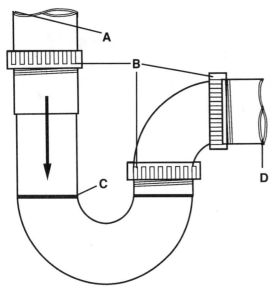

(A) Sink tailpiece
(B) Slip-joint nuts
(C) Water trap level
(D) To drain pipe

A good P-trap—notice that the slip-joint connector on the discharge (sink) side is above the water seal. This three-piece trap is a common, adjustable item sold in all hardware stores; it can be swiveled and extended to fit most sinks.

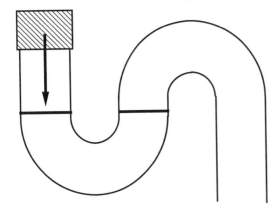

The water seal can be siphoned from this illegal S-trap; it should be replaced.

Venting

You won't see vents very often, but they are a critical part of your plumbing system because they allow air to replace the water that leaves a drain. Without a vent, you'll get a vacuum and a sluggish, gurgling drain. If your vent is plugged, you may be able to ream it out by sticking a long drain auger (also called a snake) into the round vent pipe that sticks through the roof. Retrofitting vents in an old house is strictly a pro job, but it will vastly improve the performance of the drains.

About the only bad thing about vents is that they limit the effectiveness of a plunger, which will only put pressure on the pipe between the drain and the vent. But that's a small price to pay for their real benefit—preventing the funky, unhealthy stench that results when a water trap is sucked dry by the vacuum created by water going down an unvented drain. Furthermore, vented drains stay cleaner because water flows more quickly through them.

Going Down the Drain—Fixing the Plumbing Is . . . Less Disgusting Than Ignoring It

Logically, the first step in cleaning a drain is to make sure the clog is a local problem, not a systemic one. If two or more drains suddenly plug up, I'd bet a gold-plated plunger the cause is something affecting both drains, like a major clog or a plugged vent. Because these problems can be harder to reach, they're a good reason to call for help. But if only one drain is screaming in agony, read on.

Hair and Soap Scuzz

If you're lucky, your problem is caused by something as simple as hair, soap scuzz, and other unmentionables on the strainer or just inside the drain. You can probably remove these clogs with long-nose pliers, a bent coathanger, or "mechanical fingers," a long, three-fingered tool for grabbing stuff in inaccessible places.

After you get the drain working again, resolve to keep wannabe cloggers like bobby pins away from the sink, and find someplace other than the kitchen sink to dump cooking grease. You can prevent further accumulations of soap, grease, and hair by flushing the drain with plenty of water. Put 4 to 5 inches of water in the sink or tub, then pull the plug so the water can scour the drain pipe; do this weekly if you can remember.

Drain Chemicals

If your drain is still flowing, but too slowly for your taste, you may start wondering whether a miracle chemical could solve (or should we say dissolve!) your woes. Sulfuric acid and various other preparations are sold for cleaning drains, but most experts won't use them on a totally clogged drain, because pressure can build up and the pipes can explode, or at least heat up and corrode. (And if the acid doesn't work, you'll have to work in pipes full of acid—a caustic picture.)

If acid loosens a clog, it could travel to an even worse location and get stuck there. Finally, it can also damage chrome plating and possibly metal pipes.

If you decide to use acid, use plenty of caution:

➤ Put on gloves and goggles.

➤ Read the label.

➤ Don't mix chemicals. (Did you think we were recommending a do-it-yourself Frankenstein course here? Remember, drain cleaner and bleach form a toxic combination.)

Acid is much better for preventive maintenance on drains that are starting to slow, because it eats away all sorts of organic crap. Protect metal on the sink or tub with Vaseline. This cure may work, but only if you disobey the natural urge to avoid plumbing problems until they absolutely can't be ignored one second longer.

Lye is a good preventive measure for occasional cleaning. But be *sure* to read and follow the label, because lye can solidify in a drain if left there too long. And use protective clothing and goggles.

Enzymes (chemical extracts from microorganisms that have generations of experience breaking down organic matter) are good for maintenance because they're far less hazardous than acid or lye. But keep your eye on the label—you may need to use them periodically.

Plunger (the Plumber's Friend)

Are you slightly offended by the sight of a plunger near the toilet? Not me—I take it as a sign that the homeowner knows that when things go wrong with drains, there's no time to visit the hardware store. Plungers exert a hydraulic force on the contents of a drain, and whatever is plugging it, but they are only effective up to the vent connection (which may be just inside the wall).

If you follow the advice of my friend Carl Lorentz, who makes plumbing his living, you'll get two plungers, a big one for toilets and a junior size for sinks. Use the plungers in unison on bathtubs: Use one to plunge the drain, and the other to seal the overflow (without that seal, you can't put pressure on the drain). To plunge a sink, plug the overflow with a rag, since the second plunger may not fit.

Here's how to plunge a drain:

1. Add a few inches of water to the fixture (if it's not full of liquid yuck to begin with!).

2. Roll the plunger into the water to minimize the amount of air trapped inside the bell.

3. Pump up and down as hard as you can while holding a good seal. Then give one final pull and break the plunger free. You may have to plunge for several minutes. With any luck, you'll hear a famished groan as the drain sucks down a load of filth.

If a couple of more plunging efforts fail, your choices are to disassemble the trap, use a pipe auger, or call a pro. Let's look at disassembly first.

Drain Disassembly and Replacement

P-trap removal and cleanout. Remember the rule: lefty loosey, righty tighty. But for a nut on a horizontal pipe that's facing away from you, reverse this rule.

Although traps rarely plug up, if you remove the trap, you may gain access to the clog. The good news is that new traps are quite easy to remove and replace; the bad news is that not all traps are new. You'll need a flashlight, a bucket, rag, pipe wrench, new washers for the trap (they're usually $1^{1}/_{2}$ inches in diameter), a coathanger, and a strong stomach. You may also need a replacement trap and a pipe auger (snake). Follow these steps:

1. Position the bucket under the trap and remove the cleanout, if there is one. From here, you might be lucky enough to see and remove the clog (just like you might be lucky enough to win the lottery every time! It's possible, but not likely).

2. Loosen the three large nuts on the trap (see the next photo). If you're feeling fastidious, use cloth to protect the chrome plating on metal nuts.

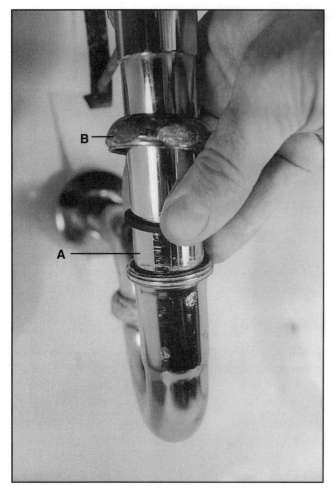

(A) Washer
(B) Slip nut

Place new washers on the pipes before reassembly.
Make sure the washer is evenly seated before you
tighten the slip nut.

3. Pull the trap apart and remove any obstruction you see.

4. If you need to, dig around in the drain with a coathanger and pull out any blockages. (Or see "The Plumber's Snake," below.)

5. Once you've removed the clog, push the washers onto the male ends of the trap (see the second photo) and assemble the trap loosely.

6. Put the trap into position carefully—if you get it right the first time, you won't need nuclear-scale force on the nuts.

The Plumber's Snake

Pipe snakes, or *augers*, are flexible tools that supposedly can be threaded into a drain to loosen and remove whatever kind of unmentionable crud is clogging it. The inexorable need for drain cleaning has spawned many inventions; the best tool for you depends on your talent, your wallet, and your luck.

➤ A simple *plumber's snake* is made of flat flexible (spring) steel.

➤ A rotating snake is slightly more expensive, and much more effective. The snake

looks like a long spring, and it's flexible enough to get through a couple of elbows before it gets jammed. It has a handle so you can rotate it as you thread it into the piping.

➤ The electric drain-reamer (you can rent one) is more effective, but make sure you're confident of using it, and don't wreck the plumbing.

➤ A special toilet-cleaning snake called a *closet auger* has a right-angle end so it can reach inside the toilet trap. But be careful not to force the auger—you could break the inside wall of the toilet.

Some people suggest using a garden hose as an improvised snake, but I'd be hesitant, since they don't seem flexible enough to get through drains.

> **Don't Screw Up!**
> For the fastidious few, there's always the chance that germs can live in the toilet. To kill them, pour some bleach into the bowl before working on it. Decontaminate snakes and tools in one part bleach to 10 parts water.

Drain Auger Techniques

For sinks: You may be able to run an auger through the trap into the drain, but it's more likely that you'll have to work through the cleanout at the bottom of the trap (if it has one), or take the trap apart and thread the auger directly into the stub of pipe leading to the drain. Or take off the cleanout plate on the drain stack below the sink and feed the auger through the opening. Turn the handle of the auger clockwise, and if you think you've hooked something, gradually withdraw the auger as you continue turning.

> **Don't Screw Up!**
> Utter plumbing purgatory is when you jam a snake in the pipes. This brilliantly converts a routine problem into a disaster that requires an expensive visit from the plumber or drain cleaner. It's embarrassing, and something you can avoid by taking care not to get in over your head. If you truly don't understand what you're doing, don't do it!

For tubs: Remove the overflow plate and the stopper and stopper linkage. Snake the auger through the overflow opening, and crank, moving the auger back and forth, to try to pick up or dislodge the clog. If your tub has a "drum trap" (look for the metal plate in the floor near the tub or inside an access panel), open the cover on the drum and run the snake in both directions from the trap. You may want to try your plunger once more before taking a drum trap apart— they're tricky.

For toilets: Feed a closet auger (mentioned earlier in this section) into the trap, being careful not to chip the china bowl. Working firmly but carefully, push the snake into the trap and feel for an obstruction. When you think you've hooked one, pull it out. If you must use a straight (sink-type) auger, be extra careful with the china—and wear rubber gloves! Because toilets are porcelain, and porcelain is fragile, you may want to go back to the all-important plunger. Pencils, toothbrushes, dentures, diaphragms, and toys can all plug toilets. If the toilet continues to plug up, it either needs repair or it has something wedged in its innards. Empty the bowl, and use a flashlight and a small mirror to inspect the trapway. Then use a bent coathanger to extract the object.

How Toilets Flush—and Other Wonders of the Modern World

Ever wonder how a toilet works? Not until it stops working. Just as the old bluesman said, "You don't miss your water till your well runs dry." So if you're still reading, I assume you have what the spies call a "need to know." So how does a toilet do its critically important task?

1. When you pull the handle, the lift arm lifts the stopper valve, and the tankful of water rushes into the bowl, pushing the putrid cargo over the water trap and down the drain (see the following figure).

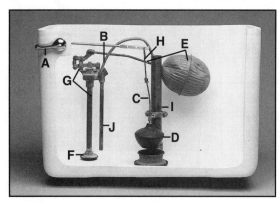

(A)   Handle
(B)   Lift arm
(C)   Lift wire
(D)   Stopper valve (or flapper in newer installations)
(E)   Float and arm
(F)   Water supply
(G)   Ballcock valve assembly
(H)   Bowl refill tube
(I)   Overflow tube
(J)   Tank refill tube

Inside the guts of an old toilet

2. As the float drops, it opens the ballcock valve, and fresh water enters the tank from the tank refill tube. At the same time, fresh water flows through the bowl refill tube and overflow tube, into the bowl.

3. When the tank empties, the stopper ball drops back into place, sealing the tank and allowing it to fill. Meanwhile, the overflow tube continues filling the bowl.

4. When the water level is high enough, the float shuts the valve, ending the cycle.

Hints for good toilet operation:

➤ To make sure the mechanism is not getting snagged on itself, watch a full flushing cycle with the tank uncovered.

➤ Check that the stopper and float are not waterlogged. The float should ride on top of the water, and the stopper should stay up during the whole flushing cycle.

➤ Check the holes under the rim and ream them with a coathanger if they're plugged (see "Hard Facts on Hard Water," in Chapter 27).

➤ Water should not circulate from the tank to the bowl except during flushing. If the toilet "runs" (periodically refills its tank), it's because water is entering the bowl when it's not supposed to. If you're not sure, test the valve seal by pouring food dye in the tank. If, without flushing, the bowl water turns color, either (a) or (b) needs repair:

(a) The ballcock valve is not shutting off soon enough, and water is rising above the overflow tube and flowing into the tank. Bend the float arm down so the valve shuts off sooner. If you have the replacement valve shown in the photo on updating your toilet's innards, loosen the clip and slide the float down the guide wire. Check that the float arm operates smoothly. And read the section on ballcock replacement, below.

(b) The stopper valve seat is damaged or dirty, and water is leaking into the bowl through the bottom. Read "Replacing Their Guts," next.

Replacing Their Guts

Toilets have come a long way since somebody first realized it would be nice not to have to march into the backyard every time nature called. Modern toilet replacement mechanisms are such a vast improvement that even operable old mechanisms should usually be replaced. First, the new equipment is mostly plastic, so it won't rust. Second, the simplified design omits many traditional trouble spots. Third, it's cheap.

And fourth, as I learned yesterday, after the old ballcock in my toilet seized up, they're incredibly easy to install. (Call it luck, fate, or coincidence; I figure my house was reading this chapter over my shoulder.)

I'll start by explaining how to replace the ballcock, then talk about the flush valve.

The ballcock refills the tank and bowl when the tank level drops during flushing, and shuts off when the tank is full. Replacing the old valve should take only half an hour. You'll need a pair of arc-joint pliers or locking pliers, a knife, and a monkey wrench. To replace the ballcock, follow these steps:

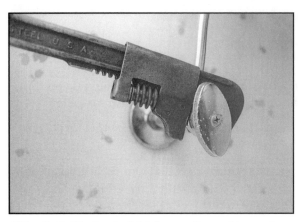

If the shutoff valve is tight, loosen the packing nut with a wrench.

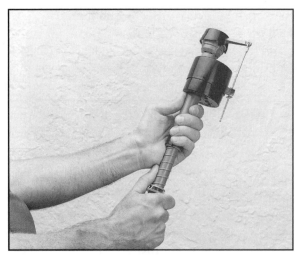

The new valve must be adjusted to the height of the toilet tank.

1. Shut off the water supply below the toilet (see the photo showing how to loosen the shutoff). Shut off the main water valve if this valve is not working or is not present. Then flush the toilet to drain the tank and sponge out the remaining water.

2. Remove the old ballcock by loosening the water supply connection and the big nut mounting the ballcock to the bottom of the tank.

3. For a good seal, clean the area around the hole in the bottom of the toilet tank with steel wool. Twist the replacement assembly to adjust its height, as shown in the photo of the replacement valve. Place the washer on the tube and insert the tube through the hole.

4. Loosely connect the water supply and the mounting lock nut. Then tighten both nuts.

5. Attach the refill tube to the valve. Cut the tube to length and clip it to the overflow pipe, as shown in the photo.

6. Turn on the water supply and re-tighten the packing nut on the water supply valve. Flush out the valve per instructions, and adjust the tank water level with the clip on the float. If you see any leaks, tighten the appropriate fitting, and you're done.

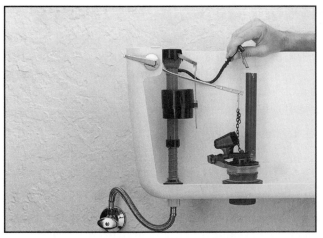

The flexible refill tube slips into an elbow that clips on the overflow pipe.

The flush valve assembly is another piece of antiquated toilet equipment that should be replaced rather than repaired. Replacement flappers simply slip down over the overflow tube. If the seat is damaged, look for a kit with a replacement seat. You'll need a sponge, steel wool, and a working shut-off to install a flapper.

1. Shut off the water, drain the tank by flushing the toilet, and sponge the tank dry.

2. Remove the old tank ball or flapper, leaving the overflow tube in place.

3. Press a mounting adapter over the overflow tube, unless one is already present (see illustration).

4. Slip the new flapper into place on the mounting adapter, positioned so it can move freely (see illustration).

5. Adjust the chain so it's slightly slack, then cut off extra chain.

(A)   The adapter supplies the mounting points for the new flapper valve.

(B)   Make sure the flapper doesn't snag against anything, and securely contacts the seat.

Replacing a flush valve

The Care and Feeding of Your Garbage Disposal

Garbage disposals, once a symbol of conspicuous consumption, are now standard equipment on new homes. They are pretty reliable, but not exactly trouble-free.

Advice for happy garbage-eaters:

➤ Keep indigestible crud like peach pits and silverware out of the disposer.

➤ The slower you feed the disposer, the fewer plugging problems you'll have.

➤ When a disposer is overloaded, a built-in circuit breaker will trip to prevent damage to the motor. If the disposer is silent when you switch it on, give it a minute to cool down, and push the reset button—it's generally on the bottom of the unit.

➤ If the grinder is stuck (you'll hear loud humming when you hit the switch), loosen it with an allen (hexagonal) wrench. If you can't find the one that came with the unit, use a standard allen wrench. Shut off the switch, insert the wrench into the socket on the bottom of the disposer, and turn until it's free; then try the power again, with plenty of water.

➤ If the disposer quits draining or springs a serious leak, chances are it's plugged near the wall. See the photo of P-trap removal and cleanout, earlier in this chapter, for advice on cleaning the trap.

➤ When you operate the disposer (which should be more often than once a week), run as much water as you can to send the crud on its way.

➤ Do not dump animal fats or byproducts in garbage disposals, especially if you have a septic system.

➤ If you're the fastidious type, grind up ice cubes or cubed potatoes, followed by $1/4$ cup of white vinegar. Then rinse with clean water to de-toxify the grinder.

Builder's Trivia

About half of U.S. sewage systems apply their treated sewage sludge to farmland in a massive, and usually beneficial, recycling project. So when you grind up the old carrot stew in your garbage disposal, you may actually be cooperating in industrial-scale composting. Can you beat that for guilt-free goulash-grinding?

The Least You Need to Know

➤ Replacing the working parts of a toilet can be easy, fast, cheap, and effective. Don't bother repairing parts that should be replaced.

➤ Chemical drain cleaners are most effective for cleaning drains that still are partially functional. Otherwise, you risk explosion or other problems.

➤ Garbage disposers can be overloaded, but between the reset button and the wrench socket, chances are you can bring them back to life without calling for help.

Nail It Down Glossary

Allen wrench   A hexagonal wrench made of solid steel, which is inserted into a socket in an allen screw or bolt.

Amps (amperes)   Units of current flow in an electric circuit or device.

Anchor   A fitting used to secure to masonry, drywall, and other hard-to-fasten materials.

Anti-rising pin   A hinge pin that cannot rise by itself out of its socket.

Auger   A springlike cleaning tool for drains and traps.

Back saw   A rectangular saw with a stiff back made for accurate cuts, usually used with a miter box.

Baseboard   Molding around the perimeter of a room that trims the junction between the wall and the floor.

Bleeder valve   A valve on top of a radiator that lets air escape so the radiator can fill with water.

Blind-nailing   Nailing so the nail cannot be seen when the work is finished, usually done on tongue-and-groove boards.

Book   To fold pasted wallpaper over on itself so the paper can "relax," or expand.

Boxing   Mixing two cans of paint to match the colors by pouring one into another several times.

Breaker box   *See* circuit breaker box.

Calcium carbonate (lime) $CaCO_3$, a component of mortar and portland cement.

Casement window Windows whose sashes are hinged vertically.

Circuit An electrical loop connecting a source, a load, and the source; allows current to flow.

Circuit breaker A safety device that shuts off a circuit if a dangerous amount of current is flowing, or if you want to work on the circuit safely.

Circuit breaker box (breaker box or circuit breaker panel) A central control panel containing circuit breakers; controls current to circuits in the house.

Circuit tester A device that lights up when current is flowing.

Concrete Portland cement, gravel, sand, and water after hardening.

Countersink bit A drill bit that removes enough wood so that the head of a screw will sit flush to the surface.

Crawl space A recess under a house that's up to 4 feet tall.

Creosote A preservative once used to protect below-grade wood, now used only in industrial applications; also used to describe a different, flammable substance that can build up in chimneys.

Crosscut To cut wood across the grain.

Cut in To prepare for rolling paint by brushing edges and corners and other places the roller can't reach.

Damper An adjustable plate that regulates the flow of air in a duct, or of smoke in a chimney.

Decking (roof) The layer of wood that holds the shingle nails.

DIY Do it yourself.

Drill chuck The rotating clamp that holds the drill bit.

Dry rot A fungus that destroys damp wood, leaving the wood looking dry.

Drywall Wallboard made of gypsum sandwiched between heavy paper.

Eave The overhang at the bottom of a pitched (sloping) roof.

Elbow A pipe fixture that changes direction.

Face-nail To nail a board so the nail head remains visible.

Fan-and-limit control A thermally 'operated switch that regulates the air blower or water-pump motor in a heating system. It also shuts the furnace down if the furnace overheats.

Fascia The eave board, usually behind the gutter.

Ferrous metal Metal containing iron, such as steel. Subject to rust.

Finial   An ornamental top on a post or column.

Finish (concrete)   To smooth concrete as it sets.

Fixture (device)   An electrical switch or outlet.

Flashing   Metal that joins various planes of a roof, or a roof to a chimney, vent, and so on.

Float   A flat tool used to smooth stucco, patching plaster, and concrete.

Flush   Surfaces that are in one plane.

Framing   Two-inch-thick lumber that forms the structure of a house.

Fuse   A device that prevents a circuit from carrying a dangerous amount of current.

Fuse box   Box that contains fuses and controls electric circuits.

Galvanizing   A zinc coating on steel to prevents rust.

Gauge   A system for measuring diameter of wires, and the thickness of sheet metal.

Glazier's points   Tiny brads that hold glass in a window sash as glazing compound is applied.

Glazing (glazing compound) or Putty   A flexible sealing material that seals a window to a sash.

Grade   Ground level.

Ground   A safety wire that gives electricity an "escape route" if something screws up with the neutral wire.

Ground-fault interruptor   A device that shuts off the power if it detects a dangerous leakage of current.

Hammer drill (or rotary hammer)   A drill that turns the bit and hammers it into the work at the same time; good for drilling concrete and masonry.

Hollow-core door   A door with two veneer surfaces and a hollow interior.

HVAC   Heating, ventilating, and air conditioning.

Ice dam   The accumulation of ice on a roof, formed by melting snow.

Inner stop   The molding that separates the upper and lower sash tracks in a double-hung window.

Jamb   The one-inch wood enclosing a door or window; holds the door hinges.

Jointer   A masonry tool that shapes and compresses the mortar joint between bricks or blocks.

Joist   Framing that supports a floor or ceiling.

Junction box   An electrical box used to hold switches, outlets, etc.

Lag screw   A heavy-duty wood screw with a hexagonal or square head.

Latch side   The side of a door away from the hinge.

Light   An individual piece of glass in a multipane sash.

Load   Anything that uses electricity in a circuit.

Mineral spirits   A replacement for turpentine, used as paint thinner, made from petroleum.

Miter   An angled cut in wood, used to form a corner joint.

Mortar   A mixture of portland cement, lime, mason's sand, and water; makes the joints between bricks, blocks and stones.

Mortise   A shallow, rectangular cavity removed from wood to allow a hinge to sit flush.

Muriatic (hydrochloric) acid   Acid that cleans up masonry by removing old mortar from the surface.

OC (on-center)   The distance between centers of repeated components, such as studs.

Out of square   Meeting at an angle other than 90 degrees.

Outer stop   The vertical strip of molding inside a double-hung window jamb; holds the lower sash in place.

Penny   System for identifying nail length.

Plate   A cover plate used to finish off an outlet or switch; also the piece of framing that sits directly on the foundation.

Quarter-round   A molding that's shaped like one-quarter of a circle (seen from the end).

Rafter   Lumber supporting the roof decking.

Rake edge   The slanting edge of a sloping roof.

Receptacle   An electric outlet.

Reducer (plumbing)   A fitting that changes the size of a pipe to connect different-size pipes and fittings.

Ridge   The horizontal line across the top of a pitched roof.

Riser   The board that connects two treads in a stairway; has a vertical face.

Romex   Plastic-wrapped cable, commonly used in home wiring.

Roof tar (roof cement)   A sticky goop used to seal holes in roofs.

Sand finish   A finish plaster containing sand; makes a regular, rough surface when floated.

Sash   The movable wood or metal element holding glass in a window.

Seat   The ledge that holds a light in a sash; also the sealing component in a faucet.

Self-priming paint   A coating that works as a primer or a finish coat.

Service panel   *See* circuit breaker box.

Shakes   Wood roofing material made by splitting pieces of log.

Sheathing   A thin structural layer used on siding; holds the nails for the surface layer; called decking on a roof.

Sinker   A cement-coated nail, thinner than a common nail; used for nailing two-inch lumber.

Sizing   A primer used to regulate the adhesion of wallpaper paste.

Snake (auger)   A springlike tool for cleaning drains.

Soffit   The horizontal underside of a roof overhang.

Solid-core door   A door made entirely of wood, usually used on the exterior.

Spall   A surface degradation of masonry.

Square   At a 90-degree angle; a tool used to mark or saw a 90-degree angle.

Stop   Plumber's jargon for a shut-off valve.

Strike off (screed)   To remove extra wet concrete and smooth the surface by pushing and pulling a 2×4 across it.

Stringer   The slanting piece of framing that supports a stairway.

Stud gap   The void between adjacent studs.

Stud   The vertical 2×4 or 2×6 framing that supports a wall.

Subfloor   The rough floor, laid directly on the joists.

Substrate   The level of material supporting the thing you're fastening.

Sweat   To connect copper pipe by soldering.

Tar-and-gravel (built-up) roof   A flat roof made of gravel on top of tar.

Tee (plumbing)   A fitting that connects three pipes in a T formation.

Thermocouple   A heat sensor that shuts off the flow of gas in a gas furnace when the pilot goes out.

Three-way switch   Switches used in pairs, to control a single light fixture.

Thumb-hard   Material that has hardened or dried enough to show the imprint of a thumb.

Toe-nail   To nail at an angle, as through the base of a stud.

Tongue-and-groove (T&G)   Board with a tongue on one side and a channel on the other, which forms an interlocking floor.

Topcoat   The last coat of paint, stain, or clear finish.

Traveler wires   Pair of wires connecting two three-way switches.

Tread   The part of a staircase you step on.

Vapor barrier   An impervious layer used to prevent humidity from migrating into a house.

VOC   Volatile organic compound, like a solvent in paint, varnish, or stain, which is usually toxic.

Volt   A unit of electrical pressure.

Water seal   A pool of water in a plumbing trap that prevents sewer gas from entering a dwelling.

Watt   A unit of electrical power (equals amps × volts).

Weatherstripping   A flexible material that seals a moving piece to a fixed piece.

Wire nut   Brand name for plastic nut that screws onto the end of wires to join them.

Index

J

I

Q-R